Beginning with a discussion of the bureaucratic imperialism of
Lord Cromer, who promoted the imperial governing doctrine of
Indirect Rule at the turn of the last century, Daniel Bivona's study
*British Imperial Literature, 1870–1940* traces the more gradual process
by which the colonial bureaucratic subject, the figure whose work
is rule, was constructed and celebrated in nineteenth- and early
twentieth-century Britain. Through insightful readings of a number of influential writers who were involved in promoting the
ideology of bureaucratic self-sacrifice, the most important of whom
are Stanley, Kipling, and T. E. Lawrence, the book then examines
how this governing ideology comes in for criticism in the novels of
Joseph Conrad and the interwar novels of imperial manners of
Joyce Cary and George Orwell. Carefully attentive both to the
complexities of individual texts and to the larger historical context,
this study makes the original claim that the colonial bureaucrat
played an ambiguous but nonetheless central role in both pro-
imperial and anti-imperial discourse, his own power relationship
with bureaucratic superiors shaping the terms in which the proper
relationship between colonizer and colonized was debated.

# BRITISH IMPERIAL LITERATURE,
## 1870–1940

# BRITISH IMPERIAL LITERATURE, 1870–1940

*Writing and the administration of empire*

DANIEL BIVONA

*Arizona State University*

CAMBRIDGE UNIVERSITY PRESS

PUBLISHED BY THE PRESS SYNDICATE OF THE UNIVERSITY OF CAMBRIDGE
The Pitt Building, Trumpington Street, Cambridge CB2 1RP

CAMBRIDGE UNIVERSITY PRESS
The Edinburgh Building, Cambridge CB2 2RU, United Kingdom
40 West 20th Street, New York, NY 10011-4211, USA
10 Stamford Road, Oakleigh, Melbourne 3166, Australia

First published 1998

Printed in the United Kingdom at the University Press, Cambridge

Typeset in Baskerville 11/12$\frac{1}{2}$ pt. [VN]

*A catalogue record for this book is available from the British Library*

*Library of Congress cataloguing in publication data*

Bivona, Daniel.
British imperial literature, 1870–1940: writing and
the administration of empire / Daniel Bivona.
p.   cm.
Includes bibliographical references and index.
ISBN 0 521 59100 7 (hardback)
1. English literature – 20th century – History and criticism.
2. English literature – 19th century – History and criticism.
3. Great Britain – Colonies – Administration.
4. Imperialism in literature. 5. Colonies in literature. I. Title.
PR478.I53B75   1998
820.9'358 – dc21
97-27249
CIP

ISBN 0 521 59100 7 hardback

*In memory of*
*Anthony L. Bivona*
*(1927–1993)*
*and*
*Roger B. Henkle*
*(1937–1991)*

# Contents

# Acknowledgments

Many people have had a hand in this book: offering their own ideas, challenging my ideas, making suggestions, steering me toward sources, and editing. I am grateful for the inspiration offered by the graduate students at the University of Pennsylvania who took my course in Imperialism and Work in the Spring of 1994. They include Anjali Arondekar, Jeannine DeLombard, Carolyn Jacobson, Sue Yom, Giselle Anatole, and Cheryl Williams. Some of the colleagues who have offered helpful suggestions along the way include David DeLaura, John Richetti, Deirdre David, Christopher Lane, and the anonymous readers at Cambridge University Press. Above all, I am grateful to two colleagues – David McWhirter and Rita Barnard – for their careful reading of earlier versions of the manuscript and their many helpful suggestions.

I am grateful to the English Department at the University of Pennsylvania for absorbing the cost of transatlantic telephone calls and faxes and to the Research Foundation at Penn for its generous summer research grant. Thanks also go to the English Department at Arizona State University for its support and, especially, to my hard-working Research Assistant Laura Nutten. I would also like to thank my editor at Cambridge University Press, Ray Ryan, for his efforts in bringing this project to fruition, and Joanne Hill, for a wonderful job of copyediting.

Parts of Chapters 4 and 5 have appeared as articles. I am grateful to *Novel* for permission to republish part of "Conrad's Bureaucrats: Agency, Bureaucracy, and the Problem of Intention," *Novel* 26.2 (Winter 1993), pp. 151–169 and to Frank Cass Ltd. for permission to republish part of "The Erotic Politics of Indirect Rule: T. E. Lawrence's 'Voluntary Slavery,'" *Prose Studies* 20.1 (April 1997), pp. 91–119.

This book would never have been completed without the generous help of all my family including my wife Jeannie and my children Laura, Michael, and Kathryn.

# Introduction

An explorer visits a penal colony one day to observe an apparatus. The guardian of the apparatus is an officer, who, without being asked, proceeds to explain the history of the ingenious machine to the explorer. The machine, it seems, was originally a product of the fertile imagination of the exalted "old Commandant," who was responsible for "the organization of the whole penal colony" in former days.[1]

As the explorer soon discovers, the apparatus itself is no ordinary engine of torture. It is, in fact, a writing machine, the "Designer." Equipped with a harrow fitted out with a sharp needle, the apparatus is designed to write into the naked flesh of the prisoner the commandment that the prisoner is charged with having disobeyed. It does so by making numerous slow passes across the body of the prisoner while he is strapped helplessly to its bed. While the first of these etchings creates superficial wounds, each time the apparatus finishes a complete sentence, the needle, which is fitted into the arm of the apparatus, returns to the beginning again to make another cut – each subsequent pass producing progressively deeper marks in the prisoner's body as the apparatus embellishes its initial sentence. By this method, the officer assures the explorer, the unwitting prisoner comes to "know" his sentence: he learns it "on his body" just before he dies – usually within twelve hours after the torture has begun. Lest the explorer worry about the humanity and legality of this form, the officer assures him "Guilt is never to be doubted."

Despite the officer's best efforts, his explanation does inspire some unease in the explorer, who finds himself in something of a moral quandary caused by his doubts about his right to intervene in a scene to which he comes only as an observer, not as an actor. Suspecting as much, the officer seeks to enlist the explorer in the cause of the apparatus by waxing nostalgic about the golden years of the old Commandant – now gone – when the apparatus was first placed into service in the colony, a time when executions were important social events, eagerly watched by young children. The officer even goes so far as to portray himself as a victim of bureaucratic machinations, at one point petulantly voicing his suspicion that the explorer may well have been sent by his bureaucratic enemy, the new Commandant, precisely to disapprove what he sees in order to provide "foreign" support for the Commandant's plan to bring the tradition of executions to an end.

Yet the explorer remains unmoved by the officer's increasingly desperate plea to preserve tradition within the colony – "help me against the Commandant!" – and instead simply reaffirms his own neutrality – "I can neither help nor hinder you." Although he treasures his political neutrality, the explorer does not remain completely indifferent to the officer's pleas, however. He does what he can to reassure the officer by telling him that, while he does disapprove of the torture procedure, he would never betray the officer's confidence. And the explorer closes with the reminder that any doubts he has about the procedure will be voiced to the Commandant only in private, not in public.

Apparently not completely reassured by this, the chastened officer proclaims, "Then the time has come," and frees the prisoner from the apparatus. He takes a new paper out of a leather wallet and shows it to the explorer. While the explorer cannot read the words written on the paper, the officer insists that the paper contains the words "Be Just." Taking this paper to the Designer, the officer then spends some minutes readjusting the controls on the machinery so that – presumably – the apparatus will inscribe this new commandment on the body of a new prisoner. He then doffs his uniform and stands before the explorer naked, resigned to take the place of the newly freed prisoner. As the text says,

Now he stood naked there. The explorer bit his lips and said nothing. He knew very well what was going to happen, but he had no right to obstruct the officer in anything. If the judicial procedure which the officer cherished were really so near its end – possibly as a result of his own intervention, as to which he felt himself pledged – then the officer was doing the right thing; in his place the explorer would not have acted otherwise.

The officer then proceeds to lie down on the bed of the apparatus and commands the soldier to strap him in. Unexpectedly, the apparatus begins to malfunction at this very moment. As the Designer box spits out its cogwheels one after another, the helpless officer is then spitted in a rather gruesome fashion on the harrow of the now out-of-control machine. The explorer notes: "this was no exquisite torture such as the officer desired, this was plain murder." As the harrow lifts the mauled body of the officer over the pit, the explorer is finally moved to take a definite action, demanding that the reluctant soldier and the freed prisoner help him to ease the body of the poor man off the arm of the apparatus:

But the other two could not make up their minds to come; the condemned man actually turned away; the explorer had to go over to them and force them into position at the officer's head. And here, almost against his will, he had to look at the face of the corpse. It was as it had been in life; no sign was visible of the promised redemption; what the others had found in the machine the officer had not found; the lips were firmly pressed together, the eyes were open, with the same expression as in life, the look was calm and convinced, through the forehead went the point of the great iron spike.

2

Kafka's story "In the Penal Colony," written sometime around 1914 by a rather gloomy clerk living in Prague during the waning days of the Austro-Hungarian Empire, is a classic story about colonization, penality, and bureaucratic manners. Like most of Kafka's stories, it floats in an allegorical free space, cut free of overt reference to any particular place or time, and consequently, evocative of many places and many times. Yet, in its preoccupation with bureaucracy, the story is recognizably the work of a twentieth-century European writer. Kafka seems to catalogue in his fiction the central anxieties of Europeans in the first half of the twentieth century: anxiety about the specter of organized, state-directed, and highly efficient terror; fear of the threat state power poses to the individual subject; the tribulations occasioned by the process of decolonization; and the unsettling belief, inherited from Christianity but soon to be discredited by the experience of World War I, that self-sacrifice ennobles whatever cause it serves no matter how corrupt or questionable.

I have briefly summarized Kafka's narrative here simply to suggest that the story encapsulates many of the main themes of this book. "In the Penal Colony" is a story about: 1) how bureaucrats manufacture a teleologically ordered history; 2) how the manufacture of this kind of history involves the inversion of the ordinary relationship of agent to instrument; 3) how the imperial bureaucrat comes to imagine his own mastery as a peculiar form of self-sacrifice – and especially, as an erotically charged, masochistically tinged, form of service to some higher power or higher ideal; and 4) how, through the alchemy of self-sacrificial abjection, he finds himself translated to a higher sphere of power.

The chapters that follow examine the narrative construction of a certain type of European bureaucratic subject – a subject perhaps now all-too-familiar to those of us who have been living in a world analyzed with such precision by Kafka. While some of the writers I examine wrote in the early part of the twentieth century, my main interest here is in the Victorian determinations of the type of subject they wrote about, a subject constructed during the high noon of European expansion to accomplish the work which is rule. While I focus my attention here mainly on writers who had some experience working in lands which were, or would eventually become, components of the British Empire, I do so to make a larger point about how an ideology of bureaucratic work was evolving toward crisis by the time of World War I. What I will call here the dual subject position of the European bureaucrat takes a number of forms, all of which are related – agent and instrument, author and character, perpetrator and victim, master and slave. While the management theories of Lord Cromer and Frederick Lugard (discussed in Chapter 1) project an ideal bureaucratic type who is somehow comfortable living within these dualities and is willing to seem to take a less histrionic part on the stage of history, and while actual imperial rule nonetheless often required the management of colonized people in what could be a brutally obvious way not envisioned by the theory, the Empire was merely a privileged stage on which England played out a larger ambivalence about the exercise of power over people. To put it another way: this book is about how the bureaucrat justifies writing on bodies by submitting his own body to be written upon.

Chapter 1 discusses the historical context in which this imperial bureaucratic ethos evolved. I argue that the politics of imperial competition at the end of the nineteenth century helped to push British society in the direction of rapid bureaucratization. My conclusions are twofold: 1) that the British Empire expanded rapidly in the late nineteenth and early twentieth centuries most directly under the prompting and through the supervision of a growing professional managerial elite; and 2) that British writers found imperial service to be the best stage for dramatizing the evolution of bureaucratic power and a bureaucratic ideology, for it was in imperial service, above all, that work became rule. In discussing Lord Cromer in Chapter 1, I mean to locate in his theorization of Indirect Rule the intellectual outlines within which the debate over bureaucratic power in the colonies was to take place. Cromer's pose of intellectual modesty and other-serving reformism helps position him as the chief spokesman for a benevolent extension of imperial rule at the very beginning of the worldwide "Scramble" for colonies officially sanctioned by the Congress of Berlin in 1885. Cromer was able to tap into the moral energy of "humanitarianism" and siphon much of it to support a project which led to a vast expansion of British imperial responsibilities. But he was able to do so by identifying the actual instruments of such a "forward" policy as self-abnegating moral heroes finally putting the world on a sound footing once and for all. Implicit in Cromer's discussion of empire as "moral" service is the idea that the self-sacrifice of the imperial bureaucrat is the chief indicator of the value of imperial rule.

Chapter 2 steps back in time from Cromer to consider one of the important ways in which an evolving ideology of bureaucratic rule comes to lay claim to a portion of the world little known to Europeans of the 1830s: Sub-Saharan Africa. In this chapter I discuss the best-known Victorian traveler/adventurers of their day – David Livingstone and Henry M. Stanley. My contention is that the younger man's eventual eclipse of the elder marks a culturally significant movement from ethnographic/missionary adventuring that is significantly independent of the exercise of bureaucratic power (Livingstone's "solitary" explorations of South Central Africa in the years 1849–1855) to that which is deeply beholden to large-scale organization (Stanley's large-scale exploration of the Congo River, 1874–1877). When Stanley published *Through the Dark Continent* on his return to Europe in 1878, his catalogue of Africa's needs – "tramways," better communications, centralized political authority – testifies to his inability to distinguish between the needs of a large-scale European exploratory safari and the needs of the African tribes among whom he moved, as well as to his convenient loss of consciousness of the disruptive impact of his own private army (at one time numbering 350 men) on the African peoples among whom he traveled. Stanley's travelogue was one of the most influential and compelling Victorian attempts to construct Africa as a space of need: a continent, in short, which lacks on a grand scale what Europe has. While it almost goes without saying now that this reinvention of Africa ultimately served European colonialist rather than African needs, the project is particularly significant for my argument because of Stanley's inadvertent demonstration of how the practical necessities of a large-scale exploratory safari determine the construction of this "needy" Africa. In this sense, Stanley's travelogue dramatizes, however inadvertently, the important loss of awareness that the bureaucratic reinvention of history imposes on Europeans, a loss which will only later on, in the twentieth century, be lamented as the loss of any alternatives to the dominant historical narratives of "modernization" and "progress."

The subject of Chapter 3 is Rudyard Kipling, arguably the most important literary celebrator of bureaucracy. Yet Kipling's notably ambivalent writings are the place in which the Darwinian thematic of "systemic intentionality" and the Cromeresque emphasis on bureaucratic invisibility are most clearly joined together under the rubric of "The Law." While some of his early "Indian stories" (and especially *Kim*) celebrate a vision of imperial harmony clearly based on the efficient functioning of a bureaucratic hierarchy, *The Jungle Books* give a deliberately biological turn to the notion of "Law" while, nevertheless, managing to promise anything but a simplistic harmony. In fact, the scale of violence in *The Jungle Books* not only sutures Darwinian law into human history (Mowgli's accomplishments are deliberately of epic proportions), but comes close to dissolving the conventional distinction between lawful and lawless behavior. In Kipling, the Darwinian thematic of "systemic intentionality" is explicitly connected with a recognizably bureaucratic model of social order projected back into an evolutionary past. In this sense, one of the most important ideological functions of works like *The Jungle Books* is to "naturalize" and thereby domesticate bureaucratic forms of social order, to make the historically contingent ideology of bureaucratic service seem a reasonable response to the imperatives of nature.

Chapter 4 discusses the work of Joseph Conrad. Arguably the most important literary critic of bureaucracy before Kafka, Conrad is important to this project, for his major novels (*Lord Jim*, *Heart of Darkness*, and *Nostromo*) examine how teleological narratives of history become institutionalized and thus resistant to change. Moreover, Conrad's attention to the limitations of individual agency in history is undergirded by a prescient insight into how the bureaucratic organization of work under European capitalism invests otherwise meaningless work with value. Conrad was aware, to an unusual extent, of how bureaucracies institutionalize historical metanarratives which then, in circular fashion, come to serve their own professional interests. Conrad's novels are thus about how professionals justify what they do by casting themselves in heroic roles in self-serving historical narratives.

In his emphasis on invisible management, Cromer constructed an archetype of colonial rule which lays stress on secret manipulation, indirect suggestion, and the exercise of power in such a way as to make it invisible in its effects: power no one has exercised can be seen as power exercised, somehow, by the victim of power. The unstated political and professional burden of Cromer's theory was to shift attention away from the conventional goals of the exercise of power and onto the means, and, by so doing, to ground the exercise of imperial power, for the European colonialist at any rate, in a self-sacrificial ethos. Thus, in Cromer's vision, the personal satisfactions of bureaucratic management for the individual manager lie, paradoxically, in the disavowal of public recognition. This self-abnegating professional ethos is simply a recirculated form of the traditional renunciatory ethos of Victorian middle-class culture. Yet, renunciation is not simply the forbidding ascetic ideal it may seem to most twentieth-century readers. Renunciation, in fact, holds out the promise of its own unique gratifications. In investing self-sacrifice with the libidinal, if purely vicarious, meanings of self-negation, it can become powerfully attractive for the "right sort" of individual, who derives an implicitly erotic pleasure from selfless service.

The problematic figure of T. E. Lawrence, who is the subject of Chapter 5, is the historical figure best exemplifying the practical efficacy of this strategy of rule and yet also the one who most clearly dramatizes the contradictory emotions – psychological and political – that Indirect Rule imposes on the ruler. *Seven Pillars of Wisdom*, Lawrence's account of his years of involvement with Prince Feisal in the creation and successful execution of the Arab Revolt against imperial Turkey, is traced by the contradictions which underlie his own self-construction as "Lawrence of Arabia": tormented by the complexities of his multifold political role in Arabia – slave to English geopolitical objectives in the wake of the Sykes–Picot accord, master/servant of the antithetical idea of Arab nationhood, and leader of men in a new kind of war – Lawrence oscillates back and forth between the libidinal and professional attractions of what he calls "happy slavery" and the harshly forbidding conditions of political and military mastery. In Lawrence, the renunciatory ethos of bureaucratic professionalism, promising a grandiose expansion of responsibility at the price of renunciation of recognition except by knowing bureaucratic superiors, is condensed in his post-war career: having returned from the Versailles Peace Conference in 1919 to attend – anonymously – Lowell Thomas's lectures about the unacknowledged "King of Arabia" – himself – he then retreats to subaltern anonymity in the guise of, first, "Aircorpsman Ross" and, then, "Private Shaw," characters ultimately recognized by their commanding officers for their important, if decidedly unheroic, abilities as good typists and morale boosters among the enlisted men.

Chapter 6 argues that during the interwar period the novel of "imperial manners" evolves into a novel of "official manners" in the work of the Modernist figures George Orwell and Joyce Cary, both of whom had first-hand experience in British colonial possessions, and both of whom were writing in a period in which the imperial optimism of Cromer's generation had been thoroughly discredited – at least among members of the intellectual class. These anti-imperial writers detach the "law" from its embedding in either the cosmos or Darwinian natural order, rendering empire as a field of conflict over what amounts to manners. Writing in the aftermath of World War I, these figures imagine the Empire in terms that help codify a recognizably twentieth-century ambivalence about the large-scale exercise of power: an ossified bureaucratic structure, resistant to change, and oppressive in its auto-cratic claim to a monopoly on modernization, the Empire both gives officials work to do and insures, however inadvertently, that that work is emptied of larger significance and value.

# CHAPTER I

# Agents and the problem of agency: the context

Mother, far, oh far from me
Is the land of my first years,
Is the land of my first tears,
Where your love and charity,
Where your faithful mother's heart
Lavished care upon your boy,
Shared all with him, tears and joy,
Prompt in healing every smart . . .
Folk might think Fate cruelly tore
In two the bond that made us one . . .
True, I stand on a strange shore
With myself and God, alone . . .
But yet, whatsoe'er the grief,
Pleasure or pain I may have had,
Mother hold to your belief
In the love of your own lad!
                    Edouard Douwes Dekker, *Max Havelaar*

Middle-class Victorians were, to put it mildly, of two minds on the subject of "bureaucracy." While the term itself was always used in a pejorative sense (it was principally associated with inefficiency, the suppression of individual freedom, and what would come to be called economic "irrationality"), Victorian Britons were nonetheless mightily proud of the accomplishments of both their efficiently-managed businesses at home and their well-drilled armies abroad.[1] By 1871, many had also been greatly impressed by the German military machine, which seemed to have demonstrated through its rapid but crushing victory over France that large-scale organization and efficiency were not necessarily incompatible things. However much nineteenth-century British culture celebrated the myth of the heroic individual (both in the "self-help" books of Samuel Smiles and in the later imperial hagiographies of such writers as G. A. Henty and Maud Diver, for example) and however much middle-class Britons professed to be repelled by the spectacle of human beings ordered to behave with the precision of machines, Victorians were actually infatuated with the power exercised by large, efficient organizations.

The middle-class public were usually able to feed this infatuation only by overlooking the incompatibility between their individualist ideology and their desire to transform the world through power, for the transformation of the world often required that others, not quite so fortunate, be reduced to mere instruments of power. Indeed, the best-known examples of this loss of consciousness appear in Britain before the Victorian age, in the early days of the Industrial Revolution in fact, when the celebration of individual initiative and autonomy was at its height. In those heady days of the reinvention of human labor power, many of the mill owners given to very public professions of faith in individual initiative were also responsible for the systematic reduction of the highly individual skills of traditional craft labor to the undifferentiated – and readily replaceable – labor power of the world's first industrial proletariat, a reduction which made the Industrial Revolution possible.[2] The sacrifice of individual autonomy by the vast majority of the working population seems to have been a necessary precondition for the success of industrialization.

That this "proletarianization" of the English working class was in obvious contradiction to the celebration of individual agency which would become the dominant note of an emerging middle-class ideology in the Victorian period almost goes without saying. Yet what is striking is the persistence of the contradictory strains throughout the century. The conceptual categories of early-Victorian middle-class culture actually fostered a highly ambivalent celebration of both industrial power and individualism. By the time Britain's industrial might was put on public display at the Crystal Palace exhibition of 1851, the celebratory voices threatened to drown out the voices of those who would try to remind Britain how much industrialization had cost: specifically, how much less personal autonomy nineteenth-century industrial workers enjoyed than their predecessors in eighteenth-century craft work. By 1851, as Britain was entering its longest period of sustained economic growth and relative labor peace, triumphant industrialism had become what Conrad would later call "a fact." Cobbett's rural rides, the Charter, and the best-laid plans of the Owenites increasingly faded from public memory.

The ambivalence about large organizations which was encoded in

Victorian middle-class ideology had roots in an Enlightenment critique of governmental power and celebration of private initiative. The liberal orthodoxy which was forming in the early-Victorian era often drew rigid conceptual lines between large-scale organizations seen as grossly inefficient and reactionary aristocratic fiefdoms (government, usually; what Weber would later call the "bureaucratic agency") and those it saw as mainly beneficent organizations disciplined by the "invisible hand" of the market and ultimately working, so it was believed, to produce a higher standard of living for the population through dedication to the miraculous incentive of private profit (industrial firms, primarily; especially, during the so-called "First Industrial Revolution," textile firms, Weber's "bureaucratic enterprises").[3] What might have grown into a more general argument among early-Victorian Britons over bureaucratic power and individual autonomy usually took the form of a more narrowly focused dispute over the value of only one type of bureaucracy – government.

In short, most middle-class Britons of the Victorian age tended to see large-scale organization in the private sphere as something good and large-scale organization in the public sphere as something bad. This now-dominant dichotomization of bureaucratic structures, which in the twentieth century takes the form of "public" and "private" sectors, had been anticipated in the founding text of political economy, Adam Smith's *Wealth of Nations*, which was published in 1776.[4] Smith's view of government as an ossified structure dedicated to preserving aristocratic privileges while stifling economic innovation has understandably been characterized as the grandfather of the Victorian doctrine of *laissez-faire*. In fact, the "science" of political economy in general had its origins in a radical political critique of "government" (i.e. of institutionalized aristocratic privilege). For the nineteenth-century heirs of Smith, men such as Ricardo, Bentham, Cobden, and J. S. Mill, the exercise of governmental power was identified as a major problem of the day, although it is important to note that Utilitarian philosophy and its "greatest happiness" principle would ultimately be used to sanction an eventual expansion of state power and responsibilities.[5] Nevertheless, most middle-class liberals of the 1830s and 40s tended to see government as a reactionary structure dedicated to preserving and enhancing the privileges of the landed classes at the expense of the middle class and the poor. Despite the modest widening of the voting franchise which the Reform Act of 1832 accomplished, middle-class suspicion of government power remained widespread during this period, becoming especially noticeable during the Corn Law controversy of the "Hungry 40s," when, despite widespread hunger in the countryside, Parliament refused to reduce the tariff on imported grain in order to preserve the economic privileges of the landed class. The behavior of Parliament during the crises of the 1840s taught a whole generation of middle-class liberals cautionary lessons about governmental power. For these liberals of Dickens' generation, government was a doubtful agent of social reform, for not only was it responsible for reinforcing the privileges of the landed class while devising new punishments for the poor through the New Poor Law, but it seemed to operate day-to-day as a "Circumlocution Office," employing aristocratic "Barnacles" dedicated to bureaucratic self-aggrandizement and the stifling of middle-class enterprise.

Yet change was in the offing. The decades immediately preceding the outbreak of World War I would see an intensification of the ideological conflict between government power and private power – what Perkin calls the "master conflict of professional society" in the twentieth century – but with what would eventually be called "the public sector" eventually accorded greater, if grudging, respectability. Although the modern welfare state bureaucracies are chiefly a creation of the post-World War II period, the first organized social welfare institutions in Britain – Trade Boards, Labour Exchanges, and Social Insurance – were created during the Edwardian era. Moreover, the Edwardian period would also see the beginnings of serious attempts by the national government to rationalize the organization of the Army in the interests of greater military efficiency, something which the German government had accomplished almost forty years earlier. Thus, the creation of the Committee of Imperial Defence at the end of Balfour's prime ministership insured the coordination of Army and Navy planning for the first time while making military management relatively independent of changes in the party in power. The formation of the first military General Staff – modeled on the German General Staff – likewise dates from 1905.[6] Not coincidentally, these rather dramatic departures from *laissez-faire* traditions roughly corresponded with the official end of aristocratic rule in Britain, as, in the early days of George V's reign, the House of Lords finally lost its veto over legislation originating in the House of Commons.

These departures from previous policy were prepared by the ripening of a new professional class ethos over the course of the nineteenth century. Perkin discusses this issue in his recent book *The Professionalization of English Society*. He argues that the first signs that "professional" class ideals are beginning to diverge from the ideals of the business class are visible as early as the 1830s, as a group of middle-class social reformers, growing in influence through an alliance of convenience with certain members of the landed class who were hostile to the abuses of industrialism, begin to question the widespread faith in the god of *laissez-faire:*

The principles of competition, individualism and *laissez-faire*, which for the capitalist class and the early classical economists had achieved the status of laws of nature as inexorable as the law of gravity, came progressively to be questioned by professional social thinkers, civil servants and even by economists, and their restrictions and reservations found their way into legislation, over the protests of the business class. The Factory and Mines Acts from the 1830s and 1840s, the public health legislation from 1848 onwards, the Food and Drugs Adulteration and Alkali (anti-pollution) Acts of the 1860s, and the state's increasing support of education culminating in the 1870 Act, can be seen as one long campaign orchestrated by (though not confined to) the professional class against the vested interests of the propertied classes.[7]

While the chief challenge to *laissez-faire* in the early-Victorian period often came from reformers appalled by how the Industrial Revolution seemed to be laying waste the lives of the industrial proletariat, the maturation of the professional class ideology at the end of the nineteenth century had perhaps much more to do with accelerating imperial competition at that time. With the dawn of the "age of national efficiency," the Victorian middle class became increasingly preoccupied with the fear that Britain was not up to the challenge of competition with its imperial rivals in Europe, especially with what was beginning to look like an increasingly menacing German Empire flush with success after Bismarck's swift victory over France in 1870. By the time the "Scramble for Africa" was inaugurated by the Congress of Berlin in 1885, many would come to see success in the game of empire as the chief indicator of economic and social health (or illness). Ironically, however, this was often accompanied by the fear that Britain's addiction to individual initiative (the original source, it was widely believed, of its economic dominance in the world) left it vulnerable to better-organized and more "efficient" rival powers. The Empire had come to be seen, finally, as the key to economic and political success, as writers as diverse and influential as Seeley, Froude, and Dilke, and political leaders not necessarily associated with traditional Toryism, such as Joseph Chamberlain, believed.[8]

But what about imperial rule helped to relax the firm grip of *laissez-faire* on the minds of the British middle class? The rapid expansion of the

British Empire meant a proliferation of new geopolitical interests, and the management of these growing interests in an atmosphere of intensifying worldwide imperial competition over the course of the nineteenth century often required the large-scale use of military power – sometimes even by committed liberals who were ideologically averse to it (Gladstone stands as the best example). Moreover, military success itself often has a way of causing the public to overlook the size of the operation responsible for producing success. When military adventures are successful, their scale can be easily forgiven – or forgotten (as Americans were to learn during the Gulf War of 1990; Britons after the Falklands conflict of 1982). By contrast, when military success is difficult to achieve or comes only at great cost, as in Crimea in the 1850s or on the Western Front in World War I, the chief complaint is often about the bureaucratic incompetence of the military hierarchy which has somehow prevented "our boys" from efficiently accomplishing the task at hand.

The British middle class, however, remained deeply divided throughout the nineteenth century over the question of how large the Empire should be allowed to grow. For much of the century, middle-class views of empire were dominated by the seemingly irreconcilable positions of the "humanitarian" movement and the Manchester School. The former grew out of the Clapham Sect, which pressured Britain to outlaw slavery at home (1807) and in its colonial domains (1833), and the mid-Victorian champion of what would eventually be called the "humanitarian" movement was the Scottish missionary David Livingstone, popularly known as an heroic figure working alone against great odds to stamp out slavery on the African continent and to bring the benefits of free trade to Africans sunk in "primitive" darkness. The best-known champion of anti-imperialist free trade in the mid-Victorian period was the spokesman for Manchester industrial interests, Richard Cobden, whose writings popularized the dogma inherited from Adam Smith: a dogma which conceives of empire as nothing but an unwarranted drain on the national treasury, and protectionism (or "imperial federation" as its late nineteenth-century exponent, Joseph Chamberlain, would call it) as the cause of economic backwardness. While few contemporaries saw Livingstone and Cobden as articulating wholly irreconcilable positions, there is no question that, despite some overlap, both ideological positions harbor strongly antithetical tendencies that would appear only intermittently on the surface.

Mid-Victorian "humanitarianism" was implicitly (and sometimes explicitly) expansionist (as I will demonstrate in more detail in Chapter 2), and its "imperialism" would become much more evident after 1850: not only in its moral aims, which would eventually require as the price of their realization a massive disruption of African ways of life, but in its economic aims as well, for free trade, Livingstone's chief prescription for the ills that plague Africa, requires the radical restructuring of pre-capitalist societies as a prerequisite.[9] The "humanitarian" movement was, in short, gradually to draw Britain into exercising power on a large scale in Africa in an attempt to remake African societies in order to fit them to the demands of a free-trading capitalism from which Africans were supposed to benefit. Livingstone's position inevitably led to the projection of a drastic "modernization" of black Africa, a position which would inevitably require the extension of the formal organs of imperial control if for no other reason than to protect the soon-to-be-free-trading tribes of South and Central Africa from white adventurers and Arab slavers.

Clearly responsive to the *laissez-faire* ideology of the mid-Victorian industrial middle class, on the other hand, Cobdenite radicals mainly opposed expansionist schemes, which Cobden himself saw as interfering with virtually the only proper function of government – the promotion of free trade.[10] Cobden's "anti-imperial free trade" ideology derived, again, from Adam Smith, who discussed sugar production in a well-known passage in *The Wealth of Nations*: primary production, he argued there, need not be monopolized, because the key to the wealth of nations lies, not in the monopolization of primary production, but in the value added to primary products by the manufacture of secondary products and the whole new industries which are created as a result. Applying this economic standard, Cobdenites could see no more reason for Britain to exercise political domination over areas of the world that produce primary products such as palm oil (to cite just one example of a West African commodity which actually did play a crucial role in the imperial politics of the late nineteenth century) than there would be in the city of Manchester exercising direct political control over the southern United States, which just happened to supply most of Manchester's cheap cotton throughout much of the nineteenth century. Manchester does not need to rule South Carolina to guarantee a continuing supply of inexpensive cotton; it need only buy South Carolina's cotton at the lowest possible price: something which will be guaranteed by South Carolina's plantation owners' following their own economic self-interest and by the existence of worldwide competition among all primary producers – by, in other words, the competitive rationality of free-trading capitalism as a system.

The Livingstonian and Cobdenite positions are ultimately irreconcilable, not only because they seem to project opposite views of future British policy toward the non-European world, but because they begin from irreconcilable assumptions about the role of governmental power. Where Livingstone assumes that British policy ought to be a disinterested – but active and ultimately large-scale – pursuit of "humanitarian" ideals requiring – if need be – large-scale military intervention, Cobden holds that British policy ought to steer away from imperialist projects and allow Britain's cheap manufactured goods to conquer worldwide markets "naturally."[11]

These antithetical tendencies in mid-Victorian ideology led to an ideologically muddled yet nonetheless gradual expansion of the British Empire in the period between the Congress of Vienna in 1815 and the Congress of Berlin in 1885 (a date with symbolic importance because it was the date on which the assembled European powers first officially endorsed the attitude that imperial conquest is what Great Powers do with their power). In fact, the dominant political figure of this mid-Victorian era, the man who stood for the most "forward" of imperial positions within British governing circles (Viscount Palmerston), is himself associated less with official imperial aggrandizement than he is with a policy of the metropolitan government following the lead of private companies and individuals and then stepping in to establish order – and doing it all on the cheap. As Robinson and Gallagher argue, Palmerstonian imperialism was a policy of deliberate compromise, an attempt to merge the concerns of free traders with those of more traditional Tory imperialists.[12] Like many Victorian prime ministers when they finally reached office, Palmerston usually acted not to fulfill some grand imperial strategy but rather to appease the contradictory political demands of the moment.

Yet the fact remains that Victorian Britain was an important military power in Europe and possessed the world's foremost empire (although only Disraeli publicly dared to call it by such a grand name until the 1880s), and neither military success nor imperial expansion could have been accomplished without a large-scale use of bureaucratic power and discipline.[13] The 1850s saw two events of signal importance in British attitudes toward its rule over its overseas domains: the Crimean War and the Indian "Mutiny" of 1857. The length and costliness of the former turned the attention of the nation toward the incompetence of the aristocrat-dominated military hierarchy; the shock of the latter would lead to the national government's assuming direct responsibility for governing India in the wake of what was widely felt to be the East India Company's manifest incompetence.[14] These two events would lead, in time, to an assertion of greater control by the national government over both the military and the empire, diminishing – eventually and only very gradually – the power, influence, and independence of aristocratic elites much as the creation of the civil service examination would eventually open up the national government to the broad middle class based on merit rather than family connection.[15] Moreover, this gradual evolution would be accompanied by a growing preoccupation among British intellectuals in the late-Victorian era with improving the "efficiency" of the Empire, part of a larger ideological transition marking the coming-to-power of the "professional class" and the maturation of its governing ideology of "national efficiency," an ideology grounded in a notion of systemic functionality. Thus, Seeley's famous call, in his 1881 book *The Expansion of England,* for Britain to assume willing responsibility for its expanding empire, many of the territories of which, he asserted, had originally been acquired in a national "fit of absentmindedness," testifies to a more general felt need emerging in the late Victorian period to systematize imperial expansion and rationalize its administration: to convert half-hearted and accidental expansionism into purposeful imperialism.[16]

The 1880s and 90s would thus see some important changes in middle-class attitudes toward the exercise of bureaucratic forms of power, prompted partly by growing competitive pressures from the other Great Powers. As Victoria's reign gave way to Edward VII's, it had become clear to many in Britain, especially in the professional middle class, that the direction of the future lay largely in the hands of efficient, large-scale organizations; that Standard Oil and the German General Staff foretold the coming age; Watt, Stephenson, Clive, and Lord Lawrence represented the past; that the future would increasingly be shaped less by the individual efforts of the Napoleonic or Carlylean hero than by the much more impressive corporate power of well-organized agglomerations, well-oiled machines. If the 1850s marked the high point in the liberal celebration of the ideology of *laissez-faire* individualism and its related critique of bureaucratic bungling, the 1880s and 90s ushered in an atmosphere more favorable to bureaucracy as a mode of social organization and a means for accomplishing large tasks – at least among the professional classes.

Of course, the popular discourse of this period – and especially popular art dedicated to celebrating the achievements of Empire – dominated as it was by the myths of individual heroism, remained hostile to this emerging bureaucratic ethos. Indeed, as I will argue later, one of the chief signs that the British social order was becoming more "bureaucratic" was the intensity with which its popular culture celebrated an anti-bureaucratic ethos of individual heroism. And this rule held, above all, in treatments of the Empire. In the latter part of the nineteenth century, the Empire was being sold to the masses as a space for the exercise of individual initiative, a space of adventure offering almost unlimited possibilities for self-transcendence. Disraeli anticipated this. His 1872 Crystal Palace speech, in which he calls on middle-class Britons to reconceive their Empire as something like an employment agency for their sons, captures perfectly this linkage of Empire and individual initiative:

England will have to decide between national and cosmopolitan principles. The issue is not a mean one. It is whether you will be content to be a comfortable England, modelled and moulded upon continental principles and meeting in due course an inevitable fate, or whether you will be a great country – an Imperial country – a country where your sons, when they rise, rise to paramount positions, and obtain not merely the esteem of their countrymen, but command the respect of the world.[17]

While Disraeli seems to have been mainly motivated by the desire to turn the attention of the British middle class away from its recent "humanitarian" preoccupation with the sorry lot of the "uncivilized" and toward the more enticing spectacle of power wielded for the sake of the powerful, his celebration of empire as a field for the exercise of individual initiative would, by the end of the century, become the dominant way in which British popular discourse would connect the middle-class ideology of "self-help" to a more ancient Tory infatuation with conquest.

Yet even Disraeli's confident assumption that England was actually free to conquer and rule as she saw fit would already seem naïve in the atmosphere of intensifying Great Power competition of the 80s and 90s. By then, a growing unease about the security of Britain's position in the world took the form of growing fears, confined, at first, mainly to the professional and governing classes, about the fitness of Britain to actually compete successfully with the other Powers – and implicitly, about the ability of an individualist society to contend successfully with its powerful continental rival Germany, which had seemed from the time of its unification to have been wholly dedicated to the cause of "national efficiency." Perhaps the most representative treatment of this theme at the time is Arnold White's *Efficiency and Empire* (published in 1901), a book which G. R. Searle has characterized as "an attempt to discredit the habits, beliefs, and institutions that put the British at a handicap in their competition with foreigners and to commend instead a social organization that more closely followed the German model."[18]

Much of Matthew Arnold's social criticism anticipates the turn-of-the-century preoccupation with national efficiency. In trumpeting a collectivist (and recognizably "continental") notion of the "state" as an anodyne to the British disease of anarchic individualism – "doing as one likes" – Arnold's *Culture and Anarchy* looks forward to later, less generous, attacks on the British "Philistine" class from within that class itself. By the 1880s and 90s, the growing distinction between business and professional class ideals would become much more visible, as the individualist ideology of the business class came more and more into conflict with the professional class ideal of "social efficiency" at home and "imperial efficiency" abroad.[19] In time, the middle-class professionals of the emerging service industries would become the most vocal critics of industrial civilization and the business class ideology of *laissez-faire*: producing the first statistically based studies of poverty such as Charles Booth's *Life and Labour of the People in London*, and offering in the place of the ideology of *laissez-faire*, "the professional ideal of an elitist society run by professional experts."[20]

The best examples of this are to be found in the work of the Fabians. Semmel discusses how the Fabian interest in affecting government policy through "permeation" led most Fabians toward a pro-imperial position by the end of the Boer War.[21] Thereafter, the "Coefficients," the Fabian dining club, would increasingly divide, not over the question of the worth of empire, but rather over the relative merits of "free trade empire" versus protectionism through "imperial federation." Sidney Webb himself was a product of the imperial bureaucracy, having spent the first thirteen years of his working life as an employee of, successively, the War Office and the Colonial Office, rising from lower-division clerk in the former to second-class clerk in the West Indian Department of the latter. He left the Colonial Office in 1891.[22]

Popular novels depicting invasions of the British homeland appear as early as the 1870s, providing evidence of growing worries about the security of British hegemony even at the very moment of Britain's economic and military predominance in the world. Yet, despite the evident anxiety, the most notable response of the "professional" class to the growing threat of Germany at the end of the century is its remarkably "positive" faith in the possibility of reforming the British social order to insure Britain's future as the most important world power. Surely, the popularity of Rudyard Kipling among the professional class tells us a great deal about the new receptiveness of this class to collective – and, ultimately, bureaucratic – solutions to a variety of social and imperial "problems" which were held to be symptomatic of this "decline."[23] As the poet laureate of the disciplinary imagination, Kipling enjoyed an enviably positive public reception which testified to a new readiness to dedicate the British social order to the newly emerging collective ideals of "national efficiency": in short, to prepare what was already the world's largest empire for continuing success in its imperial competition with the other Great Powers.

The fear of decline is not a new thing for successful empires, of course. Contrary to what it seems, a growing fear of decline is often a sign that a country has finally achieved political and economic preeminence in the world. And certainly this seemed to be the position of Great Britain in the 1880s and 90s. Although recently untested in continental warfare and having one of the smallest armies among the Great Powers of Europe, Britain nonetheless possessed the largest empire the world had ever seen, the largest and most modern navy, the most productive economy, and, as a direct result of almost a century of economic preeminence, a vast reserve of surplus capital which was being invested in everything from Indian and North American railway stocks to Argentinean cattle ranching to South African gold and diamond mines.[24]

Yet a long agricultural depression, lasting from the 1870s through the 1890s, was raising serious questions about how long Britain could sustain its economic preeminence in the world. When combined with growing fears of a long-anticipated continental war in which superior German ground forces would render British naval preeminence useless; with increasing "Social Darwinist" suspicions that the national physical "type" might well be "degenerating" (suspicions which grew widespread during and immediately after the Boer War, when the deteriorating physical condition of the British working class was documented statistically by Army recruiters); with a growing anxiety about Britain's failure to match Germany's pace of technical and scientific education and innovation (about which the British public had been warned as early as 1868 by Arnold's *Higher Schools and Universities in Germany*); and with the prophecies of intellectuals such as Seeley and Froude about the coming economic and military predominance of the sleeping giants Russia and the United States, the Great Depression worked to corrode the unblushing self-confidence that had seemed so characteristic of the mid-Victorian temper.[25]

It was in the imperial field that the liberal attitude toward the two types of bureaucracies identified by Weber would become most strained, for it was here that liberal ambivalence about the exercise of power had deeply unpopular consequences. Perhaps the most dramatic staging of this ambivalence occurred during the Sudan crisis of the early 1880s: the Gladstone government's indecisive approach to the relief of Khartoum and its own beleaguered agent, General "Chinese" Gordon, led Gladstone to lose a great deal of political capital – as Gordon lost his head.[26] Thereafter, it would be increasingly risky politically for the British government to fail to exercise decisive power in the imperial field when British agents and British interests were directly at risk. The era of unlimited imperial competition had begun, and with it, the ambivalence of the British middle-class public toward the exercise of government power would be increasingly resolved in a direction favorable, not only to the ideals of "social efficiency" at home, but to expansionism and the efficient – and deadly – exercise of military force abroad. However, as I argue below, there remained a significant gap between theory and practice, and British expansionism was by no means driven by anything that could be called a nationwide consensus on the value of imperialism. The engine of imperial expansion at this time, in fact, would increasingly become the imperial administrative class itself, which was being restructured to meet the new challenges of the era of national efficiency.

2

Many of the intellectuals who set out to explain the causes of British imperial expansion in the period from the late nineteenth century up to World War II were concerned with identifying a specific causal agent. Among writers opposed to imperialism, this process usually leads to the identification of something like an historical "villain" whose fingerprints can be found all over the business of empire-building, even when the causal agent is systemic rather than anthropomorphic. In the case of Hobson and Lenin, for instance, the "villain" is monopoly capitalism. In the case of Schumpeter, the "villain" is an atavistic aristo-military class whose martial values were unaccountably adopted by the late-

Victorian middle classes. However great the differences in political tendency between Lenin and Schumpeter, what their theories share is an addiction to a somewhat simplified model of historical intentionality. All are committed to the belief that empires, like bridges, are designed. Find the engineer and you have identified the intentional consciousness responsible for bringing the bridge into being.[27]

In focusing on the modernization of the imperial administrative class in *The Origins of Totalitarianism*, by contrast, Hannah Arendt examines the ironies that plague this relatively simple mode of historical explanation, to the "unintentional" quality of much – although by no means all – actual empire-building. Arendt argues that those European powers which were bound on a course to master the world in the nineteenth century were not even capable of mastering their own desire for expansion. While one could argue that she has her villains too (colonial bureaucracies and theorists such as Lord Cromer who supported, ran, and justified their continued existence, for instance) she hesitates to identify these in any simple way with the causes of imperial expansion. With Arendt, it becomes possible to speak of imperialism as one more manifestation of the expansive tendencies of the bourgeois state as a system, its expansion fed by the institutionalization of professional class interests in the form of colonial bureaucracies. The conversion of ideas into plans is, in fact, typically an aftereffect: "guiding intentions" are often inferred or imagined after the fact and only retrospectively assigned the role of origin or cause. To put this another way: one of the chief historical effects of expansion is the production of rationalizations for it; it is often only after the fact, and in retrospect, that these rationalizations come to be assigned a privileged role as cause. Moreover, the inversion of the actual order distorts not only the writing of later historians, who often mistake the rationalization for the cause, but the self-conception of the colonial bureaucrat himself, who conveniently comes to see himself as the mere instrument of "higher" intentions or "higher" purposes, rather than the author of them. Moreover, this kind of amnesia becomes a very effective technique for accumulating power, which typically flows downward from "god" to "disciple," agent to instrument. By displacing the source of power, in other words, by portraying themselves as mere instruments of a more powerful – if veiled – other, colonial bureaucrats were able to accumulate a great deal of personal power.

While it may be possible to trace the cause of any particular imperial project to its origin in a geopolitical idea, class or economic interests, national interests, or a growing belief in racial or technological superiority, the cause of Europe's general tendency to global expansion is much more difficult to specify. Undoubtedly Europe's own dynamic social organization played an important role in manufacturing imperial projects, much as its expanding economic power was producing not only new products and services but new needs from the sixteenth century onward. If we take this claim seriously, then it has interesting implications for my position. The cause of British imperial expansion can be seen then as chiefly an "internal" one rather than an "external" one. At least in the case of Britain, the Empire grew because empires, like capitalist businesses, need to grow. Its growth in the late nineteenth and early twentieth centuries was fostered most directly by influential bureaucratic elites whose professional mission it was both to manage a growing empire and to manufacture new justifications for its further expansion. The Empire, in brief, developed its own self-generated momentum when its servants created colonial bureaucracies dedicated to inventing or discovering reasons for further expansion.

The rationalizations which these bureaucrats offer to justify expansionist projects, though, often appear to be afterthoughts, produced to justify in retrospect what Colonial Office self-interest has already dictated is necessary to justify; produced, in short, to lend an intentional quality to actions that escape intentionality. Like the newly-appointed British Commissioner of the Cape Colony, Sir Bartle Frere, in the immediate aftermath of Disraeli's purchase of the Suez Canal in 1876, suddenly faced with the newly manufactured geopolitical "fact" that the Cape Colony no longer lay along the "road to India," the colonial bureaucrat is bound, as a requirement of his job, to justify the work that he performs. In the process of constructing these justifications, he is implicated in fostering the illusion that history can be subjected to intentional control. History, in the view of the managerial class and the educated public the members of this class sought to influence with their writings, has something like the logical concision of conspiracy: it has been (and can continue to be) managed.

While Arendt does not reject the possibility that history has, on occasion, been shaped by conspiratorial intentions, she is rightly suspicious of theories about the causes of imperial expansion that conform rather too neatly to the managerial fantasies of professional administrators of the British Empire. It is no surprise that the expansion and reorganization of imperial bureaucracies throughout the Empire near the end of the nineteenth century corresponded historically with the rise to social prominence of the professional class within England itself (a feature of late-Victorian social life to which I have already referred). Nor can it be surprising that imperial officials would seek to reinforce their professional worth back home through the same credentialing strategies which were then being adopted by the members of other professions. Perkin identifies the general process when he says, "professional society is based on human capital created by education and enhanced by strategies of closure, that is, the exclusion of the unqualified."[28]

The professional colonial administrator in the broadest sense of the term had been around since at least the time of Warren Hastings (if not since the time of Sir Walter Raleigh). Yet Evelyn Baring, Lord Cromer, British advisor to the Egyptian Khedive during the 1880s and perhaps the most influential colonial "proconsul" of the late nineteenth century, was a rather different kind of colonial bureaucrat from these earlier figures. Cromer both typified a new, late-Victorian, class of professional imperial administrator and became, later on in his career, a well-known celebrator of the virtues of the class to which he belonged and for whose interests he spoke. A theorist of colonial administration widely admired for his skillful manipulation of the Khedive, and the creator of the Sudan Political Service in 1901, Cromer offered a new ideological justification of colonial administration that would make the work of empire seem simultaneously vitally important and potentially inexhaustible. With Cromer, empire-building comes to be seen as the domain of the trained expert who is involved in the dual project of performing valuable work in the colonies and discovering the need for ever more work to be done. In Cromer, the expansive dynamic of professional expertise leads to a justification of the bureaucrat's role as the expert who both identifies his object of knowledge and intervenes to reshape it.[29]

In discussing Cromer in *The Origins of Totalitarianism*, Arendt identifies a twofold imperative governing the operation of colonial bureaucrats in the imperial field at the end of the Victorian era: the need for the bureaucrat himself to recede behind the scenes, all the better to promote the objectives of his Colonial Office while dampening and forestalling political resistance to the imperial order within the colony itself, and the need to justify publicly the possession of one part of the earth by arguing that it is essential to the possession and continued control over another part. These two imperatives, the need to govern through local instruments (an imperative given the force of exalted precept when it was codified in the "creed" of Indirect Rule), and the need to govern for an objective which is located beyond the immediate field of imperial contestation (the need, in the broadest sense, to generate new business), are associated by Arendt (perhaps somewhat oddly) both with Cromer and with the megalomaniacal father of the "Cape-to-Cairo" railway scheme in South Africa, Cecil Rhodes. As Arendt sums it up: "The outstanding similarity between Rhodes's rule in South Africa and Cromer's domination of Egypt was that both regarded the countries not as desirable ends in themselves but merely as means for some supposedly higher purpose."[30] In this sense, both Cromer and Rhodes participate in fashioning a rationale for a bureaucratic process "whose very essence is aimless process."[31] And the very absence of easily specified (or publicly admissible) aims inevitably leads to a by now familiar substitution of instrumental purposes for justifiable political goals.

Thus, it was only after he took on the job of advisor to the nominally independent Khedive of Egypt that Cromer managed to discover a rationale for Britain's management of Egypt, a rationale which is the geopolitical opposite of the dilemma faced by Sir Bartle Frere: with Disraeli's purchase of the newly dug Suez Canal in 1876, Egypt – not South Africa – henceforth lay along the "road to India." Like the other South African imperialists, Rhodes was faced at the end of the century with a dilemma created by this newly manufactured fact: the need to create a new justification for extending British power in southern Africa in light of the fact that its public reason for being part of the Empire – its place on the "road to India" – had just fled north to Egypt. As Robinson and Gallagher note, however, it did not take long for such a rationale to be found. The "official mind," which is capable of almost infinite flexibility in this regard, soon took to offering justifications for Britain's continuing to hold the Cape in order to insure the sea route to India – *in the event that the Suez Canal is blocked during war*.[32] In an atmosphere of intensifying European imperial competition at the end of the century, the originally instrumental purpose with which English imperial managers invest particular areas of the world is gradually lost sight of, as the institutional defense of what had once been purely a means tends to establish that means as end. What we have here is the systematic practice of what Conrad's Marlow will call "idolatry": the means for accomplishing some other end displacing the original end itself ("something you can set up, and bow down before, and offer a sacrifice to . . .") and, thus, the conjuring into existence of a justificatory logic potentially flexible enough to rationalize an infinite geographic expansion.[33]

Understandably perhaps, the public face of imperial service at this time was a moral one. Indeed, Cromer had more than a little to do with this. In his own public writings, he falls back on familiarly moral justifications for imperial rule as service: a vision that, nonetheless, has expansive implications, if for no other reason than that grand moral projects, in this postlapsarian world, tend to be inexhaustible. In fact, it was because colonialism was portrayed as a project of moral improvement of the colonized that it acquired such public prestige within Britain in the nineteenth century, a truth to which the popularity of the "humanitarian" movement throughout the century testifies. In his classic statement of bureaucratic paternalism "The Government of Subject Races," which appeared in the *Edinburgh Review* in January 1908, for instance, Cromer returns again and again to the claim that Britain's imperial administrators must take cognizance of the "interests" of the "subject races" in formulating imperial policy: a position which joins the notion of imperial-rule-as-moral-mission to an instrumentalist model of governing. As he puts it in a proto-Deweyan formula, "The main justification of Imperialism is to be found in the use which is made of the Imperial power."[34] However, Cromer is quick to assert that there are limits to how far imperial administrators must actually consult the wishes of the people they rule. Identifying the victims of imperial power as existing *in statu pupillari*, Cromer naturally insists that it is less important to attend to what "they" say are "their" interests than it is to rely on "our" own sense of "their" best interests.[35] The credentialed European expert, whose expertise is ideally proportional to his sense of paternal duty, is necessarily the best source to consult on the needs of "subject races." This is precisely why Cromer salutes Curzon, Viceroy of India at the turn of the century, for Curzon recognized that "the only true justification of Imperialism is to be found in the uses to which Imperial power is applied": applied, it goes without saying, according to Curzon's paternalistic sense of the "best interests" of the "subject races" he supervises.[36]

Yet this instrumentalist defense of empire is notable for the logically prior question that it inevitably forecloses: to locate the ends of empire in the proper exercise of imperial power is to disqualify the prior question about why Britain should rule distant peoples in the first place. It makes such a question unposable, or rather, substitutes a professionally self-justifying answer for the more comprehensive political and philosophical justification which would seem to be called for. The instrumentalist logic of professionalized colonialism thus exacerbates the historical dilemma in which European explorers, adventurers, anti-slavery crusaders, missionaries, and colonial officials were to find them-

selves throughout the course of the nineteenth century. Even the seemingly innocent act of exploration (if sometimes unintentionally) committed these sons and daughters of Britain to an implicit project of drastic
social transformation of the people among whom they worked.
Cromer's instrumentalist rationale for imperial expansion, which allows
the dirty work of empire-building to masquerade as highly moral activity, can now be seen as the public mask donned by naked professional
class interest in a time when colonial expansion was increasingly driven
by bureaucratic self-interest. Like the members of the "helping professions" in the late twentieth century, the professional colonial bureaucrat
has a self-interested stake in producing a certain kind of object to study,
and one of the chief public effects of his intervention, his transformation
of this object, is usually the justification of his own role — the role of the
properly credentialed professional expert. The "imperialism" of professional expertise, in other words, becomes most evident when it is staged
by experts seeking to extend their rule over literal territory. In her
reading of Cromer's rule in Egypt and Rhodes' manipulation of the
British government and the British public in South Africa, Arendt
focuses on the ideological power with which this circular logic of
justification equips the imperial manager:

What overcame Rhodes's monstrous innate vanity and made him discover the
charms of secrecy was the same thing that overcame Cromer's innate sense of
duty: the discovery of an expansion which was not driven by the specific
appetite for a specific country but conceived as an endless process in which
every country would serve only as stepping-stone for further expansion. In view
of such a concept, the desire for glory can no longer be satisfied by the glorious
triumph over a specific people for the sake of one's own people, nor can the
sense of duty be fulfilled through the consciousness of specific services and the
fulfillment of specific tasks. No matter what individual qualities or defects a man
may have, once he has entered the maelstrom of an unending process of
expansion, he will, as it were, cease to be what he was and obey the laws of the
process, identify himself with anonymous forces that he is supposed to serve in
order to keep the whole process in motion; he will think of himself as mere
function, and eventually consider such functionality, such an incarnation of the
dynamic trend, his highest possible achievement.[37]

And the contradictory nature of the colonial manager's dual subject
position – the agent who conceptualizes the goals of imperial expansion
while portraying himself as mere instrument of historical forces larger
than himself – finds expression in Cromer's model of the ideal administrator. Having surrounded himself during his tenure in Egypt with

bureaucrats willing to subordinate the natural human desire for recognition to the bureaucratic need for invisibility, Cromer later transformed this official convenience into a grand principle which could be used to justify imperial rule on self-renunciatory moral grounds, grounds which were quite familiar (and, needless to say, ideologically compelling) to his largely middle-class Victorian and Edwardian audience later in his career when he began to write and lecture about his theories in a public forum. Cromer's style of imperial management required, in Arendt's words, "a highly trained, highly reliable staff whose loyalty and patriotism were somehow disconnected from personal ambition and vanity and who were willing to renounce even the human aspiration of having their names connected with their achievements."[38] As the goal of "ruling wisely" displaces other more conventional public purposes for empire (economic, geopolitical, and so on), the worth of imperial rule comes to be measured increasingly by how much the European servants of empire must sacrifice personally to accomplish the noble ends of rule.

When Cromer established the Sudan Political Service in 1901 to replace Kitchener's military administration of the Sudan, he was able to put many of these bureaucratic ideals into institutional practice. Careful recruiting through personal interviews insured that only men of the "right sort" were sent to the Sudan. The result was a dramatic change in moral tone and administrative efficiency when compared with the rule of the old military administrators, the "Bog Barons," whom they replaced. Unlike the "Bog Barons," who refused to learn Arabic and often kept native mistresses, the new Sudanese Politicals were models of moral restraint operating under the guidance of Cromer's hand-picked governor-general, Sir Reginald Wingate:

Compared to the Bog Barons, the new civilians were models of muscular Christianity and mostly lived up to the high moral tone set by the Sudan's admirable governor-general, Sir Reginald Wingate, and his wife during their sixteen years in Khartoum. News of any liaison reaching Lady Wingate's ears could mean the coldest of receptions at Government House.[39]

As a result, the Sudan Political Service quickly acquired a prestigious reputation within the imperial bureaucracy for efficiency and ethical soundness.

Necessarily, this highly idealized version of bureaucratic service is not completely about self abnegation in the pure sense, just as – Nietzsche reminds us – altruism is never too far from egotism or self-aggrandizement.[40] Even in the mainstream Victorian novel, the cultural form in which selfless service to others is repeatedly celebrated, renunciation and self-effacement are often accompanied by other, compensatory rewards, both for the subject who gives up and for the reader who reads about these acts of renunciatory heroism. The pain of renunciation and self-effacement, in other words, can be accompanied by a refined form of psychological pleasure. The contemporary critic John Kucich identifies this pleasure as "self-negating desire," a pleasurable loss of self which, when indulged in imagination, can serve as psychic compensation for the pain of renunciation. As Kucich says of Charlotte Brontë, Charles Dickens, and George Eliot:

the experience of some form of repressive self-negation, the forceful concentration of energy against inward coherence and the breakdown of the limits of identity, is crucial in all three novelists to expand and eroticize the territory of the self, regardless of how it is produced – or, for that matter, regardless of how this exalted self is inscribed in social relationships.[41]

Cromer, we might say, implicitly holds the ideal imperial bureaucrats of his imagination to lofty standards of self-abnegating heroism analogous to those to which the literary heroines (and heroes) of Eliot, Dickens, and Brontë are held. Moreover, the "exalted, eroticized" self which is produced as an effect of the act of repression is, ironically, the aftereffect of a process which ostensibly seems designed to attenuate rather than to exalt the self. The fact that these administrators return to Britain as anonymous heroes having accomplished a job well done, but a job which typically only their immediate superiors can truly appreciate, bestows on the imperial enterprise itself a seal of moral approval, invariably the reward, at least in Victorian and Edwardian Britain, of "disinterested" behavior anonymously authored.[42] This could hardly be said to have been the case with Cromer himself, however, who became a highly visible writer and speaker; the ideal of contented bureaucratic anonymity may well be a self-serving myth promoted by highly placed imperial administrators. Central to this emerging bureaucratic ethos is the principle that disinterested self-effacement is its own reward, even if the evidence of actual rule makes imperial administrators seem anything but self-effacing background figures.

Thus, in a move which would surprise few of the writers of Victorian fiction, Cromer celebrates the anonymity of bureaucratic job performance as a guarantee of the value of bureaucratic work. Compare the advice Charlotte Brontë's character Helen Burns gives to the ten-year-

old Jane Eyre, mortified by being publicly branded a liar by Brock-
lehurst before the assembled students of Lowood School: "If all the
world hated you, and believed you wicked, while your own conscience
approved you, and absolved you from guilt, you would not be without
friends."[43] To capture the spirit of Cromer's defense of the bureaucratic
type of recognition, all one has to do is to substitute for "conscience"
here an equally lofty but avowedly secular entity – "knowledgeable
higher-ups" who can never publicly acknowledge their approval. Indeed, in Cromer and other defenders of Indirect Rule, the theory of the
proper governance of the colonized becomes homologous with the
theory of the proper governance of the bureaucratic underling.

The origins of this self-effacing style of rule go back at least to Henry
and John Lawrence in the Punjab during the early-Victorian era. A
devout Evangelical, Henry Lawrence pioneered a form of imperial rule
there which was based in a vision of the moral regeneration of the
colonized under the benevolent stewardship of British administrators.
Early on, though, this form of rule began to show the strains that would
characterize it wherever it was put into practice. Because this system
necessarily required that the administrator be given a great deal of
personal independence, the only real check to abuse of power was the
process of careful recruitment. As Lewis D. Wurgaft has argued:

The earmarks of the "Punjab Style" were heroic action, the exercise of
unlimited power, and evangelical zeal. Far from the red tape of the more settled
areas, leaders like Henry Lawrence cultivated an ideology of action and
independence as the primary instruments of imperial control.[44]

The "Punjab Style" afforded an extraordinary amount of freedom to
the individual colonial administrator to exercise his own independent
judgment. Indeed, this fact created the strange anomaly whereby a
system of rule built on a bureaucratic foundation would be eventually
undermined by the need for it to be carried out by "charismatic"
leaders. However, when the Lawrences' management of the Punjab was
compared with the East India Company style of rule in Bengal in the
1840s, the former would come to seem – at least to most mid-Victorian
British observers – not only morally but politically superior, and this
view was reinforced in Britain after the Punjab remained loyal to the
Empire during the Indian Mutiny of 1857.

A central tenet of the "Punjab Creed" was the moral efficacy of work.
Tireless workers themselves, both Lawrences insisted on recruiting
officers who shared their devotion. As one of John Lawrence's subordi-

nates, Alexander Taylor, put it, he felt "a glow of work and duty round us all in the Punjab in those days, such as I have never felt before or since. I well remember the reaction of feeling when I went on furlough to England, the want of pressure of any kind, the self-seeking, the want of high aims which seemed to dull and dwarf you."[45] Clearly the sense that one was performing a task with grand implications was what made the Punjab experience attractive to idealistic colonial bureaucrats.

Cromer's theory of Indirect Rule, presented as a new discovery of signal importance, promising, finally, the enlightened administration of colonial lands and justified, as policy, by its "disinterestedness," was thus based not only in a highly idealized vision of the British imperial mission but also in a somewhat distorted, self-flattering myth of origination. As Kathryn Tidrick has argued, the best known proponents of Indirect Rule at the turn of the century were simply offering as a new discovery what had already become a common practice within the British Empire from at least the time of the high-minded Lawrences in the Punjab in the 1840s and 50s.[46] Indeed, one might venture the claim that most British imperial administrators who eventually came to be celebrated by their peers for their successes were exponents, whether conscious of the fact or not, of one or another version of the theory of Indirect Rule. Even Curzon, known for his deliberately visible and very gaudy viceregal pageants in India, designed to impress the "Asiatic mind" with a carefully staged spectacle of imperial majesty, used the durbar principally as a practical technique for easing the exercise of his own power. The irony which persistently dogs Indirect Rule is that bureaucratic self-effacement over and over again leads to self-aggrandizement. As Tidrick notes,

the Resident's obscuration of the nature of his influence was primarily not a form of reticence or uncertainty, but of display. By diminishing the outward evidence of his authority almost to the point of invisibility, he demonstrated to the people and perhaps more importantly to himself that he could perform his duties not only without resort to force but without any discernible support at all: like Hugh Clifford's Sir Philip Hanbury-Erskine choosing to deal with rebellion not as a governor but "as a man," he was effacing not himself but his institutional context.[47]

The theory of Indirect Rule eventually found its most widely influential and explicit formulation in the writings of Sir Frederick Lugard, the conqueror of the Fulani emirates of northern Nigeria, who became the chief British administrator of these newly acquired territories at the turn of the century. Like Cromer, Lugard presents his case for Indirect Rule with the same breathless insistence that he has uncovered the key to administrative wisdom. And in the aftermath of World War I, with both Curzon and Churchill holding high authority over colonial affairs, the British government was ready to embrace publicly this ostensibly custodial theory of colonial rule, for it was widely felt then that it would bring good press in an era infected with the disease of Wilsonian self-determination. In this political atmosphere, Lugard's book *The Dual Mandate in British Tropical Africa* found a number of rapturous celebrants in Britain when it was published in 1922, among them Churchill, T. E. Lawrence, and, most importantly, the influential academic Margery Perham, who was responsible for promoting the theory to the members of the governing class.[48]

Lugard celebrates "mandate" rule because it binds imperial administrators to a lofty set of duties: the dual duty, in fact, of preserving indigenous ways of life while – simultaneously – encouraging the transformation of subject people so that they will, one day, be capable of self-rule. As Lugard puts it in *The Dual Mandate* (1922), "The responsibility is one which the advantages of an inherited civilisation and a superior intellectual culture, no less than the physical superiority conferred by the monopoly of firearms, imposes upon the controlling Power."[49] As in Cromer's formulation, the notion that the bureaucrat who rules – however indirectly – a colonized people is himself ruled by a higher code of duty (thus, the growing favor of the term "mandate" during the League of Nations era, a term which suggests that those who make the laws are themselves ruled by a higher law) situates the white district officer or Resident in an anomalous position. The British Resident in colonial Nigeria, for instance, although ostensibly the instrument of a "higher" and presumably benevolent imperial order, often found himself enjoying the autonomy and responsibility of an independent agent. Moreover, Lugard laid particular emphasis on this right of the Resident to as wide a scope for independent action as possible. Although he would have abhorred the comparison, it is clear from his formulation that the Resident's ability to carry out the aims of imperial administration is contingent on his being given the powers and leeway of, at the very least, a great chief or emir – something like, to take an ironic literary example, Kurtz in the "heart of darkness." As a result, Indirect Rule in operation was rarely very indirect. As Tidrick notes, it actually involved the Resident in an "unprecedented assumption of authority in native affairs." The only thing indirect about it was its involvement of the Resident in maintaining the "prestige of the Emir."[50] However often the theorist of Indirect Rule invokes the notion of "duty" as a curb to the administrator's potentially reckless abuse of his own independence, the Resident's ability to carry out his mission rests, finally, on his ability to personalize authority, to incarnate it in himself, in short. And when the all-too-human instrument of power is treated as the source or origin of power, as in Kurtz's fictional Congo or in Stanley's actual Congo, abuses are inevitable.[51]

Indirect Rule can be seen to serve a contradictory purpose when one examines it in light of Weber's dichotomy of charisma and bureaucracy. Indirect Rule attempts to systematize charismatic rule, to institutionalize the manufacture of leaders with godlike powers, expertise, and fields of action out of otherwise ordinary English bureaucrats. Although most writers on British imperial history tend to speak of the Empire as a place in which an anachronistic form of rule – what Weber called "charismatic" rule – was reinvented in the colonial field and imposed on people who were felt to be incapable of governing themselves by modern, democratic institutions, imposing a kind of European "Oriental despotism" at the risk of awakening, occasionally, deplorable atavistic impulses in the Europeans who ruled, I am arguing a slightly different case. My claim is that the application of the Weberian duality – "charismatic" and "bureaucratic" – in the imperial field needs to be rethought. The most notable feature of the theory of Indirect Rule, emphasized by most of its promoters, was systematic replication. Indirect Rule sought to manufacture charismatic rulers out of almost anyone English. Indirect Rule, in other words, is the bureaucratization of charisma, the systematization of personalized rule. However it was experienced on the ground, the theory of Indirect Rule was a theory for turning ordinary adventurers and bureaucrats into charismatic leaders.

Considering the issue in systemic terms, one might say that the instrumentalist logic of late capitalism inevitably produces the "charismatic" figure, for "charismatic" figures are highly useful in accomplishing work, especially in areas of the world in which personalized authority seems to be characteristic of local political authority. They are perfect instruments for the accomplishment of ultimately bureaucratic purposes. Moreover, the "nostalgia" for the "charismatic," which is implicit even in Weber's work, should itself be seen as an aftereffect of the "bureaucratization" of industrial society: the idea of personal rule is very compelling to those who have never experienced anything like absolute power. The infinite substitutability of life within a bureaucracy inevitably encourages one to dream of a different order of life and work: to dream of a utopian world in which one works for the recognition of some vastly powerful and autonomous other whose ultimate goals are breathlessly far-reaching, and whose benign recognition invests one's own paltry efforts with the glow of moral purposiveness. The Kurtz who had "immense plans," and whose powers of action seem almost un-limited within his own jungle universe, is not so much the metaphorical realization of charismatic imperialism as he is the effect – the dream – of the company man who narrates his story: Charley Marlow. And his very typicality, his unsingularity, is precisely what the theory of Indirect Rule was conjured into existence to systematize. Indirect Rule is the theory of rule which creates the necessary role of "Kurtz" and which offers the promise that virtually any properly educated European, with the right training, can fill it. Indirect Rule, in short, is the professionalization of "charisma," a strategy for enhancing the personal power of the Euro-pean administrator masquerading as a strategy for diminishing it.

3

The ideal of the selfless imperial manager in the broadest possible sense of that term had already assumed the status of well-recognized "type" in late-Victorian literature; Cromer's contribution was merely to adapt what Tidrick calls "The Punjab Creed" to a new code intended to guide the behavior of imperial bureaucrats and to justify bureaucratic rule in the colonies. Although Kipling would eventually make a career for himself by depicting these types (the popular hagiographies of Maud Diver and G. A. Henty, by contrast, tend to focus on well-recognized imperial heroes), Kipling's achievement still lay largely in the future in the 1880s. Probably the best-known figure of this type in fiction (at least in England in the 1880s) was Max Havelaar, the hero of Edouard Douwes Dekker's novel *Max Havelaar: Or the Coffee Auctions of the Dutch Trading Company*, a monument of nineteenth-century Dutch literature which created a small political furor in Holland when it was first published in 1859 (it was translated into English in 1868). Written by an embittered idealist (under the pseudonym "Multatuli") who spent three months as Assistant Resident of Lebak in the Dutch East Indies and whose experiences there resemble somewhat the events of the main narrative, *Max Havelaar* was once described by D. H. Lawrence as a higher-order *Uncle Tom's Cabin*.[32] Like Stowe's novel, it is a tract novel dedicated to exposing social ills – in this case, the crime of Dutch imperial misrule in the East Indies – by offering the example of a hero whose self-sacrifice sanctifies his failed attempt to reform the Dutch imperial administration. But unlike Stowe's novel, which sermonizes against slavery, Dekker's *Max Havelaar* argues a case for the reform rather than the abolition of Dutch rule over Java. For this reason, Dekker's views on empire are much closer to Cromer's than they are to the views of an anti-imperialist. Dekker is a reformer with an insider's view of the operation of colonial bureaucracies within a system of indirect rule.

Yet *Max Havelaar* is also – it is important to point out – quite a bit more than a simple tract novel. It makes intriguing use of narrative voices, most interestingly the frame narrator, Batavus Droogstoppel, the pedestrian coffee broker who, although the unwitting beneficiary of continued Dutch rule over the East Indies, somehow remains obtusely innocent throughout the novel of the clear connections between Dutch rule over the East Indies and his own economic prosperity. By way of fanciful analogy, imagine, if you can, *Uncle Tom's Cabin* as an earnest dramatization of the evils of slavery cast in the form of a narrative framed by a largely unselfconscious, but voluble, Simon Legree (with a generous amount of politically cautionary annotations).

The multiple voices of the novel create multiple irony, and, indeed, this is the feature most celebrated by critics. The novel consists largely of Havelaar's narrative, dramatically reconstructed by the impoverished intellectual Scarfman, and presented with much tendentiously naïve commentary by Droogstoppel. Interestingly, the three narrators are strongly marked as representatives of their social classes: "Dry-as-dust" Droogstoppel, the middle-class coffee broker; Havelaar, the dueling aristocratic hero; and Scarfman, the poor intellectual who comes initially into possession of the original manuscript of Havelaar's adventures which is subsequently appropriated by Droogstoppel. In Droogstoppel and Havelaar, the novel inscribes a familiar European class difference into the terms of a conventional opposition between materialist rationality and idealistic nobility. Thus, despite the fact that Dekker's own political loyalties clearly lie with Havelaar, Droogstoppel is presented as the most artistically interesting character in the book: the unselfconscious butt of Dekker's satire. Although Havelaar's selfless reformism is ostensibly what is chiefly celebrated, the novel insists, through its use of irony, on the connection between middle-class trade and imperial rule. In other words, unlike most nineteenth-century literary treatments of empire, the book poses its oppositions in such a way as to locate middle-class business clearly within an imperial system as the chief beneficiaries of colonial rule, beneficiaries who, like the unwitting Droogstoppel, are given to ignoring the clear connection between Dutch rule over a farflung empire and the coffee-trading prosperity of fellow Dutch brokers (indeed, Dekker even lampoons bourgeois unconsciousness by having Droogstoppel unwittingly "territorialize" Java by identifying place names such as "Padang" with brands of coffee beans with which he is familiar). While juxtaposing middle-class attitudes with aristocratic ones, *Max Havelaar* refuses to pry the world of Dutch business free of its responsibility for a farflung empire, meanwhile making a novelistic "argument," not for granting Insulinde independence, but for making Dutch rule more humane and – not incidentally – more efficient. Dekker's own political views are avowedly reactionary and involve him in a bizarre celebration of paternalistic aristocratic rule, yet, apropos of this study, the book offers a prescient critique of the system of Indirect Rule as a bureaucratic system which actually prevents reform by preventing accurate information from reaching the seat of power in the European metropolis.

Dutch imperial history plays an important role in making this blunted critique possible. The Dutch colonial empire was largely a product of the seventeenth and eighteenth centuries and the Dutch themselves had usually seen their colonies principally as cash-crop lands (this system came to be known as the *cultuur-stelsel*). Unlike India, which became both a major consumer of Manchester textile goods and an important field of investment for British capital in the nineteenth century (especially in its railroad), the East Indies were treated by the Dutch not as a promising market for manufactured goods so much as a place for the production of basic commodities for the European market. Even Droogstoppel's role as coffee broker marks him as a seventeenth-century figure, a survival of the preindustrial commodity capitalism that made Holland the wealthiest country of seventeenth-century Europe.[53] Yet, despite the fact that Dekker's novel poses its conflict of values in dichotomous social class terms, Dekker's selfless aristocratic hero actually conforms quite neatly to Victorian conventions of bourgeois domesticity: Havelaar's family, familiarly nuclear, is cloyingly Dickensian in its sentimental intensity; his wife Tina (a Victorian "angel in the house" if ever there was one), at one point, is even acclaimed for perfecting her own form of domestic heroism by dispensing with the family's "babu" in order to raise her child – "Little Max" – by herself (*Max Havelaar*, p. 94). The class distinction, in other words, threatens to evaporate with the unfolding of the narrative itself, and thus has to be re-foundationalized by Dekker himself. This he does by having his narrator Scarfman indulge in some rather odd-seeming digressions on the origins of aristocratic titles which, he claims, demonstrate that men bearing the title of "count" actually had administrative duties to perform in the Holy Roman Empire (i.e. that aristocrats, far from being social parasites, have actually earned their social privileges in the past by performing valuable imperial work). Having thus demonstrated that aristocrats once actually worked to oversee the homeland, he then feels justified in slipping in the claim that aristocracy is "rooted in nature itself" (*Max Havelaar*, p. 68).

While the novel's controlling ideology is clearly bourgeois (the tirelessly energetic Havelaar is the consummate disciple of the Victorian "gospel of work"), it is a bourgeois ideology of an unusual type, requiring the invention of a class of betters and the celebration of an idealism, held to be characteristic of this class, which is antithetical to bourgeois instrumentalist rationality. Like the Victorian ideal of the gentleman in England, derived from originally aristocratic models but gradually pried free of the aristocratic ideology of blood, Dekker's aristocratic ideology is every bit the middle-class invention, but a middle-class invention fraught with anti-bourgeois implications. In this sense, Dekker can be seen as one of the earlier instances of Perkin's professional, producing a critique of bourgeois culture and economic imperialism that is, nonetheless, safely contained within the structure of middle-class moral norms and structures of feeling (see, for instance, the poem quoted at the head of this chapter). Moreover, although the book is critical of Dutch imperial rule, its criticism is confined within the limits imposed by an instrumentalist logic: it is very much a novel about how to make an existing system more humane rather than about how to abolish it altogether.

The most striking thing about Havelaar's attempts at reform, however, is the fact that they are futile. Dekker depicts his hero as a quixotic figure attempting to convince the Dutch Resident to abandon his allegiance to the local Regent (a local Javanese lord given a measure of autonomy by the Dutch colonial regime and, consequently, given to exploiting his subjects by forcing them to perform free labor for him) in order to put imperial administration on a sound and just footing. Despite that fact, the novel sets up the melodramatic undoing of its idealistic hero as a means of dramatizing why true reform of the Dutch colonial system is actually impossible. Naïvely believing that the Dutch Governor-General will listen to his complaints about lack of action from the Dutch Resident against the corrupt Javanese Regent, Havelaar is too idealistic to calculate the bureaucratic reasons why no action will be taken: he fails to realize (what "Scarfman," a.k.a. "Dekker," knows) that bureaucratic self-interest at every level of the colonial hierarchy guarantees that no Regent will be seriously challenged on his right to exact tribute from the people, for no higher-up in the Dutch colonial bureaucracy is willing to write the critical reports necessary to do so. Such reports falling into the hands of reformers or critics of empire in Holland might well endanger their own comfortable positions as supervisors of what is – admittedly – a fundamentally corrupt system. As Dekker convincingly demonstrates, Dutch rule is enduring precisely because it makes effective use of the political insulation that Indirect Rule provides, and thus would be undermined by the kind of reform Havelaar seeks. Regents are supposed to exact tribute; it is precisely these exactions that make the Regents the most visible rulers of Insulinde, thus insuring the relative invisibility of the Dutch imperial hierarchy by deflecting the people's anger onto local despots. The very failure of the idealistic reformer Havelaar, then, can be recuperated as a success for Dutch colonial administration, a theatrical success through which a mildly sympathetic Dutch imperial regime stages its ultimate powerlessness to curb the excesses of the Javanese Regents, thus promoting a misleading myth about the source of true power in Lebak. In short, Indirect Rule in the East Indies ultimately serves the goal of protecting the jobs of Dutch administrators.

On the other hand, the Dekker who so presciently details the reasons why reform is futile cannot plausibly be the victim of the same naïveté which afflicts his main character. Yet in depicting Havelaar as a Christ-like reformer doomed to failure on this earth, Dekker seems to confine the very possibility of reform only to an unrealizable Utopia, while nonetheless insisting on the necessity of "benevolent" administration over a people clearly in need of being ruled by the "best." In short, the novel asserts the necessity of reform in the interests of a lofty ideal of rule-governed justice, but can only represent that possibility as self-defeatingly quixotic.

*Max Havelaar* thus inadvertently depicts the reform of Dutch rule over Java as an impossibility precisely because it depicts the Dutch administration as a very efficient, self-enclosed bureaucratic system. Its efficiency can be measured in ways that all colonial bureaucrats can understand: Java produces wealth, in the form of exportable cash crops for the home country, and the Dutch rule Java indirectly, through

Regents who, because they are natives of the Indies, guarantee the effective invisibility of the actual structure of rule itself. *Max Havelaar*, in short, is an ironically anachronistic commentary on the theory of Indirect Rule, but one which, inadvertently perhaps, demonstrates the impossibility of the very reform for which its author yearns.

# CHAPTER 2

# Why Africa needs Europe: from Livingstone to Stanley

Africa's need: tramways!
Henry M. Stanley, *Through the Dark Continent*

Sub-Saharan Africa in the years before the "Scramble" was a place about which Europeans knew comparatively little. While centuries of European and Arab slave-trading left both West and East coasts dotted with slaving stations, Europeans seldom ventured far inland from the coasts in the sixteenth through the eighteenth centuries, principally because they lacked detailed maps of the interior and feared the threat posed by tropical diseases. These two conditions of African exploration would remain largely unchanged until the nineteenth century. The African interior (and especially the Congo watershed, covered as it was with forbidding jungle punctured here and there by majestic rivers) would remain largely uncharted until the invention of the steamboat made upriver travel practical. And the best-known tropical disease – malaria – would remain an unmasterable threat until quinine came into widespread use during the Victorian age. For this reason, the steamboat and quinine were probably the two items of material culture most responsible for making the nineteenth-century European exploration and exploitation of the African continent possible.[1]

Britain's role in Sub-Saharan Africa in the early nineteenth century was shaped by its position as the world's most important sea power. Having been awarded the Cape Colony by the Congress of Vienna in 1815, Britain was, in the following decades, the only important European power with extensive imperial interests in southern Africa. The British government tended to treat possession of the Cape as crucial to the security of the Indian Empire, for obvious reasons, until de Lesseps' completion of the Suez Canal in the 1860s abruptly altered the geopolitical meaning of South Africa, requiring the manufacture of newer "economic" and "humanitarian" reasons for holding it. While possession of South Africa could be justified (at least initially) in the language of geopolitics (and the argument clinched by the brute fact of Britain's dominance of the world's sea lanes), Britain's gradual and deepening involvement in the affairs of West and Central Africa in the nineteenth century was prompted by something other than purely geopolitical motives. There, the reasons had much less to do with geopolitics than with humanitarian (and economic) concerns, as Britain cast itself in a new role on the world stage as the chief enemy of the slave traffic.

Despite some evident successes in disrupting or closing down once-profitable transoceanic slaving routes in the nineteenth century, early British anti-slavery efforts had little impact on the slave trade in the interior of the continent, which seemed to be flourishing. Indeed, it did not take long for even the most devoted abolitionists to realize that any campaign against slavery within Africa waged purely on moral grounds would be doomed to failure unless it included plans with economic incentives. Recognizing early on that the campaign against slavery threatened to stamp out trade in the most valuable African product of the time – its people – influential English "humanitarians" such as Thomas Fowell Buxton favored substituting trade in legitimate non-human goods for the illicit trade in people, as this seemed the only practical way to procure African cooperation in curtailing it. Ironically, however, this same "humanitarian" movement, which set itself the lofty moral goal of freeing Africans from bondage, would eventually be prodded into *de facto* support for the less obviously moral project of extending the formal boundaries of the British Empire into the interior of the continent during the latter half of the nineteenth century. And this change in focus was a direct result of the attempt to put into practice "humanitarianism's" central beliefs: first, that the slave trade could only be stopped if trade in other goods were substituted for the trade in human beings (if, in other words, Africans could be reconceived as a market rather than a commodity), and second, that African "savagery" would persist until Africans were converted to Christianity on a large scale.[2] While most of the British missionaries drawn to Sub-Saharan Africa during the first half of the nineteenth century arrived eager to suppress slavery and Christianize the continent, they eventually drew in their wake a diverse group of traders, adventurers, and imperial administrators, few of whom were as fervently committed to the originally "moral" goals of the "humanitarian" movement.[3]

Yet the first half of the nineteenth century was a period of great optimism in "humanitarian" circles. Such was the atmosphere at the time that even after disaster befell the Niger Expedition in 1841 (an expedition planned and led by Buxton himself) support for the Christianization of Africa within England remained unabated. Moreover, within a few years of the disaster on the Niger, the most important African missionary of his day, Buxton's best-known disciple, arrived in South Africa to take up work among the Bechuanas, a black African tribe long victimized by Boer slave-raiders. Soon after his arrival, David Livingstone managed to cement firm connections with many different black African tribes and to begin to preach the gospel throughout the southern part of the continent. Not long content with the mere work of conversion, though, Livingstone soon found himself involved with providing guns to the Bechuana to help them to protect themselves against the Boers, with exploring and mapping vast stretches of the southern third of the continent heretofore unmapped by Europeans, with describing in detail for European readers the exotic flora and fauna of Sub-Saharan Africa, and with opening up lines of trade for the African tribes among whom he traveled. His first book-length account of his explorations, the modestly-titled _Missionary Travels and Researches in South Africa_, which tells the story of his travels from South Africa to Loanda in Portuguese Angola and then down the Zambezi River to the Indian Ocean from 1849 to 1856, was an immediate bestseller when it was published in 1858, solidifying his reputation as a devout Christian missionary and anti-slaver, and demonstrating to an eager British audience his abilities as a fearless explorer and scientific investigator.[4]

While the publication of _Missionary Travels_ made Livingstone's name something of a household word in Britain, his reputation did not achieve truly mythic dimensions until he was "lost" and subsequently "found" by the Anglo-American journalist-explorer Henry M. Stanley in 1871. Although already a figure of renown in Britain in the 1850s, Livingstone was transformed into the subject of popular legend, a "lone white man, turning his back on thoughts of home," by Stanley's newspaper accounts of his journey through Central Africa in pursuit of him. These accounts of their meeting in the wilderness, later published in book form under the title _How I Found Livingstone_, were written at least as much to establish Stanley's credentials as an African explorer (and to garner publicity for his employer Gordon Bennett's newspaper, the _New York Herald_) as to magnify Livingstone's selflessness and physical courage.[5] Yet Stanley's journey to find Livingstone (who was by no means lost) marks an important historical moment in which a relatively unknown disciple, ostensibly possessed by the same ideals as his master, uses the medium of print to seize metaphorical possession of both his master's reputation and the experience of Africa, and to transform that legacy significantly in the name of carrying it on. As Tim Youngs argues in a recent essay on *How I Found Livingstone*, Stanley's journal of his encounter with Livingstone becomes the medium for the construction of a certain kind of imperial self, a self constituted through the gestures of ownership – particularly the ownership of experience. Identifying Stanley as both "capitalist and journalist," Youngs notes how Stanley converts both "experience" and "story" into property.[6] Not only does he present an Africa populated by natives given to amazed exclamations about this "white man's" (Stanley's) practical wisdom, but he constructs a certain kind of Livingstone, a Livingstone who, by being made to stand for the "humanitarian" past, confirms Stanley's self inscription as the represen tative practical man of the future:

The differences between Stanley and Livingstone, as suggested by the former, are ones of action and reflection. Livingstone is the relieved; Stanley the one that brings the relief. Stanley is the practical man, unhappy when languishing in camp instead of being on the move; Livingstone is the patient diplomat who will delay his travels to satisfy Africans' requests and customs. Livingstone's geographical explorations have been hampered by the refusal of his men to proceed with him . . . Livingstone is the embodiment of moral, Christian ideals; Stanley is the physical achiever, and it is in this relationship that *How I Found Livingstone* has its most profound historical and cultural significance. Livingstone is portrayed as belonging more to the Romantic age and Stanley to the modern, commercial, practical one.[7]

This difference between the two men as African explorers and Victorian cultural heroes develops a compelling metaphorical resonance in British imperial history in the nineteenth century. I will argue that, in designating his difference from Livingstone in this way, Stanley forecasts a larger historical change in Britain's mission in Central Africa in the nineteenth century: a change from a limited commercial and missionary penetration, justified largely in moral terms during the age of "humanitarianism" (the Age of Livingstone), to a more aggressive exploration and search for economic opportunities prefatory to the official beginning of the "Scramble" instigated by the Congress of Berlin in 1885 (the Age of Stanley).[8] Borrowing his authority from a widely revered figure he has himself consigned to a mythic – if recent – past, Stanley reinvents Africa as a land of economic "need" (and consequently as a land promising enormous economic opportunities for Europe). Moreover – my central point – in constructing Africa as land of need, Stanley reveals how deeply implicated the illusion of charismatic individualism is in the historical reality of bureaucratic power. Stanley is the self-styled individual hero whose deeds are enabled in large measure by the massive scale of his enterprise, and thus his travelogue reveals the tendency of "charisma" to forget or disguise its own origins in "bureaucracy."

Although Stanley's "needy" Africa may seem little different from the Africa Livingstone wished to see transformed by "Christianity and commerce," it is actually conceived along rather distinct lines. While one needs to be wary of overdrawing a distinction which conforms all-too-neatly to Stanley's own narrative self-portrayal as the "son" who must, even at the risk of overstatement, emphasize his difference from the "father" who authorizes his exploration in the first place, the question posed is an important one: does the displacement of Livingstone by Stanley represent an emblematically significant shift in the exercise of representational power over Africa?

Besides the obvious personal contrast between the modest Scottish missionary and the brash American journalist, larger differences in outlook suggest themselves. The Stanley who undertook the management of Leopold's "Free State" of the Congo in the 1880s, for instance, is a figure much more deeply beholden to the ideology of economic modernization than his mentor Livingstone. His way of conceptualizing Africa's needs suggests closer parallels to the thinking of the Agency for International Development in the late twentieth century than to the evangelical moralism governing the beliefs of the best-known abolitionists of the early nineteenth century. A close look, consequently, at their most representative works – Livingstone's *Missionary Travels* (1858) and Stanley's *Through the Dark Continent* (1878) – reveals significant differences in the scope of the respective exploratory projects, in the form of the narratives, in the construction of narrative subjects, and in the ideological implications of each narrative.

Some of these differences may be traced to differences in the scale of each exploratory project, and these differences in scale are telling. The Livingstone who crossed South Central Africa over a period of seven years, seldom accompanied by more than a small group of native bearers, was engaged in an exercise in power/knowledge on rather a vastly different scale from that of Stanley, who departed from Zanzibar in 1874 with a party of 350 and who engaged in dozens of large-scale military confrontations (thirty-two on the Congo River alone, he reports!) before he and what was left of his famished party staggered into Boma near the West Coast three and one-half years later. Moreover, the contrast between the "mild missionary" Livingstone and Stanley the "Breaker-of-Stones" tells us a great deal about how a drastic change in the scale of European "penetration" of Africa coincides with, and is encouraged by, the production of a different kind of Africa in European discourse: a new Africa coming to be defined as less in need of moral transformation by Christian missionaries than of economic and political transformation by colonial bureaucrats and economic imperialists, an Africa offering plenty of confirming evidence of its own "need" for economic modernization and political centralization. If Stanley's disciplinary methods seem designed to produce him as a familiar charismatic figure, his construction of Africa as space of need, nevertheless, reveals a modernizing, bureaucratic consciousness at work behind the scenes. More so than Livingstone, Stanley explicitly addresses himself to an audience of would-be imitators, ready to benefit from the sound, practical advice contained in the pages of his book. As I have already pointed out in Chapter 1, this is one of the chief signs of a bureaucratic consciousness at work: the bureaucrat fills a role in a system designed to be immortal rather than personalized, individualized, and historically limited – even when, as in the case of Indirect Rule, the system is designed to shape charismatic leaders out of the unpromising clay of ordinary Englishmen (or Americans). Stanley ultimately projects an Africa in need of being tamed by other Stanleys, an Africa ready to reward those who discipline themselves in the act of taming it, and writes a travelogue which is both one of the most exciting examples of the "survival" genre, and a handbook offering detailed advice on managing a preindustrial workforce.[9]

I shall discuss here, first, Livingstone's "humanitarian" mission in Africa before moving on to consider Stanley's reinscription of Africa as space of economic need.

2

Livingstone's *Missionary Travels* is remarkable in the way it seems to refuse dramatic possibilities that a skilled journalist like Stanley would never forgo. In part, this may be due to the fact that the narrative remains closer in form to the original journal taken down in Africa. Even though, as Livingstone reveals, he lost his first journal on the way to Loanda and was forced to reconstruct it later from memory, the reconstruction bears few of the expected markers of intentionalized narrative construction. His daily notations are remarkably free of portentous anticipations of the end, of a final goal which, because of its immanence in the beginning, organizes the seemingly random succession of events into a teleological *processus* of meaning. Like a journal which has never been reread or rewritten before being published, *Missionary Travels* is set mainly in the present of immediate experience rather than, as Stanley's travelogue so clearly is, in the dual temporality of immediate experience reconstructed through the ordering process of memory. His readers are not even told until many pages into the book that Livingstone has any intention of traveling to Loanda (his "destination" in the first half of the book), and he presents the initial plan to follow the Zambezi east to the Indian Ocean, a momentous feat of exploration in its own right that gives some sense of direction to the activities of the second half of his book, in a remarkably offhand way.

The impression this creates uncomfortably confirms the one publicized by Stanley: the impression of an explorer/missionary essentially wandering through Africa. The Livingstone of Stanley's *How I Found Livingstone* is not unlike the main protagonist of *Missionary Travels*. He is a man so attentive to the needs and desires of the Africans among whom he moves and so wary of the exercise of coercive force as to be unwilling and unable to keep his mutinous bearers with him. The effect of Livingstone's failure (or reluctance) to convert his journal into a clearly marked journey toward a goal is to leave his readers with the sense that the steps along the way possess their own peculiar finality of meaning for him. The space of Africa becomes, in *Missionary Travels*, a dilatory space, a place ultimately of providential wandering, we must infer, but by no means a narrative space mapped out in overtly teleological form.[10] A *telos* is there in Livingstone, we are led to assume, but it is a non-material one – the Christianization of Africa – a utopian goal that will never be reached by the main protagonist. Yet, when read against Stanley's travelogue, which invests the goal of reaching the West Coast with something like the meaning of a Conradian "idea" (or an "Ahabian" obsession), Livingstone's journal seems to be organized around multiple, competing purposes.

One could say that this difference between the two travelogues simply marks a difference in literary mode. While neither book fits neatly into generic categories, Stanley's text clearly owes much more to the conventions of what Mary Louise Pratt calls "survival" literature than does Livingstone's *Missionary Travels* – a work of "anti-conquest" strongly flavored by the twin projects of "natural history" and geographical exploration.[11] While travel writing of the "survival" genre typically

makes extensive use of the dramatic possibilities inherent in the narrativization of the daring exploratory journey, "anti-conquest" refuses
many of these possibilities, seeking instead to dramatize the European
subject's scientific fascination with nature and the landscape as well as
(certainly in this case) his religious and moral concern for the welfare of
non-Christian people. Where Stanley, as a result, tells his readers much
about himself and his role as leader of men, Livingstone gives much less
emphasis to that conventional role, proffering instead a remarkably
self-effacing subjectivity that nonetheless barely masks a different form
of European mastery – that of the detached, scientific observer and
moralistic reformer.

However, the ideological consequences of this difference in structure
are telling. Stanley the "Breaker of Stones" (*Bula Matari* is what he was
called) first marches his initially reluctant army into the Congo rainforest, then fights his way down the length of the Congo River to a Boma
portentously mapped out as his ultimate destination from the very first
pages, meting out harsh justice to his own "troops" along the way to
forestall any threat of mutiny. The mild man of God Livingstone, by
contrast, at times presents his modest-sized party to African headmen as
helpful visitors, at other times throws himself and his party on the mercy
of local despots. Moreover, Livingstone often suspends his journey for a
week or a month at the pleasure of the local leader, and acquires a
reputation for fending off threats of violence against his party with a
mild fearlessness matched by a principled unwillingness to engage in
battle if it can be avoided. Where Stanley literally battles his way across
much of Central Africa, Livingstone fights no battles at all, not even
against Zambezi tribes which had previously been victimized by the
minions of Chief Sekeletu, his prime benefactor and protector who
furnishes him with guides for the eastern part of his journey. Although
clearly aware of the historical importance of his explorations, Livingstone refuses to engage in conventionally heroic self-characterization.
He simply does not cast himself as the hero of the kind of epic adventure
narrative into which Stanley so readily inserts himself, despite the fact
that his narrative contains the materials for one. In that sense, the modal
differences between Livingstone's *Missionary Travels* and Stanley's
*Through the Dark Continent* correspond in some degree to those between
the earlier African explorers John Barrow and Mungo Park, whose
travelogues are discussed by Pratt in *Imperial Eyes*.[12]

It would be wrong to overstress the modal distinction, however, for
unquestionably *Missionary Travels* was read by Livingstone's English

readers as an epic narrative. Indeed, Livingstone's own narrative reticence can be (and was) read as lending an important dimension to his
heroism: a kind of heroic reticence which the American journalist
Stanley was professionally and personally incapable of sustaining.
*Through the Dark Continent* appears regrettably immodest by comparison:
the self-conscious self-assertion of a lesser-known disciple whose epic
self-construction bespeaks an overly-loud ambition to outdo his master,
both in his own deeds and in his vivid (indeed, sensationalistic) memor-
ialization of them.

Necessarily, these differences in literary form give rise to significant
differences on the level of representation of the African continent itself.
Stanley's Africa is a land of savage beauty and rude wealth but mainly of
savage resistance to civilization and progress: it needs to be whipped
into shape, as a horse-trainer would his colts or a stern Victorian father
his children. Livingstone's Africa, by contrast, is a land of astonishing
wealth populated by wayward "heathens" who are, despite their faults
and a certain irreducible cultural otherness, remarkably reasonable and
consequently quite susceptible to the seductive message of self-transformation contained in the gospel of "Christianity and commerce."

Because Stanley publicly cast himself in the role of disciple of Livingstone, he has often been credited with being the man most responsible
for attempting to carry out Livingstone's plan for the transformation of
Africa through trade. Yet, despite Stanley's claim to Livingstone's
legacy, it is difficult to credit him with being quite the worthy disciple he
claimed to be. The reasons lie at least partly in differences in the way
each conceived of the "African." Livingstone's "African" is essentially a
"reasonable" adult in need of persuasion rather than, as Stanley's
"African" so obviously is, a wayward child in need of sometimes harsh
discipline. Consequently, Livingstone treats the Africans he visits with
the respect due to European adults, devoting a great deal of his time to
attempting to persuade his African listeners of the benefits of free trade
and the immorality of slavery and other "savage" practices.

Like his mentor Buxton and British "humanitarians" generally,
Livingstone invested commerce with morally transformative meanings.
He believed fervently that the importance of his trips to Loanda and to
Mozambique lay in the possibility that he might thereby help to open up
trade routes for indigenous goods such as ivory, which could substitute,
he hoped, for the then-profitable trade in human beings. It perhaps goes
without saying that, like British "free traders" generally, from Adam
Smith to Richard Cobden, Livingstone was incapable of imagining the

cost actual free trade would eventually impose on Africa, a cost all too obvious now to twentieth-century readers familiar with the European legacy in the "developing" world. To put it succinctly: Livingstone's devotion to free trade as an anodyne for African backwardness goes along with an inability to examine critically how "freedom" operates in a context in which global differentials of power threaten to make a mockery of the very possibility of free trade.

The very notion of "free trade," however, like the concept "slavery," is enmeshed in a set of assumptions about property that are, to say the least, rigidly ethnocentric. The Livingstonian notion of "slavery," in fact, cannot be detached from the play of conceptual contrast with types of coerced labor familiar to his Victorian readers which Europe has never acknowledged to be forms of slavery in the strict sense (examples run from apprenticeships to the duty children owe to parents). Yet because his language lacks a category for naming the corporate nature of many African societies (for recognizing their alterity in this sense), Livingstone universalizes a rigidly English notion of property in *Missionary Travels*, and is – not surprisingly – shocked to discover that "slavery" remains a widespread practice throughout the southern half of the continent, practiced extensively by both black African tribes and white Boer farmers. Regardless of how widespread slavery actually was in nineteenth-century Africa, it is interesting to note that Livingstone's alarm seems to have been rather easily triggered by his personal revulsion from the traditional power most African chiefs claimed over the bodies of their subjects, for he invariably reads such practices as the forming of political alliances with other tribes through the exchange of chiefs' daughters, for example, as forms of "slavery." By this broad standard, the European Habsburg monarchs could be convicted of "enslaving" members of their own family. As Dorothy O. Helly reminds us, "slavery" in this particular European sense rests on notions of "commodity" and "property" that are not easily translated into a nineteenth-century African context, except by dismissing out of hand alternative conceptions of property.[13]

Livingstone's confessed inability to understand the moral difference between the African convention of paying *hongo* ("bribe," "toll," or "tribute," depending on one's point of view) to local chiefs for the right of passage through their lands and the familiar English criminal practice of extortion provides another example of the ethnocentric rigidity of his conception of property. Given to moralizing African customs, he invariably interprets the demand for *hongo* as a peculiarly individual moral failing – a symptom of personal venality. His usual response when African headmen demand payment for passage is to refuse it and then to take his revenge by sermonizing against the moral characters of individual chiefs in the pages of his book. One could argue that the demand for *hongo* should instead be seen as an inevitable effect of the decentralization and diffusion of political power in the Central Africa of the 1840s and 50s. One might also claim (and there is a great deal of evidence for this claim in the pages of Livingstone's book) that Livingstone's uncompromising resistance to paying *hongo* amounts to the shrewd strategy of a wizened bazaar bargainer holding out for the lowest price. What better way to resist paying a high toll than by condemning toll-collecting itself as a deeply immoral activity? In fact, Livingstone relates many instances when, despite refusing to pay *hongo*, he was allowed to proceed anyway. One can only surmise that, in cases like this, he is released when the headman with whom he is dealing decides that his excessive resistance is a sign he actually has little to give.

But Livingstone's dislike for paying *hongo* also stems, he would have his readers believe, from a principled commitment to the ideal of free passage. An essential precondition to free trade, free passage is a commercial value raised to the status of moral value in *Missionary Travels*. Thus, after dwelling on one chief's "extortion" (Chief Sekomi's), at one point, Livingstone inadvertently passes rather quickly to the strikingly ethnocentric assertion that passage should be "free":

Sekomi's ideas of honesty are the lowest I have met with in any Bechuana chief, and this instance is mentioned as the only approach to demanding payment for leave to pass that I have met with in the south. In all other cases the difficulty has been to get a chief to give us men to show the way, and the payment has only been for guides. Englishmen have always very properly avoided giving that idea to the native mind which we shall hereafter find prove troublesome, that payment ought to be made for passage through a country.[14]

The assumptions underlying this passage are worth considering: 1) that rights of way are not property and thus cannot be owned and rented out; 2) that reciprocity is established only by paying for labor power (the services of guides) not for the right to cross territory; 3) that such reciprocity can and should be enforced. Moreover, this latter assumption is embedded in a larger assumption about power: that the British traveler/missionary comes on the scene as the implicit representative of higher political powers – the high chief Sekeletu, most immediately; the British government, ultimately – that possess the power to punish "extortion" if only they would exercise it. What makes Livingstone politically acceptable to his English readership is largely the fact that these assumptions remain at the level of assumption; their implications never brought to the surface. The result is a carefully crafted impression that Africa contains, regrettably, too many individual "savages" who refuse to play by universally accepted rules.[15] The ideological power of this kind of discourse stems directly from the refusal to critically examine these assumptions, a refusal which has the effect of naturalizing and universalizing a rather limited and ethnocentric model of reciprocity and which occludes the necessary role of power.

Although there is no question that Livingstone realized on some level that "free trade" (and its crucial precondition – "free passage") could be established in Sub Saharan Africa in fact only through the exercise of coercive political and military power, he almost never admits this publicly. His tendency to romanticize "the African" for his readers has its counterpart in a tendency to mystify the exercise of power. In contrast to Stanley, who seems not only to enjoy overmuch the display of force but to delight in moments of self-congratulation for his many successes as leader of men, Livingstone disdains public discussion of such amoral behavior. Although aware that his skills as an English-trained doctor invest him with great potential power in Africa, he prudently refrains whenever possible from doctoring Africans, fearing that if he loses a patient to death or incurs the jealousy of tribal medicine men he will jeopardize his protected position. When he does discuss the use of power directly, it is usually in the context of a reassuringly abstract discussion of Britain's "humanitarian" mission. Consider, for instance, his discussion of "free trade" in his *Cambridge Lectures*, a lecture cited by historians such as Thornton as a crucially important indicator of how Victorian "humanitarianism" was subtly recrafted into an exercise of power that bears the benevolent public face of a moral mission:

By encouraging the native propensity for trade, the advantages that might be derived in a commercial point of view are incalculable; nor should we lose sight of the inestimable blessings it is in our power to bestow upon the unenlightened African, by giving him the light of Christianity. Those two pioneers of civilization – Christianity and commerce – should ever be inseparable; and Englishmen should be warned by the fruits of neglecting that principle as exemplified in the result of the management of Indian affairs.[16]

A striking statement for the age of *laissez-faire*, this claim – typically of Livingstone – is notable less for what it asserts than for what it assumes:

that the metropolitan government can be the agent of economic "progress," that Christianity and commerce share some sort of moral equivalence, that the promotion of trade requires the political transformation of
Africa (i.e. that political integration through state [or imperial] power is
the precondition for economic transformation). In a decade when the
Manchester School was arguing, with some evident success, against the
further "unnatural" and expensive extension of British imperial fron-
tiers and in favor of allowing the market for British goods to grow
"naturally" across the globe, Livingstone was making an antithetical
case for the deliberate creation of markets and the promotion of trade in
African primary goods aided by the deliberate extension of imperial
power.[17] Yet he does so caressingly, by deliberately underplaying the
role of power.

That Livingstone failed to convince the British government of his day
to take a more active role in African affairs (beyond sending a few more
warships to intercept transoceanic slavers), testifies both to the popular
appeal of *laissez-faire* ideology in the 1850s and 60s and to the lack of any
clear consensus within the British governing class about the value of
expensive imperial projects in Sub-Saharan Africa at that time.[18] Although the "humanitarian" discourse on Africa had clearly constructed
a powerfully responsive domestic ideological consensus by the 1860s and
70s (Robinson and Gallagher note how even attempts to abandon
colonies such as Gambia brought out thousands of "humanitarians" in
protest in the 1870s[19]), Livingstone's generation of "humanitarians"
would spawn a second generation, of whom the "Breaker-of-Stones"
Stanley was the most outrageous example, much less interested in the
religious and moral transformation of Africa than in its economic and
political reinvention. A product of the "Second Industrial Revolution,"
Stanley spent much of his early life in an America whose economic
modernization was proceeding at a breakneck pace, in large measure
because of massive investments in new infrastructure (waterways, the
transcontinental railway, the telegraph) and large public investment in
the extermination of those native Americans who stood in the way of
economic "progress" and continental homogeneity. Perhaps because of
this history, Stanley was more conscious than the generation of Cobden
and Livingstone of the importance of political and infrastructural transformation as a precondition for trade. By imagining Africa as a place of
economic need at the historical moment when the interior was being
mapped and other European powers were growing decidedly interested,
Stanley set the stage for the bureaucratic reinvention of Africa in such a

way as to make inevitable its partition among the Powers and the destruction of its previous ways of life.

3

Stanley's *Through the Dark Continent* was written in 1878 to publicize his adventures in tracing the Congo River from its source to the Atlantic and to promote Central Africa as a legitimate sphere of interest for imperial Britain. What makes this travelogue interesting in this context is its peculiarly "Marlovian" identification of imperial purposes: Stanley envisions Africa as a factory for the manufacture of imperial purposes – themselves determined to a large extent by the explorer's own practical needs in undertaking a large-scale expedition through Central Africa.[20] Not only do Stanley's instrumental needs in making a journey of exploration through the heart of the continent (most notably, his need to "manage" hundreds of Zanzibari porters and gun-bearers) condition his projection of Africa's need for modernization ("Africa's need: tramways!"), but Stanley's travelogue celebrates Africa as, finally, a place of infinite possibilities because, paradoxically, both infinitely needy and infinitely rich, and therefore, a place which will always return an answer to Europe about why Europe ought to be there. His two major preoccupations in this book – constructing his own charismatic subject-role as *Bula Matari* ("Breaker-of-Stones") and constructing Africa as space of need – are both signs of a bureaucratic logic set to work on Africa. The book becomes simultaneously a textbook offering detailed suggestions for managing Africa, a persuasive dissertation on the reasons why the continent needs to be managed, and a rhetorically compelling utopian vision of the rewards that the successful management of Africa will bring to Europe.

Stanley's journey across Central Africa was a venture on a large scale (like his earlier expedition to "find" Livingstone, this trip was also funded by Gordon Bennett of the *New York Herald*). While the spectacle of Arab trading (and slave-trading) caravans was a familiar one to the people of the interior of Central Africa in the mid nineteenth century, white explorers were still few enough to be memorable. There can be little doubt that the hostile reception with which Stanley often met had much to do with the size and, consequently, threatening appearance of his expeditionary force: unlike Livingstone, who often traversed Africa with relatively small parties, Stanley set out initially with over 350 men (and a small number of women and children) from Zanzibar in 1874, trooped through Uganda, where he established friendly relations with Emperor Mtesa, who allowed his expedition to explore and map Lake Victoria, moved south to Lake Tanganyika, which he also circum-navigated, and then followed the Livingstone River northward and westward through the dense rainforest for its entire length in order to prove his hypothesis that the Livingstone must be the Congo. When he reached the village of Nsanda in the western Congo finally on August 4, 1877 with a tattered force much reduced in number by disease, malnu-trition, and death in battle, and dispatched a plea for food from "any Gentleman who speaks English at Embomma" (a letter famous for its self-memorializing postscript: "I am the person who discovered Living-stone in 1871"), he had long since realized that he had succeeded in proving his geographical hunch correct. By the time Stanley reached Boma in 1877, a significant number of the major rivers and lakes of Central Africa, their shape not to mention their very existence unsus-pected by the Europe of 1848, had just been mapped; many of the "white spaces" on the map of Central Africa had just recently been filled in through the work of European and American explorers and missiona-ries such as Livingstone, Burton, Speke, Grant, and Cameron (not to mention Stanley himself on his earlier expedition). And the impetus this mapping gave to subsequent European penetration of the last significant part of the African landscape yet to find itself the victim of European depredation has been, by now, much discussed. Indeed, Stanley made a career for himself which condenses the main stages of this European penetration: although he claimed he wrote *Through the Dark Continent* in order to interest Britain in taking a more active imperial role in Central Africa, upon his return to Europe he was seduced and won, not by Britain, but by King Leopold of Belgium, who sent him back to the Congo as his agent in 1879 – with an even larger party of workers and heavily armed troops – to begin preliminary work on the railroad for which he so ardently wished.[21]

While Stanley's own description of his expedition across Central Africa as an "exploratory safari" would seem to suggest an innocuous surveying activity (all perfectly innocent observation and mapping), it was, like all such expeditions, necessarily far from innocent. Stanley's travelogue typifies the operation of the logic of mapping in the history of European expansionism, for to map the course of a mighty river which, in the minds of many of the natives of the Congo rainforest he meets, emerges only twenty miles upstream out of a land of mythic wonder, flows through the heart of the known world, and empties, twenty miles downstream, over a cataract in a land populated by all-powerful but distant cannibals or "dwarf-men," is, of course, to impose, over against their way of understanding the landscape of Africa, a radically alien way of seeing the landscape itself. It goes without saying that European maps of previously unknown territory tend to feature those aspects of the landscape which facilitate or hinder the traversing of the landscape – rivers, mountains, lakes, and so on – for mapping presupposes that the mapper sees a value in traveling great distances, that the psychological centrality of the local has yielded to a larger, global, symbolic vision. Not surprisingly, then, Stanley begins his expedition under the assumption that what Africa needs above all (because, of course, what Stanley could use above all) is knowledge of Africa's terrain, which will enable him (and others) to travel beyond the narrow psychological horizons confining the natives of the Central African rainforest. Although his bearers occasionally raise the question with polite indirectness, what is never subject to direct question here is the value of this global perspective.

Yet mapping is only one of the means used by Stanley to suture Africa into European structures of meaning. *Through the Dark Continent*, like most of Stanley's books, is also a highly dramatic adventure story which offers its European readers detailed ethnographic descriptions of unfamiliar but curiously exotic people. More important than ethnographic description for its own sake is the practical benefit of certain basic ethnographic categories to the manager of men. A small number of the Zanzibari *Wangwana* (freemen) Stanley employs are individualized and repeatedly praised for their courage under adverse conditions, but most of all for the virtue most useful to the white explorer – "fidelity." In hiring porters and gun-bearers for his journey in 1874, for instance, Stanley sorts Zanzibaris into two classes, the *Wangwana* (i.e. Zanzibari "freemen") and the *Wanyamwezi* (literally, "pagan" people of Unyamwezi on the mainland; to the *Wangwana* of Zanzibar – "slaves"), in order to suggest that Africa already offers a fortuitously useful characterological dichotomy readily adaptable to the necessary division of labor on an exploratory expedition. The *Wanyamwezi*, inherently less "civilized" than the *Wangwana*, make better porters; the *Wangwana*, on the other hand, better escorts. As Stanley says of the *Wanyamwezi*,

Naturally, being a grade less advanced towards civilization than the *Wangwana*, they are not so amenable to discipline as the latter. While explorers would in the present state of acquaintance prefer the *Wangwana* as escort, the *Wanyamwezi* are far superior as porters. Their greater freedom from diseases, their great strength and endurance, the pride they take in their profession of porters, prove them born travelers of incalculable use and benefit to Africa. If kindly treated, I do not know more docile and good-natured creatures.[22]

Despite this fortunate "fact" of African life, Stanley inevitably finds himself engaged anyway in remaking African character through his role as disciplinarian. Attributing Livingstone's years of wandering to his excessive mildness as a leader and determined to march resolutely to the accomplishment of the goals of the expedition, Stanley puts on a face of "gentleness and patience" that nonetheless signals clearly the presence behind it of "strong, unbending force" (Stanley I: 56). When fifty of his men desert at the very beginning of his journey he even posts "detectives" to catch them, worried that unless he does so he will not have sufficient numbers to command the respect of the tribes he will be moving among. What's more, he seldom hesitates to impose a harsh military discipline on his employees, although he is given to describing the actual scene of punishment in circumlocutions familiar to Victorian public school teachers: "whipping," for instance, is always displaced by the more polite and innocuous-sounding "chastisement" ("chastisement," in fact, even works overtime in this book as a euphemism for "slaughter": most notably in the scene in which Stanley and his party join the *Waganda* in a fight against their local enemies whom they fire upon from the water [Stanley I: 229]). Despite his use of euphemism, however, Stanley frankly confesses to using a level of violence proportional to the African violence it is designed to curb, for he insists that the measures he takes against his unruly men should be seen as "inoculating the various untamed spirits . . . with a respect for order and discipline, obedience and system" (Stanley I: 55). What is inoculation, after all, if not infection for prophylactic purposes? In Stanley, the disease that is African disorder can only be cured by the administration of judicious amounts of the infectious agent. The taming of one's porters is not merely a metaphor for the taming of the wilderness but a practical training for it.

But how will the exercise of violence, even in the interests of the "black brother's" long-term good, inculcate respect? For inculcating respect, it would seem, should be necessary for successful management. Here Stanley falls back on the metaphor of colt-breaking so familiar from later Victorian discussions of the twin enterprises of childrearing and *mission civilisatrice*:

The dark brother, wild as a colt, chafing, restless, ferociously impulsive, super-stitiously timid, liable to furious demonstrations, suspicious and unreasonable, must be forgiven seventy times seven, until the period of probation is passed. Long before this period is over, such temperate conduct will have enlisted a powerful force, attached to their leader by bonds of good-will and respect, even, perhaps, of love and devotion, and by the moral influence of their support even the most incorrigible *mauvais sujet* will be restrained, and finally conquered. (Stanley I: 58)

The cure, in short, for the undisciplined behavior of the opium-eating, betel-chewing, cannabis-smoking *Wangwana* of Zanzibar is a disciplinary regime designed to encourage the construction of psychological interiors equipped with consciences capable of memory – in fact, the memory of pain. Moreover, memory itself, on this model, is called into existence by a metonymical displacement of experiential "effect" by inferred "cause." While punishment is the traumatic (and necessarily memorable) "effect," to achieve true interiority, in Stanley's sense, one must be able to infer a "cause" – the "offense" – which then subsequently must inhabit memory as the origin of punishment. And if the violence of *Bula Matari*'s punishments is proportional to the enormity of the inferred cause (the offenses which merit punishment in the first place) then surely punishment itself can be taken as a sign of love, and the punisher viewed with the respect appropriate to him who dispenses love only apparently disguised in the clothes of hate. Moreover, the morality of this kind of punishment is somehow guaranteed by the pain it causes the punisher: it is Stanley, after all, who is forced to bend his own will to the discipline of punishing others, to the punishing demands of the role of leader. The theme of shared sacrifice, a standard one in travelogues of this genre, becomes the almost ludicrous means by which the leader justifies his own indulgence of disciplining power. By assuming the role of the "god" or "chief" who suffers from having to inflict suffering (he prefers the more modest term "white father"), Stanley attempts to justify his own project and his privileged role to his employees – and readers.

As with most travelogues of the "survival" type, the geographic destination is invested with central metaphorical significance. The ultimate purpose of the leader's strategic use of discipline is to insure the insertion of his newly disciplined subjects into the same narrative of discovery which confers meaning on the leader's own apparently aimless trek through the wilderness. However, his employees must be so inserted only at a lower level, as instruments. Thus, *Through the Dark Continent* reveals how Stanley tries to balance his practical need for standing at a godlike remove from his Zanzibaris against the need for insuring that the Zanzibaris see themselves as engaged in the same, historically significant, project as the "Master" – serving history by serving the "Master." Incapable, though, of appreciating the geographic, economic, and political significance that their trek has for their American leader, but bound nonetheless to a project which demands of them an extraordinary amount of personal risk, Stanley's Zanzibari porters and bearers must be offered some motive beyond simple monetary compensation to keep them on course. Aware, in other words, of the obvious limitations of the role of simple employer on an expedition which requires of all its members a constant readiness to run great personal risks and to make, perhaps, the ultimate personal sacrifice, Stanley knows that he can only maintain his role as leader if he strategically uses charismatic force over his African porters, if he appropriates the power and commands the deference of a great chief. In short, the function of charismatic leadership here is to make each step along the way an act of meaningful service rendered by the porter to a personalized authority, because the more distant – and abstract – goal of the entire trek is necessarily beyond his powers of understanding.

Like many white explorers of Africa, then, Stanley pretends to deplore (at least for his white audience) the fact that Africans invest him with abilities and powers that are more properly those of gods than of men (his mentor Livingstone, by contrast, usually made a point of demonstrating his fallible humanity publicly in order to avoid such ascription with special powers, which he found impious and thus a bar to the effectiveness of his missionary work). But, like countless later white explorers and adventurers, Stanley also describes for us how he eventually comes around to understanding the practical benefits of commanding great deference, especially while he has to force his Zanzibaris to hack their way through the dense underbrush of the rainforest under constant threat of attack from local cannibal tribes.

This transition in Stanley's self-conception occurs early in *Through the Dark Continent*, although one wonders if he is actually conscious of how grand is the role he has adopted. While traveling through the relatively "civilized" Uganda ruled by the Emperor Mtesa, a land which Stanley (and other European explorers) could not resist describing in Edenic terms, Stanley finds himself exploring Lake Victoria (he established on this journey that Victoria was not comprised of five different lakes, as Speke and Burton suspected). One day in April 1875, while on Musira Island, he places himself in the metaphorically significant place of transcendental subject – he who sees but cannot himself be seen – and dilates on the beauties of a scene into which he has already intervened, at least symbolically, by having named one of the islands "Alice" after his betrothed:

It is a spot from which, undisturbed, the eye may rove over one of the strangest yet fairest portions of Africa – hundreds of square miles of beautiful lake scenes – a great length of grey plateau wall, upright and steep, but indented with exquisite inlets, half surrounded by embowering plantains – hundreds of square miles of pastoral upland dotted thickly with villages and groves of banana. From my lofty eyrie I can see herds upon herds of cattle, and many minute specks, white and black, which can be nothing but flocks of sheep and goats. I can also see pale blue columns of ascending smoke from the fires, and upright thin figures moving about. Secure on my lofty throne, I can view their movements, and laugh at the ferocity of the savage hearts which beat in those thin dark figures for I am a part of Nature now, and for the present as invulnerable as itself. As little do they know that human eyes survey their forms from the summit of this lake-girt isle as that the eyes of the Supreme in heaven are upon them. How long, I wonder, shall the people of these lands remain thus ignorant of Him who created the gorgeous sunlit world they look upon each day from their lofty upland! How long shall their untamed ferocity be a barrier to the gospel, and how long shall they remain unvisited by the Teacher! (Stanley I: 222)

Despite the reversion to a pious tone in the invocation of a God-who-is-not-Stanley in the conclusion to this reverie, the significance of this passage lies in its implicit conflation of bird of prey, God, Nature, and explorer. Stanley is the explorer who sees from God's perspective, and whose act of seeing carries portents of a disciplinary project soon to be enacted on the bodies of God's wayward children who, as yet, do not know Him. Moreover, these Victoria islanders feel free to engage in "savagery" only because, so it seems, they do not yet see themselves being seen (unlike the well-behaved prisoners in Bentham's Panopticon, for instance). By contrast, the explorer, who is also not seen, is thereby free to commit himself to the discipline of disciplining them, like Moses coming down from Sinai. Again and again, the explorer who acts in the name of God finds himself in God's place – seeing with God's eyes and punishing in God's name. By his godlike behavior will you know the instrument of God.

Stanley insists that his role as disciplinarian is far from a purely negative one, however. He wants his readers to take seriously his self-presentation as a formidable "white father," as much noted for his benevolence as for his ruthlessness and determination (the "man with the open hand" is what "his" *Wangwana* would call him).[23] And he measures his success in this self-portrayal by the laudable behavior of his *Wangwana* at the end. Thus, when the bedraggled expedition finally arrives at Boma in 1877 and the *Wangwana* are finally properly fed and housed, they plunge into a state of anticlimactic "brooding" broken only by the consolations of the dying: " 'We have brought our Master to the great sea, and he has seen his white brothers, *La il Allah, il Allah!* – There is no God but God!' they said – and died" (Stanley II: 470). Although Stanley treats these exclamations as poignant tributes to the success – and worth – of his mission, they are also remarkably pathetic: the final cries of a people who have given their all for the relatively pointless task of accompanying their "Master" across the continent simply to shake hands with other white people. Like much of Stanley's journey, these moments emblematize the bureaucratic displacement of end by means: the journey itself, whose significance the "white father" must construct for his bearers, has been invested by them with "pseudo-religious" or purely ritualistic meaning because it makes no other sense that they can surmise. And that investment is encouraged by Stanley himself as an efficient means of accomplishing the goals of the expedition. Thus, unlike other Victorian travelogues (and certainly unlike Livingstone's work), *Through the Dark Continent* reads very much like a mid-Victorian textbook in management, containing the whole science of how to discipline an unruly Africa, and including even 1874 price lists sufficient to give any European traveler who wishes to follow in Stanley's footsteps a clear sense of how much it will cost to outfit a complete expedition.[24] The instrumental displacement of end by means, of ultimate goal by technique for reaching it, finds its fullest expression in this adventure novel which is also a handbook.

Stanley does a great deal more here than reveal his management techniques, however. *Through the Dark Continent* is also a paean to the promise of Trade, and an anticipatory celebration of a utopian Africa pacified by commerce. The disciplining of Africa, metaphorically prefigured here in the disciplining of the expedition itself, is presented as both a precondition to effective trade and a hoped-for result of the universalization of trade through the connection of Central Africa to European trading networks. Needless to say, Stanley's mission is thus undergirded by the unremarked paradoxes that implicitly threaten the integrity of both his ethnographic "discoveries" and his promise of an Africa transformed by trade.

One of these paradoxes runs as an unstated theme through much of the European exploration literature of the nineteenth century. It might be formulated as follows: static ethnographic description of the "people without history" combined with the strategic deployment of a transformative or "modernizing" discipline guaranteed, in the long run, to reduce the very "difference" the grasp of which is the putative source of the white man's power/knowledge. When taken one historical step further in the twentieth century, this attitude evolves into what Renato Rosaldo calls "imperialist nostalgia": the attitude of nostalgic regret for the passing of a way of life which one has oneself helped to destroy.[25] Although Stanley pays lip service to the ideals of the Livingstonian moral mission, even going so far as to attempt to convert Emperor Mtesa of Uganda to Christianity (although he thinks he is successful at this, Mtesa's subsequent behavior leaves much room for doubt), he gives, if anything, greater emphasis than Livingstone did to the transformative power of commerce. "Trade," in Stanley's book, develops a broad metaphorical significance that encompasses, among other meanings, nothing short of the moral transformation of Africa, for, like Livingstone, Stanley becomes convinced over the course of his almost four years of traveling through Central Africa that the tribes with the greatest trading contacts with the outside world are less given to repulsively primitive practices. Of course, the evidence he cites for this claim inadvertently reinforces the impression that Stanley's whole project is irredeemably self-enclosed: he often measures the degree of a tribe's primitiveness by that tribe's willingness to trade food for his cloth and to allow the peaceful passage through its territory of his expedition, an expedition which, on the evidence of the text itself, inspired a great deal of unease among Africans accustomed to associating such large groupings only with invasion forces or with slave-trading caravans come to depopulate the countryside.

A related symptomatic contradiction runs through Stanley's discussions of the importance of trade in this book, a recognizably Victorian contradiction which crystallizes in his comments on the abundance of Uganda. It might be formulated in the following way: if trade is the source of peace and progress, assuring contact and communication with the outside world and thus opening Africa up to enlightened ideas while ultimately diminishing the hostility to outsiders of the more isolated tribes, then an increase in trade will be the foundation for the moral and economic rejuvenation of Africa, as Livingstone argued. Yet trade presupposes a conception of need, and since much of Equatorial Africa is a land of abundance, as Stanley so vividly demonstrates, its people can hardly be said to "need" in the usual sense of the term. To stimulate trade, Stanley must somehow convince Europe that Africa's needs are immense. (It almost goes without saying that in writing a European bestseller Stanley was not setting out to convince Africa that it needs to trade.) Africa's eventual compliance will be guaranteed (i.e. coerced), presumably the same way that Stanley insured African compliance throughout his journey – by assisting the most powerful local rulers or slave traders, especially those like Emperor Mtesa who are given to a laudable curiosity about European ways and European arms, to consolidate and extend their domains.

The problem Stanley faces in convincing Europe, though, is that the Kingdom of Uganda (at least as he often represents it in some lyrical passages) is a self-enclosed paradise, a place which does not need Europe in any obvious way. But unlike earlier European representations of the New World, as "Oroonoko," for example, which were designed to critique European manners and ways of life, Stanley's representations of Uganda are designed not so much to critique overcivilized Europe as to represent Africa as a land afflicted by the paradoxical disease of overabundance: a disease for which Europe and America can offer a cure.[26]

From a geopolitical point of view, Stanley tends to treat what is really a problem for Europe (why won't Central Africa agree to become part of the world trading system?) by converting it into an African problem which Europe can then solve. The problem then becomes Africa's, but an African problem which is promisingly susceptible to technocratic and imperial solutions originating in Europe and America. Despite its natural abundance, then, Africa lacks much of what Europe has: railroads, navigable rivers, the telegraph, in short, the infrastructure of the modern industrial state – all those "things" ("relations" might be a better word) which act as spurs to the kind of commerce Europe has in abundance. Africa can be "opened up" when it is awakened to its need for what Europe has. Not surprisingly, then, what Stanley most appreciates about the Emperor Mtesa is his laudable "openness" to things European (signified, above all, by Mtesa's "need" for Stanley).[27] At this general level of analysis, Stanley's argument flirts with what one might call the tautology of otherness: Africa lacks almost everything which would make it not Africa but Europe.

But the ideological power of Stanley's text lies less in its geopolitical argument (which is never completely fleshed out, in any case) than in its detailed representation of how scarcity, the *sine qua non* of economic relationships, is essential, paradoxically, to prosperity. Scarcity is – implicitly here – treated as the foundation for good individual character, and the manipulation of scarcity as the necessary foundation of commercial prosperity. The problem of Uganda's abundance, as Stanley sees it, then, lies in the fact that that abundance blinds Ugandans to the necessity of setting up extensive trading contacts with the outside world. In short, Uganda's greatest need is to be convinced that it needs.

The difficulty which occasions Stanley's resort to tautology here is a difficulty of measurement. Abundance or wealth, he seems to assume, can be measured by willingness to sell at a low price. While this may be true, *ex hypothesi*, according to one of the tenets of political economy, the experience of Central Africa makes this kind of measurement problematic. For one thing, in measuring abundance in this way, one has to suspend consideration of the relational aspect of exchange. While low prices might well argue the existence of an agricultural surplus, Stanley here is inattentive to the more germane question of who owns this surplus, assuming rather too hastily that all must have too much and thus be willing to trade it for cloth (in Uganda, Stanley is trading American-made cloth, a commodity the locals both know and desire, for food). Moreover, his experience later on in the Congo rainforest suggests that Africans trade (or refuse to trade) for a variety of reasons that often defy understanding by the standard of rationality used in an exchange-ridden economy such as Victorian Britain's, which is characterized by a high degree of specialization of economic function, and consequently, by a highly predictable and widespread need for complex exchange relations. For this reason, low prices in and of themselves can be a suspect measure of abundance: a commodity, for instance, may not be a universally accepted currency and thus cannot effectively index prosperity (although it may). As anyone who is familiar with the history of farm commodity prices in industrialized societies in the twentieth century is aware, very low prices can index overproduction – and thus poverty – as readily as prosperity.

While Stanley claims that the tribes which have more extensive trading contacts tend to be less given to savagery, the evidence he cites for this is rather suspicious. Quite often, he simply infers the existence of extensive trading contacts from the evidence that certain tribes do not mistreat his own expedition. In short: according to Stanley, if you are peaceful, you must trade; if you war on us, you must be dangerously self-enclosed and cut off from the pacifying influence of trade.

The failure to trade is nonetheless treated as the prime signifier of the myriad infrastructural deficiencies of Africa. This becomes especially clear when Stanley is in the Congo rainforest – the most difficult part of his long journey. Because trade, in his sense, requires effective means of transportation, it cannot be easily carried on here where the land is covered with virtually impassable jungle and the river is marked by extensive cataracts. Despite uncovering palpable evidence that the tribes of the rainforest do somehow trade, Stanley nonetheless finds them deficient in their trading practices because they do not use middlemen. The rainforest tribes seem to exchange goods only with contiguous tribes rather than with trading caravans traversing the entire countryside.[28] Geographical and political barriers understandably prevent the dissemination of caravans which might otherwise cross the entire region of isolated tribal groupings, linking them in a web of bartering relations. This preoccupation with middlemen is given an ironic twist later when, on his return to Africa in the 1880s, he discovers that the success of his safari across Central Africa in the late 1870s had the unintended effect of opening up new and profitable slave-trading networks for one of the most infamous middlemen in Africa, his erstwhile ally Tippu Tib, the notorious Zanzibary slave trader, who had assisted him for part of his journey up the Congo River in 1876.[29] Ironically, given Stanley's public avowal of his intent to help wipe out the slave trade, his expedition itself seems to have had the effect of stimulating rather than diminishing the trade in human beings.

The failure of Africans to trade also betokens a failure of communication, in Stanley's estimation. One of the main problems of Sub-Saharan Africa, in Stanley's view, is that information there is carried only along lines of traffic, and this makes impossible the achievement of what one might call the experience of historical simultaneity. Thus, at one point, he laments the fact that while the natives of Karangwé might quickly hear news of the arrival of white men at Victoria Nyanza (the arrival of white men is always a newsworthy subject in Stanley's estimation), the natives of Komeh, 300 miles closer to the Lake, might only hear of it long after the whites have departed (Stanley I: 119). That this problem of misinformation likewise afflicts, not only Victorian England in the 1870s, but most notably the United States with its vast frontier (despite the completion of the transcontinental telegraph in 1861), goes without remark. Africa is deficient in information and the means for its transmission, he implicitly concludes. Although he notes the widespread use of drums in the rainforest, and is impressed by the speed with which African tribes can mobilize thousands of warriors in response to the threat he represents to them (an achievement only possible if an extensive indigenous communications network already exists), he does not link this fact with his lament over Africa's lack of the telegraph.

Of course, it almost goes without saying that Africa lacks a common currency, as well. Although Stanley is able to use American-made cloth to trade for food during a good portion of his journey, the final hundred miles or so of his journey down the Congo finds his expedition gradually succumbing to the effects of malnutrition because they are unable to find natives willing to trade food for their cloth. The acceptable "currency" in this part of Africa is, it seems, not cloth (here relatively abundant due to the extensive trading links these tribes have with the Europeanized West Coast), but rum (which is greatly desired but in scant supply). Without rum to trade for food, Stanley and his force are whittled down to skeletons before finally being rescued by the Europeans of Boma. They become, ironically, victims of an indifferent local population who ought to exemplify the beneficent effects of free trade on Africa. The final irony of Africa is that nowhere is it in greater need of drastic moral reformation than here, only a few miles inland from the West Coast, where it comes closest to conforming to Stanley's prescriptions.

The self-enclosure of Stanley's discourse on Africa's needs is perhaps not surprising in such a thorough-going disciple of the Victorian faith in progress. Yet Stanley's almost systematic construction of Africa's needs along the lines of his own practical exigencies does throw some light on a similar process of substitution occurring more self-consciously in the "official" discourse of an imperial manager such as Cromer. The ideological power of this transposition lies in its deferral of the question of ultimate purpose through the substitution of instrumental purposes. He who constructs Africa's future need not answer any ultimate questions about why it must be so constructed: the doing substitutes for consideration of ultimate purposes. In this type of exploration narrative, the confrontation with alien forms of life in an alien land provokes, not so much the moral disgust of the missionary, as the practical disgust of the "man of action" who is bound to a project of exploration the worth of which is measured largely by its practical difficulty. Yet Stanley's instrumentalist rationality engenders a utopian vision of an Africa pacified by commerce and, especially, by the infrastructure of the capitalist state: a vision which, he certainly believes, is fundamentally moral. As improved communication and transportation will doubtless promote trade, it must then follow that improved trade will foster peace and a laudable openness to civilized values somehow so evident in the Europe of the 1870s. It is perhaps not surprising that Stanley should have been taken in by Leopold's philanthropic pretenses for the Congo: railroads carried moral meanings for Stanley long before he first met Leopold in 1878.

Yet if Stanley's preoccupation with the morality of infrastructure is perhaps understandable in such an unselfconscious instrumentalist, it commits him, nonetheless, to something like what Marx would call "fetishism" (perhaps we might refer to it as "infrastructural fetishism" rather than "commodity fetishism").[30] Stanley's fascination with infrastructure and the management of a preindustrial workforce is fundamentally a fascination with techniques which ultimately are to serve the moral goals of African prosperity and progress. That process of divination, however, sets Stanley on a course of infinite instrumentalist regress, with the rather abstract goal of civilizing Africa yielding its place to instrumental goals of seemingly increasing concreteness. As the precondition for civilization and progress is trade, the precondition for trade is infrastructure (means of transportation and communication) and social discipline. But why arrest the regress at this point? Indeed, Stanley eventually does not. What he discovers when he returns to the Congo to build a railroad and finds himself beset by a variety of practical difficulties (including the political difficulties created by his rivalry with the French explorer de Brazza and his service to Leopold) are the preconditions for infrastructure and social discipline: political reorganization and military pacification. In other words, empire.

While it would be foolish to argue that Europe did not need Africa in the nineteenth century, for the evidence of Africa's economic importance to an expansive capitalism is too weighty to be ignored, there is also no question that the commercial/humanitarian construction of Africa's needs played possibly the most important part in creating the ideological preconditions for "the Scramble."

By the 1880s Stanley was directly involved in propaganda for the "Free State" on behalf of King Leopold. In the immediate aftermath of the Congress of Berlin in 1885, Stanley published his book *The Congo and the Founding of Its Free State*, a book which dedicates its second-to-last chapter to inventorying the vast natural riches of the Congo and its last to examining the rich political opportunities for Europeans in Central Africa which the Congress itself seemed to have authorized for them. Having summarized the decisions of the Congress, Stanley then goes on to welcome the "merchant adventurer" to a land which, through Stanley's efforts and those of the assembled powers of Europe, has been made "safe" for his work:

These philanthropic views have been realised. The merchant adventurer is fenced all around with guarantees against spoliation, oppression, vexation, and worry, and his Consul, the representative of his Government, is charged with the jurisdiction over his person and property. At the gateway to the free commercial realm the commissioner, with his colleagues, will take position, and will remain there close at hand to protect his interests. These officials will constitute a Court of Law called the International Commission, to whom he can always appeal for redress and protection. Only on the exportation of the produce he has collected can a moderate sum be charged, sufficient to remunerate the riveraine Government for its expenditure. The liquor traffic may not be abused; slave-trading is prohibited; the missionary is entitled to special protection; and scientific expeditions to special privileges. To all these numerous privileges in behalf of commerce and humanity, the European Powers, and the United States, as well as the International Association, otherwise the Congo State, unanimously gave their approval, and every political Power left the Conference with unqualified satisfaction.[31]

No longer merely an explorer and commentator on the deficiencies and beauties of Africa, Stanley has become after 1878 the agent of King Leopold assigned the task of "selling" a false vision of a pacified and politically-organized Free State to some of the same readers who were presumably entranced by his narratives of the perils of exploration. Beginning with an invocation of "philanthropy" in this passage, he exhorts the European businessman to come to a part of Africa already prepared to receive him. He will be well received precisely because this "commercial adventurer" will not, so the passage implies, have to behave like an adventurer. His personal property rights are protected by laws guaranteed by nothing less than the assembled Powers of Europe. Should he suffer "spoliation, oppression, vexation" he has means of legal redress. Even "worry" has been ruled out as a possible experience for the European business "adventurer" in the Congo. Evoking the very anxieties about "savage Africa" it seeks to put to rest, the rhetoric of this passage seems to be attempting to conjure away not only the lawlessness of Central Africa but the lawlessness of the imperial rivals of Europe. The passage's metaphors of enclosure (from the merchant's being "fenced all around" to the "gateway" where he will be greeted by his attendant consul) are ambivalent on at least two planes: on the horizontal plane, by evoking too immediately the threat of "untamed" Central Africa without the "fence" which menaces and helps create the experience of "safety" and enclosure within; and on the vertical plane, by suggesting that the "merchant adventurer" will find himself in a law-governed space, his great importance – indeed, the commercial pioneer's singularity – signaled by his ability to command the personal attention of the highest of government representatives – "his Consul" – who will (note the military metaphor) "take position" to greet him at the gateway. Coming as it does at the end of another of Stanley's bestselling "survival" narratives, this welcome to European business cannot help but charge the prospect of European trade in Central Africa with the meaning of dangerous adventure, precisely because Stanley is at such pains to deny it. Stanley welcomes the businessman into the experience of his books – an experience fraught with the vicarious perils (i.e. the purely imaginative pleasures) of the individual hero successfully tackling an untamed Africa – but assures him that he will arrive via a comfortable steamer. Whatever the risks (we will only allude to those), the rewards, he promises, will consist not just of profit, but of recognition. The European trader will find himself in Stanley's shoes miraculously relieved of the necessity of confronting the dangers he did. Like much of Stanley's work, this passage couches a utopian vision in implicit self-congratulation: a vision of peaceful, law-abiding, commercial prosperity, in which open trade is somehow reconciled with the best interests of both European businessman and African native.

# CHAPTER 3

# Kipling's "Law" and the division of bureaucratic labor

For when the gentiles, which have not the law, do by nature the things contained in the law, these, having not the law, are a law unto themselves: Which shew the work of the law written in their hearts, their conscience also bearing witness, and their thoughts the mean while accusing or else excusing one another.

Romans 2: 14–15

Although not a colonial official himself, Rudyard Kipling, when he returned to India in 1882 to become sub-editor of the *Civil and Military Gazette* in Lahore and begin his career as a serious writer of fiction, found himself among hordes of English who were.[1] In fact, the note of defensive self-assertion which sounds through Kipling's "know-it-all" attitude in his early writing seems to serve a dual purpose: to represent in fictional form the attitudes so common among the types of English officials he knew in India, and to express a more complicated, if somewhat transparently desperate, longing for the expert knowledge usually available only to credentialed bureaucrats. Not only do many of Kipling's tales center themselves on the figure of the solitary administrator, a bureaucrat who is essentially alone yet the center of a complex web of power and information systems, but his work often presents an "official" view of the cosmic order as a seemingly suitable metaphor for cosmic order itself.[2]

There is an oft-cited passage in his story "The Conversion of Aurelian McGoggin," for example, directed ostensibly against intellectual atheism, in which Kipling seems to be celebrating the bureaucratic hierarchy of the cosmos while implicitly distancing himself – through irony – from "official wisdom" of this complacent sort:

But in India, where you really see humanity – raw, brown, naked humanity – with nothing between it and the blazing sky, and only the used-up, overhandled earth underfoot, the notion somehow dies away, and most folk come back to simpler theories. Life, in India, is not long enough to waste in proving that there is no one in particular at the head of affairs. For this reason, the Deputy is above the Assistant, the Commissioner above the Deputy, the Lieutenant-Governor above the Commissioner, and the Viceroy above all four, under the orders of the Secretary of State, who is responsible to the Empress. If the Empress be not responsible to her Maker – if there is no Maker for her to be responsible to – the entire system of Our administration must be wrong; which is manifestly impossible.[3]

However well this tongue-in-cheek statement epitomizes the banal "truths" by which imperial bureaucrats live (or, rather, the "truths" they manufacture to justify their work to the public), it certainly would be a mistake to identify Kipling's own views too closely with the opinions voiced in this passage. Indeed, the tautological structure of the argument, a tautological structure characteristic of similar arguments from cosmic design going back at least to Pope's "Essay on Man," suggests that Kipling is placing himself at an ironic remove (Pope can hardly be said to have been treating Bolingbroke's views with irony). If hierarchy has a justification, the passage implies, it lies in the fact of hierarchy.[4] As an argument, the passage reduces to the tautological claim that the cosmos must be hierarchically ordered because, if it were not, imperial hierarchies would lose their justification. In other words, the claim the syllogism is designed to support is already assumed in its premises.

If transparently specious, the argument nonetheless does cast some interesting light on Kipling's own, more deeply skeptical, views. Kipling's doubts about ultimate purposes, one suspects, often lead him to make a vociferous pledge of allegiance to the bureaucratic purpose of the moment.[5] Certainly the classic example of this is "The Great Game" in the novel *Kim*: although British political objectives within a game of European Great Power rivalry are presented in that book as the ultimate sanction for Kim's own actions on behalf of the British Secret Service, Kim's accomplishments can only be termed "epic" if one stretches the meaning of the term considerably. The "Game" itself in *Kim* never loses the connotation of "trivial child's play" (the French and Russian agents whom Kim and Huree Babu "defeat" in the Himalayas are but ignorant buffoons). Moreover, the other father figures in that book – Lurgan Sahib, Huree Babu, Mahbub Ali, and even Colonel Creighton – are depicted essentially as boys engaged in "playing" for "its own sake." Given these facts, it is hardly likely that Kipling invested the actual goals of the Secret Service (as opposed to the process of playing itself) with ultimate importance. The work of empire, for Kipling, is finally a substitute instrumental goal hypostatized to ultimate purpose (much like Marlow's notion of "work" in *Heart of Darkness*). And this hypostatization produces the rhetorically satisfying (if ideologically suspicious) effect of quietly ushering off the stage inconvenient questions of ultimate purpose which, in any case, Kipling's corrosive skepticism cannot abide.

Despite Kipling's preoccupation with the psychic and social value of "work-as-end," his focus in his fiction is seldom on just any form of work. Work, in Kipling, is usually a complex form of social endeavor featuring – indeed, requiring – a complex division of labor which, in turn, is treated as the glue holding a society together.[6] Thus, Kipling's early stories often make a point of identifying and dramatizing the complex division of labor which grounds all social endeavor. Moreover, unlike most of his Victorian contemporaries, Kipling does not attribute uniqueness to industrialized societies in this regard – nor, for that matter, to human societies. Because of the universality he attributes to it, the division of labor passes out of the realm of culture (it is by no means unique to industrial Europe) to become a constitutive feature of nature. For this reason, Kipling's preoccupation with imperial work in "adult" stories like "The Bridge-Builders," "William the Conqueror," and "At the End of the Passage" and in the novel *Kim* is of a piece with his focus on the "work" of hunting (and vengeance) in animal parables like *The Jungle Books*, ostensibly written for children.

Rather than seeing Kipling as the apostle of "work," then, I propose seeing him as the apostle of "division of labor." For Kipling, a complex – and hierarchical – division of labor is the foundation of social order everywhere.[7] The interdependency such work fosters ultimately helps to glue the social order together in a complex web of interrelationships, founded on inequalities of power and ability. Social order, in Kipling, is most often an effect of bureaucratic ordering of work – the "rationalization" of human relationships – that makes the human social world of India subserve imperial ends (in *Kim*, most obviously) and the sociality of the animal world subserve the ends of evolutionary "fitness" (in *The Jungle Books*).

It should be added that "order," to Kipling, means disciplinary interdependency, or rather, that "order" is the name he usually applies retrospectively to the effects of disciplinary interdependency. Despite his infatuation with engineering and the toys of modern technology (he was especially fond of motor cars in middle age), Kipling is not quite accurately seen as a late-Victorian apostle of "progress," however. For him, the justification of bureaucratic modes of order is ultimately to be found in bureaucracy's ability to bestow value, to bridge the gap between instrumental and ultimate purposes – manufacturing something to do and offering itself as a means for doing it – thus bestowing a sense of almost godlike agency on certain individuals which is accompanied by the positing of strict limits to individual autonomy as well as a self-conscious skepticism about the "ends" thus manufactured.

For this reason, social hierarchies in Kipling (at least among his human characters and animals) tend to feature less the racial rigidities of caste than efficient (or inefficient) divisions of labor and thus tend to serve utilitarian rather than cosmically authoritarian ends. Unlike the relatively rigid caste structure of traditional Indian society (which was deliberately given a renewed emphasis by the British *Raj* in the nineteenth century), bureaucratic hierarchies of this sort ought, ideally, to be flexible enough to change as the "work" of the particular society changes.[8] Nevertheless, because Kipling does hypostatize this order, his works have an ideological effect akin to Cromer's justification of imperial rule: the Kipling text is busily involved in manufacturing the ideological justifications for the bureaucratic order it represents and reifies on its own pages. Like Cromer's theory of administrative efficiency, Kipling's representations of Indian life perform the trick of inverting the conventional relationship of instrumental goals to final or ultimate goals, thus implicitly dismissing the latter as unimportant. One of the remarkable features of Kipling as a writer is his ability to dramatize for his readers the dilemma of the bureaucratic underling, while insisting, like others "in the know," that we readers remain knowledgeably skeptical about the worth – or durability – of the ultimate goals for which such bureaucrats work.

I would like to examine this aspect of Kipling's work as it reveals itself in one of his most impressive early achievements, *The Jungle Books* (1894–1895) – a collection of stories in which "nature" is reinvented as a bureaucratic order characterized by a high degree of specialization of function (a cross between an efficient business firm and a military organization, in fact). But before doing so, I wish to look at two other works of his from the 1890s – "At the End of the Passage" (1890) and *Stalky and Co.* – which foreground social and cosmic order, not so much as a feature of the world, but as individual praxis, a process of deliberate and necessary ordering in which the individual subject is bound to engage in order to preserve his own sanity. In focusing on these stories, I take for granted the common claim that Kipling is the literary apostle of imperial officialdom – the celebrator of "the white man's burden" carried on by an efficiently operating network of well-trained experts such as the spies of Colonel Creighton's "Ethnological Survey." Thus, I give much less emphasis than I might to the stories which underline that well-known side of his career as a writer.9 What I am primarily interested in here instead is the Kipling who connects bureaucratic order to a late-Victorian model of "nature," the Kipling who naturalizes and domesticates bureaucracy.

The contrast in tone is stark, then, between the early story "At the End of the Passage," which peddles dark "adult" truths about a cosmic bureaucracy's indifference to human desires, and the two *Jungle Books*, written a mere five years later, which address an audience of children with the comforting illusion that "nature" is always already governed by a code of "laws," and that the human world of bureaucratic work is metaphorically identical with the natural order.

2

"At the End of the Passage" presents itself initially, at least to twentieth-century readers, as a classically "Kiplingesque" rumination on the tragic stakes in the solitary "white man's burden." The four English subalterns and civil servants who meet weekly to squabble while playing whist are represented as needing these "holidays" in order to manage, however tenuously, to "pull themselves together." As Kipling says, "They were lonely folk who understood the dread meaning of loneliness."10 Their need for each other's company is described as being as "ardent" a need as the desire to drink is for "men without water." Their day-to-day work consists of a variety of politically grand yet finally thankless tasks: one character, Lowndes, is assigned the Cromeresque job of managing the ruler of a "native state" in the interests of the British *Raj*; another, the doctor Spurstow, is charged with trying to stem the spread of cholera during a particularly oppressive dry season. The anonymity of these large tasks, the general thanklessness of imperial work, as well as the manifold personal risks to which the characters are exposed by administrative higher-ups who treat them as readily replaceable cogs, occasions the need for socializing with fellow bureaucrats and trading insults which reassert confraternity by paradoxically testing its boundaries.11

The story implies that the characters seek out the recognition denied them by higher-ups through substitutes: specifically, through a male bonding ritual with their own "kind" in which insults substitute for more direct tokens of respect and affection, and in which the fantasy of childish dependency can be indulged, however apologetically, to alleviate the strain of playing the "adult" in their working lives. Although a familiar theme in Kipling's early work, "At the End of the Passage" turns the homosocial group, driven back upon their own community-in-small because denied recognition from "above," into a metaphor for human work and the construction of value.[12] Unlike some other pieces of his writing, though, "At the End of the Passage" poses, but cannot answer, the question of whether there is an overarching "order" – a cosmic "Great Game," for instance, or a solemn order of "duty" – which might guarantee the ultimate efficacy of sacrifice, bestowing meaning on individual death and a progressive trajectory to the individual life, and, by extension, to the imperial project which he supervises. While the comic novel *Kim* assumes the existence of a larger (and largely benevolent) imperial system for Kim to serve and a rule-governed, if contestatory, political order – the "Great Game" – which both limits and enables his successes as agent of the *Raj* (that is, after all, the ultimate source of most of the comforting illusions the novel peddles), the tragic story "At the End of the Passage" raises questions about the very existence of such an order, or, at the very least, that order's ability to ground identity and meaning (as, for instance, the *langue* determines meaning for an individual utterance – a *parole* – within it). "At the End of the Passage" is ultimately about the refusal of initiation, the emotional ambivalence that underlies the very attractive wish to "sleep back" into "terrified childhood" in order to escape the unbearable emptiness of bureaucratic subjectivity. Yet, in this story, bureaucratic subjectivity comes to be equated with identity itself, as the official bureaucracy of the *Raj* becomes a metaphor for the cosmic order.

The grim discussions of the men playing whist underline the psychological difficulty of performing the job of imperial official in what Cromer called "unofficial" empire. Like Cromer himself, who was sent to Egypt to exercise authority only indirectly by advising the nominally independent Khedive, the British officials in this story either have been themselves advisors to native states' rulers or are familiar with the bureaucratic difficulties in advising rulers only nominally independent of the British *Raj*. A figure like Lowndes, for instance, finds himself in exactly this delicate political position. His job requires him to "manage" a native states ruler without any public show of management. Thus, he exercises what is only a potential authority in the name of a government which deliberately sends subaltern officials to do work for which the Colonial Office can disclaim responsibility any time it so wishes. Like T. E. Lawrence on his first mission to Feisal, men placed in this position find themselves in the position of "boys" doing "men's" work, but without the security that full public authority confers. The whole point of Indirect Rule, after all, at least as far as the Government of India is concerned, is to bully "Old Timbersides" while evading the messy political consequences that the spectacle of public bullying will inevitably bring on. Underpaid, unrecognized, overworked, and forced to conform to a relatively rigid standard of sexual abstinence as a requirement of their jobs, the white characters in "At the End of the Passage" find a temporary respite from the ideals Cromer celebrates by trading in insider gossip about the depravity of native states' rajahs and by singing sentimental music hall songs which evoke an imaginary home country they will never see. It almost goes without saying that the ideological burden of this species of Kipling's work is to celebrate the ethic of self-sacrifice in a way that avoids questions about what England is doing in India to begin with, for in this respect Kipling's basic political assumptions seem at one with those of the members of the Anglo-Indian Club.

The story itself, however, is a bit too subversive to be talked about comfortably over drinks at the Club. The central metaphor – "the passage" – carries multiple but closely related connotations which suggest its ambivalence: "the passage" refers most obviously to a process of initiation, a "rite of passage" (which connotes the possibility of mastery implied in the everyday honorific meaning of "adulthood"); to the crossing of boundaries (from life into death, waking into sleep, while implicitly refusing the conventional position of privilege to either "life" or "waking rationality"); and to birth itself (ironically pointing to the horrors of individual subjectivity awaiting the newborn at the end of the birth passage, to the castrating loss of fullness that is the price of subjectivity and identity). The latter connotation is especially interesting, because it suggests that Kipling's story toys with a fantasy of regression in which birth is projected as a peculiarly horrifying form of metaphorical death. What lies at the end of the passage is "birth" imagined as death or extinction. The ambivalence behind this fantasy is the psychological root of "self-negating desire": in its "publicly acceptable" form, the foundation of the self-renunciatory ethos; in its "unacceptable" form, the root of the desire for self-negation. In this tale, the negative side to self-extinction is principally what is emphasized. As I have argued in Chapter 1, it is Cromer who most baldly aligns the self-renunciatory ethos of Victorian culture with the day-to-day requirements of imperial management. But it is Kipling who most clearly stipulates the tragic cost such an ethos imposes, while hinting at its attractions. "At the End of the Passage," then, focuses mainly on the tragic dimension to bureaucratic rule, the cost which ruling imposes on those who work for the ruler, the harsh discipline to which those who discipline others must themselves submit. And this tragic cost is dramatized in the "going out" of Hummil.

Hummil, we readers discover, is rapidly coming undone. His cynicism seems to exceed the ordinary grumbling expected from overworked employees who have not been getting enough sleep. In fact, the other three characters treat his attitude as an implicit threat to themselves, at least partly because Hummil frankly admits his own attraction to suicide, an attraction which the others share but will not admit. Thus, at one point, Hummil loudly praises another British official, the "luckier" Jevins who, he says, recently "went out," using a phrase which, with obvious irony, identifies the assumption of imperial duties with death itself. While all four characters freely insult each other, Hummil's aggressive abuse of the others at dinner one night exceeds even their rather liberal standards of "fair play":

Throughout the meal Hummil contrived laboriously to insult directly and pointedly all his guests in succession, and at each insult Spurstow kicked the aggrieved persons under the table; but he dared not exchange a glance of intelligence with either of them. Hummil's face was white and pinched, while his eyes were unnaturally large. No man dreamed for a moment of resenting his savage personalities, but as soon as the meal was over they made haste to get away. ("Passage," p. 87)

Lowndes, Mottram, and Spurstow expand the ordinary bounds of "fair play" immeasurably by performing monumental acts of self-suppression under the "benevolent" discipline of Doctor Spurstow, busily kicking each of the other two under the table to prevent them from responding to Hummil's importunities in kind. Yet the story implies that Hummil's failure to provoke a directly "savage" reaction from his fellows contributes to his loss of psychological mooring: Hummil's verbal violence is meeting no resistance to speak of; his fellow bureaucrats are denying him the therapeutic experience of a punch in the face. Having already lost a sense of his human limits, signified by his barely jocular identification of himself with one of Satan's despairing minions ("It's an insult to the intelligence of the Deity to pretend we're anything but tortured rebels" ["Passage," p. 86]), Hummil takes refuge in a desire for a sleep which, ironically, he cannot attain. Sleep promises both relief from the physical tortures of everyday existence in India (underlined by the stifling atmospherics of the story) and the fulfillment of the logic of self-renunciation: a loss of self viewed, not negatively (as self-sacrifice), but positively (as desire to die, to be released, to stand beyond desire). Like Hamlet, Hummil has sought sleep but discovered, to his despair, that it can be accompanied by nightmares – the prolongation of consciousness beyond the threshold of consciousness. His ambivalence is perfectly captured here when he first begs Spurstow, like a child, to give him a soporific; then confesses that he originally brought his sleeplessness on himself by placing a spur in his bed to prevent himself from "going off" (Passage, p. 92). The measures taken to forestall death are ironically those which accelerate its coming. Sleeplessness, in the hot climate of this part of India, puts one well along the road to death. Moreover, despite Spurstow's commitment to therapeutic ideals, even he finds it necessary to pay a tribute to the attractions of death/release by offering a general thanks to "Heaven who has set a term to our miseries" ("Passage," p. 93).[13]

Yet the important role that bureaucracy plays in this tragic tale is underlined in the passage in which Hummil explains to Spurstow why it is that he will not take a vacation. Were he to do so, he would have to be replaced by Burkett who would inevitably be accompanied by his wife. For Hummil, a regress of official relationships opens up the possibility of an infinite regress of tragedy: thus, he imagines Burkett's wife "murdered" by accompanying Burkett, who would himself be "murdered" by the very physical conditions from which Hummil would be taking a holiday ("Passage," p. 94). And this realization is conditioned by the imagined universality of the self-renunciatory ethic among Anglo-Indians: the predictable spectacle of Burkett's wife, the loyal *memsahib*, surrendering her own comfort to be at her husband's side once her husband is ordered to die in Hummil's place. The anxiety which this vision occasions underlines the point that Hummil finds himself governed by conflicting codes: he cannot take leave without abandoning his successor and wife to almost certain death; he cannot stay without implicitly accepting the inevitability of his own death. To do his job is to die. Moreover, given his clear ambivalence, Hummil's refusal to take a vacation may also be read as the exercise of the selfish desire to monopolize for himself the joys of the ultimate "holiday."

Martin Green refers to this element in Kipling's work as an attempt to re-motivate an eclipsed ethic of loyalty and self-sacrifice once felt to be characteristic of the "aristo-military caste" in English society.[14] While this is undoubtedly one of the ideological burdens it shoulders (although we have already made the point earlier that this "aristo-military" ethos should actually be seen as the product of the imagination of middle-class professionals), it is striking how far Kipling is willing to go in the direction of offering, not simply a plea for the shouldering of self-sacrificial burdens, but an appeal to the libidinal satisfactions implicit in self-negation for its own sake.[15] On the artistically more interesting side of self-sacrifice for Kipling, lie the subversive but publicly inadmissible pleasures of self-obliteration or self-negation. These pleasures are, it must be said, dramatized in more socially acceptable forms elsewhere in his fiction: at the end of *The Light That Failed*, for instance, in the mortally wounded Dick Heldar's embrace by his male "mother" Torpenhow on the battlefield in the Sudan; or in *Kim*, in the form of the Lama's search for his river and release from the burden of desire. In any case, self-sacrifice is seldom without its attractions for Kipling.

Hummil's dilemma in "At the End of the Passage" is compounded by the difficulty of distinguishing between "identity" and "place" in a bureaucratic hierarchy. When Spurstow leaves Hummil to return to his own job for a week, Hummil begins to have serious auto-hallucinations. The "splitting" of Hummil which follows the departure of Spurstow is the literalization of this paradox of bureaucratic identity. That the departure of the English "other" coincides with the liberation of a mirror-image "spectre" of the self is hardly accidental. Hummil has already "given birth" to this "spectre" in his discourse with Spurstow, in his imagination of the bureaucratic "place" of death filled by anyone English and therefore victim, like himself, of self-renunciatory disci-pline. Its literal realization in the narrative suggests a moment of "Imaginary" identification of self with its "place," self with representa-tion, that is simply the fantasmatic realization of Hummil's desire to fill the empty place of death. He finds his "place" at the price of discovering that what he is is nothing more than a structural node in a disciplinary network, a network which is implicitly identified both with an histori-cally contingent form of bureaucratic work and with the cosmic bureau-cracy.

But it is the reaction of the returning friends on discovering Hummil's body a week later which reinforces Kipling's point about identity and bureaucracy here, and marks "At the End of the Passage" as one of the finest stories about professional anxiety. Lowndes, for instance, is immediately spooked by the "look" in the dead Hummil's open eyes, and he identifies the fear he feels with the problem of representation, the problem of the "likeness":

"I can't face it!" whimpered Lowndes. "Cover up the face! Is there any fear on earth that can turn a man into that likeness? It's ghastly. Oh, Spurstow, cover it up!"

"No fear – on earth," said Spurstow.

Mottram leaned over his shoulder and looked intently. "I see nothing except some grey blurs in the pupil. There can be nothing there, you know." ("Passage," p. 97)

Mottram's claim that there can be "nothing" in a dead man's eyes actualizes the fear rather than assuages it. What does one see in the eye of a dead man? Oneself, of course, reflected back: or rather, another pair of eyes reflecting yet another pair of eyes and so on, *ad infinitum*, an infinite regress of mirroring representations without point of origin. Yet the very identification of the subject with the other, the image on the eye of the other, is accompanied by the disturbing realization that that image entails the loss of what it represents. In death, Hummil does not "look like" Hummil; in death, he "looks like" Mottram, Spurstow, Lowndes, and anyone else who identifies with the image in his open eyes – in short, anyone who has eyes. The "place" he once filled is their "place," yet to identify with him on that basis is to risk identifying with an empty "node" in a bureaucratic structure, potentially assignable to anyone and therefore the place of no one in particular. The "spectre" which Hummil's isolation liberates, finally, is the "spectre" of mirroring representations without origin, empty places in a symbolic order which promises to confer identity on the subject and value on his work, but which actually confers nothing but the empty identity of the bureaucratic role – after all, dying is a job for which anyone is well qualified – within a larger structure organized along the lines of strict division of imperial labor.

Despite the seeming promise that bureaucratic ambition makes – the promise that success (and identity) will be bestowed and measured by one's march up its carefully differentiated ladder rungs – inhabiting the very promise of bureaucratic "identity" is the threat of de-individuation. Thus, when Spurstow returns from his bathroom confrontation with "nothing" near the end of the tale (it was clearly "something" which causes him to destroy his camera), his own "whiteness" recapitulates the "whiteness" of the "spectre" he did/did not see, much as Mottram's earlier "whiteness" duplicates the whiteness of the dead Hummil upon whom he gazes. Kipling's point seems to be that death is infectious because it is bound up with the process of representation itself, conferring identity at the price of sacrifice.[16] Yet "whiteness" here is also a signifier of the collapse of individual differences. In terms of the political allegory, "At the End of the Passage" identifies "whiteness" itself (the "whiteness" of "whites") as the empty "place" in a disciplinary order "filling" an "empty place" in history. What is the cost of ruling? Acceptance of self-obliteration.

However much this story may reinforce the classic Anglo-Indian belief that imperial service was a necessary, albeit thanklessly noble, act of self-sacrifice, there is no question that few writers of the period ever subjected its darkly tragic implications to an analysis as stark as Kipling's. Nor does Kipling admit here the conventionally Victorian consolation that usually accompanies celebrations of the ideal of self-sacrificial service: the conceit that one has left behind a permanently better world, a much "improved" India.

### 3

A much less grim set of tales, the stories of *Stalky and Co.*, most of which were written during the 1890s, together comprise one of the best schoolboy novels of the late-Victorian era. Many of the main characters in *Stalky* were drawn from Kipling's memory of his own experience at the United Services College at Westward Ho! in the late 1870s and early 1880s, and the three main characters in these stories – Stalky, McTurk, and Beetle – constitute a metaphorical society-in-small, whose vengeful pranks are usually organized to make the most efficient use of each individual's particular strength.

The stories also trade in an interesting myth about discipline and punishment. When one compares the almost loving way corporal punishment is meted out to the main characters by the wisely benevolent "Head" with J. A. Mangan's description of the brutality of actual public school discipline in the Victorian age, one wonders at Kipling's ability to transform his own past in the interest of publicly palatable myth. As Mangan argues, "Too frequently [during the Victorian age], there was an ideology for public consumption and an ideology for personal practice; in a phrase muscular Christianity for the consumer, Social Darwinism for the constrained."[17] Certainly, the treatment of bullying and corporal punishment in *Stalky and Co.* suggests that the author had to work overtime to reconceptualize the everyday brutality of upper-class education as a metaphorically valuable upbringing: corporal punishment that leaves its victims with no regrets and with nothing but loving memories of the chief brute – the Head (Kipling dedicated *Stalky and Co.* to Cormell Price, his beloved Headmaster at the United Services College, who died five years before the book was published).

Indeed, the first story – "Stalky" – dramatizes the chief pattern for many of the others: Stalky and Co. triumphing over one of the housemasters by outfoxing him. As in all the stories, the punishments the Head metes out here in response to the boys' misbehavior are tinged with a great deal of ambivalence. Thus, when the Head hears the true story of Mr. King's being dressed down by Colonel Dabney for trespassing on his land and then gives each boy six licks for embarrassing the housemaster, he leaves them in paroxysms of gratitude, precisely because the Head has admitted to them that he is "perpetrat[ing] a howling injustice."[18] The boys' gratitude stems from the delighted glimpse they have been given into the Head's constraints: like a larger schoolboy, the Head himself, they discover, is bound by rules. One of these rules requires him to maintain discipline among the housemasters by supporting their authority up to a point, even if it means that, in order to do so, he must dispense a few unwarranted beatings to the boys. In other words, the beating scene is one which universalizes the notion of constraint through a complex displacement: the Head beats the schoolboys in order to maintain discipline among the housemasters, not among the boys. Being beaten "unjustly" secures the boys' symbolic triumph over the housemaster King. In fact, beating in all these stories is depicted in a strangely non-physical way – an act of recognition that is miraculously free of pain. Like the moment of death in the mainstream Victorian novel, the moment of beating in *Stalky and Co.* is a moment of loving recognition: the teleological culmination of narrative action, the ritual act of scarification that marks the passage into manhood, the repeated moment of literal violence that confers identity and subjectivity on the victim by metaphorizing the passage into adulthood as a passage through loss and disfigurement.

Moreover, the boys usually treat the pain of an unfair beating as a fair trade-off for the momentary experience of equality with the beater. As the 1917 story "Regulus" reveals, it is important to Kipling that the moment of discipline be an implicitly democratic one. The beater and beaten must, in fact, become, not simply equals through psychological identification, but mirror images of one another. The beating scene in Kipling typically produces a moment of self-distantiation in which the subject learns to play the roles of both victim and victimizer. Thus, at the end of "Regulus," Winton, who has submitted to being caned by his form-mate "Pot," is rewarded with an appointment as Prefect. For Kipling, the route to rule is through the experience, not of justice, but of injustice seen from opposite angles. One could go so far as to say that Kipling finds injustice to be a far more important educational experience than justice. While the latter presumably teaches one the valuable lesson of what it feels like to be a victim of discipline, the former teaches one the delights of victimizing in the name of justice – or, in the name of something one cannot justify. Discipline, in other words, is the violence one ultimately learns to take pleasure from inflicting on one's self. Identity is confirmed when one is recognized by "higher-ups" as a body worth beating. Moreover, heroism involves mastering the impulse to conceive of oneself as victim, despite the abundant bodily evidence encouraging one to do so.

The symmetrical relationship between victim and victimizer, subject and object, is reinvented in one of the most interesting stories of *Stalky and Co.*, "A Little Prep." At the beginning of this story, we discover that the boys of the school have had their bounds restricted by the Head because of the threat of an outbreak of diphtheria (although only one boy, Stettson Minor, has actually contracted the disease). Breaking these bounds as usual one day, Stalky and Co. are surprised by the Head, who comes upon them "fantastically attired in old tweeds and a deerstalker" and immediately orders them punished for their disobedience of his rules (*Stalky*, p. 268). The scene in which he discovers them develops an ambiguous meaning because of Kipling's suggestion that the Head seems to have been dallying with some women whose voices the boys hear in the background. The judge – so the story initially seems to suggest – may well be pleasuring himself and hypocritically punishing the boys for their inadvertent blundering onto the scene of his pleasures. Moreover, the way the Head liberally dispenses another form of punishment – "extra tuition" – to many of the key older members of the school's rugby team at the end of term suggests that he quite possibly takes delight in punishing gratuitously.

Interwoven with this main plot is a subplot about imperial heroism and rank. A graduate of the school named Crandall has returned to the school to heroic adulation. Crandall, it seems, had performed an act of public bravery during one of the Afghan Wars by rescuing the body of another school graduate, "Fat-Sow" Duncan, who had been killed in a skirmish. The story of Crandall's bravery makes him the object of schoolboy awe when he returns to the school at the end of term to tell his story himself (and he eventually does so with graceless unease). It is only fitting that a "real subaltern" such as Crandall be conspicuous for personal bravery, for "A Little Prep" places much emphasis on the hierarchy of popularity among the graduates returning for end-of-term ceremonies. The story even has the graduates process across its pages in ranked order, from the most exalted – "real subalterns" – down to Sandhursters, to militia subalterns, to businessmen and bankers, respectively – the last-named standing on the lowest rung of the ladder of schoolboy popularity at United Services College.

Yet there are two main links between plot and subplot in this story: heroism and lungs. The Head, we and the boys discover, has not been "breaking bounds" to dally with women (although the insinuation early in the story that he was manages to "sexualize" the feat of heroism before Kipling reveals the truth to his readers), but rather has been at the home of the only victim of diphtheria, Stettson, saving his life by sucking fluid from his lungs. The women murmuring in the background in that early scene, we discover, are Stettson's mother and sister. The Head's heroic act was accomplished under the rule of reticence (he told no one at the College that he had risked his life to save a schoolboy), while Crandall's, by contrast, is a public feat for which he is publicly celebrated by the younger boys (although Crandall too observes the niceties of the rule of reticence by reluctantly telling the story in as awkwardly unadorned a fashion as possible). To reinforce the symmetry of Head and Crandall, the story reveals that both "victims" have lung problems: Stettson has diphtheria and Fat-Sow Duncan was shot, we are told, through the lungs.

Because of its starkly symmetrical plotting, the story manages to suggest, not only the obvious point that the Head's personal bravery is parallel to Crandall's, but that saving the signifier of the dead – the body – as Crandall does on the battlefield, is equivalent to saving the living from death, as the Head does in risking infection himself by draining Stettson's lungs of fluid. In equating the two acts of heroism through structural symmetry, the story implicitly equates the objects of heroic action – the dead body and the live body – both of which have become signifiers, nodes in a disciplinary network, possible places – roles – to be eventually filled by any of the other boys, the common fate of all.

Moreover, the public adoration showered on both the Head and

Crandall is interesting here. When the Head reminds Crandall "you'll never get such absolute adoration as you're getting now," he is forecasting the adoration to be bestowed upon him once Stalky passes word of his heroism to the rest of the boys at the school. Yet this type of adoration suggests a mirror-style collapse of individual differences: you'll never get such adoration as the adoration of your narcissistic other, for such adoration is, in a strange way, self-generated. The celebration of heroism is enabled by the successful disciplining of the schoolboys themselves. At United Services College, there is an almost universal consensus of value that is itself the chief effect produced by education at the place. The boys' rowdy celebration of the Head's own unconfessed heroism at the end of the story seals his success as an educator, and he ironically celebrates that success through his favorite ritual: by recognizing each individual boy in an "epic" orgiastic whipping at the end of the story. As Kipling says, by this feat the Head "dealt faithfully" with Stalky, McTurk, and Beetle.

When all is said and done, *Stalky and Co.* remains a collection of stories about the training of imperial rulers or heroes – the conflicting codes by which the boys who will one day rule are taught to live. Concerned with more than the inculcation of stoic virtues, though, these stories seek to reinvent pain as pleasure, punishment as recognition, and reticence as full speech. Yet the stories about Stalky, McTurk, and Beetle devote surprisingly little attention to actual learning itself. To the contrary, the main characters are presented as, in many ways, always already disciplined, always already trained in the codes of imperial service (themselves identical with the codes governing the mis-behavior of the cleverest schoolboys). In fact, the final story, "Slaves of the Lamp, Part II," underlines the equivalence of school and imperial service by staging a reunion of the now-thirtyish school chums, who gather to tell stories of the post-scholastic heroics of the absent Stalky.

While the grown-up Stalky is represented as Burton-like in his linguistic abilities and Clive-like in his leadership qualities, the deeds for which he is celebrated here are closely symmetrical with his schoolboy antics: now a charismatic leader of an Indian Army company of Sikhs, Stalky achieves immortality during the Afghan War by performing deeds of bravery that involve breaking bounds, sowing discontent among his enemies to turn them against themselves, pacifying the countryside by installing a captured Afghan prisoner as ruler, and having his deeds recognized negatively by the Anglo-Indian bureaucrats at Simla who – appropriately – punish him for his success. In breaking the rules, Stalky pays implicit tribute to the rule-governed structure that will recognize him as hero/outlaw. His rebelliousness has not been tamed; instead it has been channeled into the service of the structure against which he has rebelled.

The systemic nature of this form of *Bildung* is emphasized at the end of the story by Beetle, who is usually held to be a representation of the writer Kipling. Responding to Dick Four's claim "There's nobody like Stalky," Beetle insists that Stalky is not individual but common:

"That's just where you make the mistake," I said. "India's full of Stalkies – Cheltenham and Haileybury and Marlborough chaps – that we don't know anything about, and the surprises will begin when there is really a big row on."

"Who will be surprised?" said Dick Four.

"The other side. The gentlemen who go to the front in first-class carriages. Just imagine Stalky let loose on the south side of Europe with a sufficiency of Sikhs and a reasonable prospect of loot. Consider it quietly." (*Stalky*, p. 446)

If, as Beetle claims, Stalky is just one of many, it is because heroism is not a function of special qualities that reside in special individuals. It is an effect produced by an efficiently-operating disciplinary structure. Heroism – indeed, individuality itself – is manufactured by hierarchical structures – public school, Army – to fulfill a corporate or systemic function that is, nonetheless, antagonistic to its other main function – to maintain order through a unitary disciplinary code. Heroes are always the exceptions to the rules, and their heroic acts – at least in Kipling – seem to be designed to confirm through transgression the importance of the rules they break. Moreover, as this passage reveals, heroic action always participates in savagery, a savagery which is appealing precisely because it conforms to an instrumental logic which, in turn, encourages us to suspend any consideration of the larger value of the goals for which Stalky fights.

4

Like most of the best of Kipling's writings, the two *Jungle Books* (1894–1895) are collections of short stories rather than coherent novels. The most celebrated of these stories – the Mowgli stories – are responsible for giving the books their names. While each story can stand on its own in literary terms, the Mowgli stories as a group can be analyzed as a novelistic unit of sorts: a *Bildungsroman* like the later *Kim*, set in a defamiliarized locale which suggests analogies with historical settings, actual societies; and, like many *Bildungsromanen,* a story about a disciplinary project. In fact, the very "timelessness" of these stories (they are certainly not "timeless" in any radical sense, since Kipling explicitly locates Mowgli in the jungles of central India in the time of the British *Raj*) offers Kipling the opportunity to construct a parable about law, order, hierarchy, and human interrelationships by displacing it in the "jungle" – geographically outside of, and temporally in the very earliest days of, human history. Thus, the implicit doubleness of the characterizations here is required by Kipling's intentions: all the animals are constructed in a state of animal otherness, yet all are also human in a number of significant ways, not the least of which is the fact that they all communicate by language. *The Jungle Books* comprise Kipling's most comprehensive statement on social order, and their central organizing motif – "The Law" – is deployed in a way which suggests Kipling is attempting a farreaching generalization of the notion of bureaucracy and the societal division of labor on which it rests.

Although presented in contradictory fashion, Kipling's notion of "The Law" has led critics to search for its sources in the history of ideas and in the Indian cultures he knew so well. Noel Annan, to take one example, associates Kipling with continental sociology (especially Durkheim, Weber, and Pareto) and its notion of rule-governed structure. For him, Kipling's "Law" is parallel with twentieth-century anthropology's emerging notion of "culture." By contrast, Shamsul Islam emphasizes the prescriptive and morally coercive side of "The Law" rather than the morally neutral, relativistic side: for him, Kipling's distaste for Hindu aesthetic religiosity led him to embrace Islam's contrasting ethical "stress on positive action, devotion to duty, discipline and order."[19] Kipling's "Law," to Shamsul Islam, seems to owe its ethical stress to Islamic practice, its comprehensiveness to the "synthesizing power" of Buddhism,[20] and its focus on ritual as ordering principle to Kipling's experience with freemasonry.[21]

Whatever its intellectual roots for Kipling himself, Kipling's "Law" clearly combines prescriptive and descriptive functions in a way that brings it very close to the classic meaning of "ideology." Kipling's "Law" is both an ethical code prescribing how people (or animals) ought to behave and an explanatory code accounting for how people (and animals) inevitably have behaved in organized societies (and nature). It blurs the line between the ethical notion of "law" and the morally neutral or relativistic anthropological notion of "culture," thus generating the fantasy of a rule-governed order which – luckily – is somehow found to be the order of the natural universe as well, a social order which is identical with or analogous to the order of nature. Like mathematics to Kant, Kipling's "Law" is a theoretical construct with a serendipitous relationship to the Real. Kipling's "Law" marks the point of attachment of the human order to the natural world.

The notion of "Law" here has a further complexity. Although invariably invoked in *The Jungle Books* as a singular entity ("The Law"), its singularity is nonetheless implicitly contested. Kipling agrees with Blake up to a point ("One Law for the Lion and Ox is Oppression!"), yet he reserves the right to assign universal coherence retrospectively to "The Law" in a way that is reminiscent of Darwin's somewhat elastic use of "law" in *The Origin of Species*. "Law," in Darwin, is an inference that accounts for, or provides an adequate description of, the way species have evolved. It is, in short, the set of rules the existence of which allows one to infer a totality, a "system" served by "law."[22] The Law of natural selection, for instance, is a theoretical construct which accounts for how species have evolved in the past. But, as a scientific law, it continues to operate in the present: in that sense, species continue to be "governed" by it. Although he made great strides in prying his notion of "law" free from anthropomorphic assumptions, Darwin was not completely successful in doing so, however. His law-governed natural order is designed, but not by a designer; it has the coherence of law, without the lawgiver. Darwin dispenses with the notion of a divine intention formerly held to be responsible for creating the species, but he cannot dispense with a "systemic intention" which accounts for the ultimate rationality of natural selection as a process. As Darwin's *Origin* purchases its intellectual power at the price of remaining uncritical of its own status as coherence-bestowing narrative (design with a designer – Darwin; teleological structure – argument – designed to challenge teleology), so Kipling's notion of "The Law" compels his readers to imagine a larger order or disciplinary system whose purposes are served by "The Law," while paradoxically discrediting just such a procedure by suggesting that such reification is all-too-characteristic of the questionably superstitious patterns of thought of despicable humans like Buldeo (hated by Mowgli because he is haunted by the very ghosts, his own instruments, he conjures up to reinforce his privileged position as the village's chief hunter). What is at stake here, in other words, is the epistemological status of a theoretical construct which seems, somehow, to be immanent in nature: something like what Kant referred to as the problem of "synthetic a priori truths."[23]

The story "Mowgli's Brothers" contains perhaps the clearest statement of what Kipling means by "The Law." The story opens with Father Wolf expressing disgust that Shere Khan has recently broken "The Law" by hunting man. While this transgression might imply that Kipling accepts a traditional (and non-Darwinian) hierarchy of being, a less grandiose practical exigency lies behind Father Wolf's disgust: indiscriminate killing of this sort will inevitably bring down upon the heads of the "jungle folk" the indiscriminate vengeance for which humans are notorious. By killing man, Shere Khan has created the conditions for a disruption of "equipoise" in a world governed by the law of vengeance. As in the stories we have already discussed, the problem of symmetry and balance in Kipling is bound up with the problem of "law." No sooner does Mother Wolf (Raksha, "the Demon") threaten Shere Khan with a more-than-commensurate vengeance at the hands of a grown Mowgli, then Kipling's narrator describes the "Law of the Jungle" in a way that establishes Law as the paradoxical means by which lawlessness can be exercised more "efficiently":

The Law of the Jungle lays down very clearly that any wolf may, when he marries, withdraw from the pack he belongs to; but as soon as his cubs are old enough to stand on their feet he must bring them to the pack council, which is generally held once a month at full moon, in order that the other wolves may identify them. After that inspection the cubs are free to run where they please, and until they have killed their first buck no excuse is accepted if a grown wolf of the pack kills one of them. The punishment is death where the murderer can be found; and if you think for a minute you will see that this must be so.[24]

The clear implication of the final sentence of this paragraph is that the Law protects the immature wolves in the long-term interests of the pack itself: the "cooperative" hunting for which wolves are famous would be impossible if something did not restrain individuals from making easy prey of immature cubs. Moreover, the allegorical function of this passage as a statement of moral precept is clear: the larger societal order has the moral right to claim the loyalty of the immature regardless of the proprietory feelings of the "parents"; the rights of the community supersede those of the nuclear unit once the immature have reached a certain stage of growth. And the authority for this claim of right derives from a larger evolutionary "logic" or "design," a systemic intention: the efficiency of the killing machine that is the wolfpack rests, finally, on its capacity for self-renewal, ultimately guaranteed only by the continuous operation of this Law which protects the young until physical maturity.

For this reason, *The Jungle Books* give a clear pride of place to animals which hunt cooperatively (such as wolves) over animals which are solitary hunters (tigers and jackals, for instance). For these books seek to teach their readers the contradictory disciplinary lesson that identity can be achieved only through the surrender of a certain degree of individual autonomy; that agency is enhanced not, as "common sense" might lead one to expect, through the free exercise of individual impulse, but rather through the curbing and channeling of individual impulse, the disciplining of the self. Self-discipline becomes something more than a tiresomely reiterated Pauline moral precept here because it is put in service of the goal of evolutionary efficacy within a larger natural order which has taken on the appearance of a rule-governed bureaucratic hierarchy. Moreover, to take this argument one step further: in Kipling the individual acquires an enhanced sense of personal agency precisely by submitting, as Conrad's Stein will say, to "the destructive element." The price one pays for individual power is submission to the risks of self-negation.

The logical difficulty, though, is an obvious one which menaces almost all the social prescriptions for improving the "fitness" of the national "type" offered by Social Darwinists as diverse as Spencer, Lombroso, Nordau, and Pearson: why bother prescribing what nature will inevitably drive individuals to do? Kipling's answer seems to be that the coercive aspect of law – in fact, childrearing itself with all its emphasis on what the child should do – is itself a product of evolutionary history. In teaching the young to obey the law, adults are acting on instinct. The question of precedence – which came first, law or instinct? – is held in suspension. Like other such questions of origin in Kipling, it can only be treated through myth (although, as we shall see, mythicization usually does not resolve the problem of precedence but only makes the issue more problematic).

The dual nature of Kipling's "Law" is also underlined in this story's use of ritualistic practices. Thus, Bagheera teaches Mowgli that he is subject to seemingly arbitrary totemic prohibitions: because his life was "paid for" with a bull, he must never touch cattle (*Jungle*, p. 18). Yet the reason for this particular restraint is dubious, to say the least, for Bagheera's killing of the bull does not restore equipoise; rather it unbalances a tenuous order of reciprocity which will not be restored to balance until Bagheera kills another bull at the end of "The Spring-Running" and claims "All debts are paid" (*Jungle*, p. 342). Unlike that other anomalous child in Kipling, Tota in "Without Benefit of Clergy,"

Mowgli is given a place in the symbolic order. His symbolic place in the Seeonee Pack is signified by his assumption of his jungle name, but his baptism is accomplished only by surrounding him with totemic prohibitions. While meant to appeal to the fascination with the peculiarly "nonutilitarian" customs of the "primitive" prevalent among Kipling's late-Victorian readers, these totemic prohibitions do serve an identifiably practical disciplinary function in the story. By prohibiting certain types of meat, Bagheera offers Mowgli the opportunity to restrain himself in order to learn the value of restraint itself.[25] Purely "ritualistic" prohibitions, however arbitrary, do teach a lesson about power: both about the power of "parental" figures to enjoin certain practices to the young and about the power which the subject may himself eventually command once he learns how to practice self-restraint. Submission is the paradoxical price one pays for eventual command. In fact, lessons about power are more easily taught when considerations of "practicality" are suspended. In this sense, the text proposes another significant difference between those who know and practice restraint (Bagheera, the wolves, the man-cub) and those who do not (the jackal, the tiger Shere Khan), and this difference is implicitly the enabling condition for the kind of bureaucratic disciplinary regimentation which will enable the more efficient killing of the mature Mowgli (as well as the foundation for the political hierarchy of the jungle in which the solitary killers are marked as anti-social "outlaws"). *The Jungle Books* celebrate, then, not only the evolutionary superiority of communal hunters, but the delightful gratifications in store for those who learn to defer gratification.

Once having shown he can curb his own violent impulses, Mowgli can be trusted as a leader; having shown he can acknowledge the authority of others (Akela), Mowgli is presented as capable of donning the mantle of leadership when his time for leadership arrives. The purely symbolic appearance of the gratifications he refuses himself is deceptive, though. They are implicitly invested with a "systemic," albeit indirect, function, much as the "lawlessness" of *Stalky and Co.* (is it not clear now why Kipling bestowed the name of a company on that book?) is channeled and enabled by the "lawfulness" of the society-in-small – the bureaucratic hierarchy founded on disciplinary restraint which will acknowledge, in the end, the supremacy of Stalky himself.[26]

Kipling's preoccupation with language here makes language central to his notion of discipline. In "Kaa's Hunting," for instance, Mowgli is kidnapped by monkeys, creatures much despised by Kaa, Baloo, and Bagheera – Mowgli's chief "fathers." Oddly enough, the monkeys seem to be despised chiefly for the fact that they possess very "human" traits: they cooperate, they eat indiscriminately, they are gifted mimics who can speak a variety of tongues, and they desire recognition for its own sake (in Hegel's view, that which distinguishes the "human" from all other creatures; in Freud, the realm of "sexual" or "libidinal" energy which humans, he believes, possess in greater abundance than all other creatures). Their deficiencies might best be understood as deficiencies of a parodic sort. The "ape" becomes a privileged figure of fun in Victorian culture precisely because he is seen as so "humanlike." But once having identified apes as gifted mimics, one must then address the problem of how to articulate the difference between humans and apes. Victorians generally solved this problem by simply redefining the nature of the ape's abilities: the ape's mimicry testifies to merely parodic, second-order, signifying abilities. The idea of apelike mimicry – repetition without meaning – then contrastively testifies to the signifying "depth" of human language, which necessarily escapes the condition of empty imitation, achieving instead a depth only possible when conscious creatures utter words which point to concepts. As a corollary, the ability to generate new words is said to guarantee the existence of consciousness – indeed, self-consciousness. In other words, the ape doesn't "know" the meaning of what he is doing; the human, somehow, does "know."

On the one hand, Kipling's own anti-foundationalist tendencies would seem to align him with the monkeys rather than against them. On the other hand, this Victorian *Bildungsroman* is ultimately concerned with vaunting an order of discourse which escapes the mirroring of the Imaginary and accedes to the representational power of the Symbolic in Lacan's sense. Pure mimicry closes off access to the metaphorical power of language. Those who can only repeat cannot master the repetition-with-difference that is characteristic of metaphorical representation.

Lacking such representational power, the *Bandar-log* thus necessarily lack memories, as Baloo reminds us. Their discursive universe is self-enclosed; they can appear to "be" anyone but cannot accede to a limited, bounded way of being in the world (the self-disciplining which creates the preconditions for mastery; the practice of disciplinary techniques which creates the illusion of a "subject" which is self-disciplined) because they are uncontrollable by a larger discursive order, or by the memory of pain inflicted for their own good in the past (as Hathi the elephant is, for instance). Where Mowgli uses "master words" he learns from Baloo to command aid from Chil the Kite, the monkeys cannot be

bound by any "master words." They lack a sense of limits, the guarantee
of identity within a narrative disciplinary order:

> Sore, sleepy, and hungry as he was, Mowgli could not help laughing when the
> *Bandar-log* began, twenty at a time, to tell him how great and wise and strong
> and gentle they were, and how foolish he was to wish to leave them.
>   "We are great. We are free. We are wonderful. We are the most wonderful
> people in all the jungle! We all say so, and it must be true," they shouted.
> (*Jungle*, p. 46)

After having summoned their bards to entertain Mowgli with paeans to
monkey-greatness, the listening monkeys then respond with similar
logic: "This is true; we all say so." Thus, the monkey-Imaginary is an
echo chamber much like the nightmare realm of Hummil: in a world
constituted by mirroring representations without point of origin, there is
no exit from continual self-reference. Monkey language cannot sum-
mon up an "outside" which would establish its limits. Monkeys, in other
words, cannot learn, because their language has no symbolic or metaphorical power. Lacking limits, the monkeys lack psychological interiority, and thus their every utterance connotes the hollow mockery of
empty braggadocio (and, not surprisingly, their social structure is deplorably anarchic).

By contrast to the monkeys' empty mimicry, "Kaa's Hunting" celebrates Mowgli's acquisition of the power of what one might call
"disciplinary communication" – the ability to master others through the
use of what the text calls "master words." While Mowgli is described as
learning the various "master words" in a way that is strikingly like the
monkeys' mimicry (all he does, after all, is imitate Baloo), the story has a
clear ideological stake in differentiating the use of master words from the
empty mimicry of the *Bandar-log*. "Master words" function in these
stories much like secret passwords among the spies in *Kim* or like the
masonic formulas in "The Man Who Would Be King": forms of
disciplinary communication; words which bind. While all "master
words" are translated by the text as reiterations of the same semantic
formula "We be of one blood, ye and I" (and notably signify a profession
of physical, albeit purely metaphorical, community), they differ as
individual utterances by how they are pronounced. They are effective,
we are told, only if pronounced with an "accent" appropriate to the type
of creature being addressed. While the formula would seem to assume a
generalized, and implicitly democratic, community of speaker and
listener, the one who uses master words actually exercises power over his

listener by imposing a duty which no listener may shirk (the one notable exception in *The Jungle Books* is the white snake, a spectral presence who, like Haggard's She-who-must-be-obeyed, is carefully treated as external to nature). In that sense, "master words" function as orders, producing obedient behavior from the members of a community always already disciplined. Unlike the ceremonies of "blood brotherhood" which Victorian explorers such as Stanley repeatedly engaged in in Africa, ceremonies meant to pacify by asserting relationships of equality among the parties in the absence of common language or common customs (or, indeed, common interests), the proclamation of blood brotherhood in *The Jungle Books* involves the invocation of inequality, by imposing a duty which the listener must render to the speaker upon having heard what the speaker has to say. In that sense, the "master words" suggest a childish linguistic utopia in which the use of magical signifiers forestalls all resistance because of the preexistence of a disciplinary/bureaucratic order – an unseen power – which can and will enforce obedience. Words can only bind if there exists a power to punish those who refuse to be bound. Kipling himself is bound, therefore, to generate a power to punish. In "How Fear Came," thus, Hathi the elephant identifies that disciplinary power – fear – traced, of course, by Hathi to a transgression of the Law by the primeval tiger (a "cultural" event yet also, clearly, a condition of life in a natural order governed by the "law" of natural selection).

A parable ostensibly told to account for the tiger's "right" to kill man on one night of the year, Hathi's tale is told during a time of drought, when the anomalous "water-truce" suspends temporarily the ordinary antagonism between predators and prey. Above all, Hathi attempts through parable to fold the necessity of transgression into the order of law in a way that is underlined by the story's setting at a moment in history when the Edenic "original" conditions of peace have been reconstituted temporarily through the "water-truce."

The aboriginal tiger, the Cain-figure in Hathi's parable, first brings death to the Jungle by killing a buck. In response, Tha the elephant brings "fear" into the world in the form of a man who lives in a cave. When "fear" subsequently spooks the tiger and calls him a "shameful name," Tha gives the tiger permission to inspire fear in man on one night of the year, but with one qualification: that the tiger, who has known fear himself, show "mercy" to man on that night. When the tiger ignores Tha's warning and instead kills the man, thinking he has thus killed fear, Tha warns him that he has, as a result, taught man to kill, thus disseminating fear generally throughout the jungle. In other words, the tiger's failure to identify with man on his night of fear inaugurates a generalized reign of fear necessitating the imposition of the Law of the Jungle, which must now be enumerated and taught to the young cubs. As in the Eden of Genesis, transgression of the one law inaugurates a process which multiplies new restrictions and imposes the awful necessity of work: in this case, the necessity of painful learning of what once came "naturally." Moreover, transgression conjures law into existence (or precipitates its conscious articulation: they amount to the same thing in Kipling) to curb the anarchic impulses which have been themselves generated by transgression. What Hathi's tale is about, in other words, is the process of coming-to-consciousness of law. Why must Mowgli learn the Law? Because he has a memory, and "memory" is the chief effect of living within a narrative which supplies motives from the past and projects a fantasm of the future in which the subject is assigned a specific role to live out. A "natural" human response to the ubiquity of fear, narrative disciplines the subject by allowing him to project himself through the bodily reflex of fear in the present to envision triumphing over it sometime in the future.

As a myth intended to explain the origins of rule-governed order, Hathi's tale is notably circular in its assumptions, allowing Kipling to refuse to commit himself to seeing either law as the origin of transgression or transgression as the origin of law. Transgression provokes the promulgation of law, but law has no meaning in the absence of the possibility of transgression. Like the fabular book of Genesis, Hathi's tale of the origins of law narrativizes and historicizes an origin which cannot originate because of the logical impossibility of conceptualizing either transgression or law as primary. Like many myths of origin, Hathi's tale serves to put an end to questions of origin by narrativizing them: by turning them into a story which purports to account for the demonization of the solitary hunter. In that sense, Hathi's tale is a transparent exercise in ideological power over those with limited memories. Rather than persuasively justifying the demonization of the tiger, it simply asserts the existence of a community of law-abiding listeners defined in opposition to the outlaw – the tiger – whom they hate and fear.

*The Jungle Books*, of course, do much more than simply accommodate subjects to the rule of law. Like epic literature in general, these stories are also structured by a logic of wish-fulfillment. Thus, the pleasures of authorized and legitimized violence – the vicarious pleasures of vengeance – must be articulated, somehow, with the fantasy of rule-governed order. Kipling, thus, will attempt the difficult task of balancing his celebration of ordered, rule-governed, reciprocity against his delight in the pleasures of lawless violence. He does this most notably, in fact, in two of the late stories in the *Second Jungle Book* – "Letting in the Jungle" and "Red Dog" – which are explicitly linked in "story" time (although interrupted in "narrative" time by "The King's Ankus").

As Mowgli's vengeance against the village in "Letting in the Jungle" demonstrates, organized vengeance is much more pleasurable than vengeance which is limited to the powers of the solitary individual. The libidinal pleasures inherent in vengeance are enhanced when it is of epic scale, when it is well organized and carefully planned. Where the later books of the *Iliad* presumably delighted the ancient Greeks with the spectacle of an angry hero – Achilles – become an uncontrollable killing machine, *The Jungle Books* offer the delightful spectacle of righteous fury enabled only by the discipline of planning and initial restraint. The Mowgli of *The Jungle Books* finds his true epic analogue, though, not in the heroic but finally almost supernaturally brutal Achilles, who at the height of his vengeful fury even redirects the flow of mighty rivers, but in the efficiently self-restrained Odysseus, who only begins shooting down Penelope's suitors one by one after he has first carefully attended to every detail involved in reimposing his authority over his household. Odysseus' epic-scale vengeance is notably "efficient" because brutally individualized and carefully planned and organized: the appropriate response of a killer famous for his ability to both compose and then live out his own narratives of vengeance.

"Letting in the Jungle" picks up the story after Mowgli is driven from the Indian village, having been accused by Buldeo of being a sorcerer for having organized the trampling of Shere Khan in "Tiger-Tiger!" (one of the stories in the *First Jungle Book*). It is a story about the vengeance which the jungle takes on human society, a vengeance orchestrated by a liminal figure who is neither completely human nor completely animal, neither completely of the village nor completely of the jungle.

In the beginning of this story, Mowgli returns to the village to find that his human mother, Messua, and her husband have had their property confiscated by the villagers who, instigated by Buldeo's tall tales, are convinced that the couple harbored the "Devil-child" Mowgli in order to bring ruin on the village. That Kipling's own notion of reciprocity does not involve a simple balance of payments is indirectly revealed when Messua's husband, in his fury at losing all his property, vows that he will extract "twice" what has been stolen from him in a great lawsuit:

I will bring such a lawsuit against the Brahmin and old Buldeo and the others as shall eat this village to the bone. They shall pay me twice over for my crops untilled and my buffaloes unfed. I will have a great justice. (*Jungle*, p. 220)

Although his rage is certainly understandable, Messua's husband is obviously using the term "justice" as a synonym for "revenge" here. The conventional notion of balanced reciprocity which underlies the everyday notion of "justice" has clearly fled the scene. Yet this passage raises a larger question about Kipling's own notion of reciprocity. Perhaps justice does equal vengeance in *The Jungle Books.* Perhaps the moral wrong committed by the villagers in taking Messua's property would not be simply righted by a restoration of the value of that property. Perhaps some additional "payment" is necessary to compensate the wronged for their suffering, a compensation over and above the simple value of the property which was stolen. Perhaps, even the "justice" which Mowgli does in orchestrating the destruction of this village which wronged his "mother" is, in some understandable sense, reciprocal. If it is to be seen as reciprocal, if equipoise is restored, Mowgli's actions must be judged by a different standard than the usual. If so, what is that standard?

In some respects, Kipling's standard is simply power. Mowgli makes his actions right by exercising them, and by being around at the end to write – or remember – the history of what went before. Thus, "Letting in the Jungle" is a psychologically powerful fantasy steeped in a celebration of technique. That we as readers are asked to take something of a moral holiday, to suspend our conventional considerations of justice and reciprocity, is clear from this focus on technique. The story goes into a great deal of detail about how Mowgli organizes the letting in of the jungle. He works with military precision, sorting the various jungle creatures who constitute his army into different, hierarchically ordered classes ranged according to their ability to conceptualize time and accomplish certain physical tasks. He thus gives pride of place to the elephant Hathi who is blessed, like a human being, with a long memory. Moreover, he manipulates Hathi through his knowledge of Hathi's story – the story of his wounding. Like Stanley in the Central African jungle or Dr. Monygham in Conrad's *Nostromo*, Mowgli recognizes the central practical importance of narrative in bestowing value on individual actions by allowing individuals to conceptualize a future goal as the fulfillment of the past: thus, he tells Hathi his own story as a means of manipulating him to aid him in his project and awakens Hathi's dormant memories of his abuse by humans in order to motivate him for the destruction of the village which is the project of the moment. As Hathi's narrative traced the demonization of the present-day tiger to his ancestor's "sin" in the distant past, so Mowgli's tale-telling supplies a motive – drawn from the story of Hathi's mistreatment in the past which led to the "sack of the fields of Bhurtpore" – and projects a future of which an epic vengeance will be the fulfillment. Far from being reciprocal, however, Hathi's repetition of the "sack of the fields of Bhurtpore" at the behest of Mowgli is an implicitly gratuitous act, for his vengeance on the humans who once wronged him was already completed in the past. Once again, reciprocity is implicitly identified by Kipling, not with the restoration of equipoise, but with successful, because excessive, vengeance. The focus of the story then is not on the balanced righting of wrongs but rather on the ideological technique to be used to give excessive vengeance the appearance of a justification.

The scale of Mowgli's project, suitable to an angry Old Testament Yahweh, actually frightens Bagheera, who can understand "a quick rush down the village street, and a right and left blow into a crowd," but who, unlike the elephant, cannot fathom "this scheme for deliberately blotting out an entire village from the eyes of man and beast" (*Jungle*, p. 227). When the destruction is over, the fields of barley have been trampled, never to bear fruit again, and the jungle has reclaimed the village, Mowgli is described as satisfied for he "had the good conscience that comes from paying a just debt; and all the Jungle was his friend, for all the Jungle was afraid of him" (*Jungle*, p. 298). Clearly, reciprocity has become something which the powerful can define as they please. Like the God of Genesis, whose notion of justice is flexible enough to rationalize banishment, unceasing labor, and death as the appropriate payments for eating one forbidden fruit, Mowgli is free to define injustice as justice because he is free to do anything he pleases now that he possesses sufficient organizational ability and social prestige. The implication is that Mowgli has become morally indistinguishable from the "unclean" Shere Khan of "How Fear Came," who taints the water with grease from a fresh man kill while proudly proclaiming that he killed man "for choice – not for food" (*Jungle*, p. 173). The important moral distinction which Kipling seemed to be at pains to erect between the solitary killer who hunts, not for need, but for pleasure, and the cooperative hunter who kills only for need has been revealed as illusory, finally. What differentiates Mowgli from Shere Khan in the end is simply Mowgli's possession of organizational ability which the solitary tiger cannot command.

No doubt, Kipling wishes simply to entertain his readers with the fantasy of a jungle boy who progressively develops the powers of Dionysus and who, accompanied by his companion panther, commits, finally, an unjustifiable vengeance of wronged nature against the human: an act meant to defy understanding in ordinary human terms. Unlike Euripides' *Bacchae*, however, which carefully places its god beyond human standards, "Letting in the Jungle" associates its "Dionysus" figure with highly rational planning in the interests of restoring an "order" somehow disrupted by human transgressions. While "vengeance" becomes coterminous with "justice" here, the story's fanciful focus on technique and organization situates Mowgli very much as a human rather than a god. Moreover, however slippery his use of the term, the question of justice matters to Kipling in a way it does not to Euripides' Dionysus, or, at least, so one should infer from the prominence given Bagheera in the narrative.

The *Jungle Book* stories ultimately appeal to a psychological need of the bureaucrat which is rooted in emotional ambivalence. They articulate the pleasures of lawless vengeance with the rather Lenten pleasures of disciplinary organization. In the spirit of wish-fulfilling fantasy, *The Jungle Books* implicitly promise that the pleasures one gives up to become part of a hierarchical organization are not given up at all; rather they return to be reexperienced with even greater intensity. Moreover, the desire for revenge, which can find gratification only in breaking all bounds, answers somehow to a rule in nature: carefully orchestrated revenge, narrativized as the righting of a wrong committed against the subject in the past, is "lawful." "Law," like reciprocity, is the term we use to justify retrospectively what serves finally only psychological gratification. "Law" is a rather flexible end, conveniently offering its services to us so that we may define what we want to do as what we have to do.

CHAPTER 4

# Cromer, Gordon, Conrad and the problem of imperial character

He was not running a great enterprise there; no mere railway board or industrial corporation. He was running a man! A success would have pleased him very much on refreshing novel grounds; but on the other side of the same feeling, it was incumbent upon him to cast it off utterly at the first sign of failure. A man may be thrown off.
                                                        Joseph Conrad, *Nostromo*

When the Gladstone government dispatched General Charles Gordon to Khartoum in January of 1884, it assigned him a confusing mission that was the inevitable outgrowth of incoherent policy. Convinced that the Mahdist uprising was not worth the cost of suppressing, the British government seems to have envisioned the impossible: that Gordon, renowned for exceptional powers of "personal influence," would be able to stage a withdrawal of Europeans and Egyptian troops without needing a costly imperial army to keep the Mahdi at bay during the withdrawal. To be sure, the government took its time in approving the mission, for Gladstone himself ordered it only after the public outcry in Britain, carefully nurtured by W. T. Stead's *Pall Mall Gazette*, which editorialized that the triumph of the Mahdi would inevitably lead to the reestablishment of slavery in the Sudan, had become too politically powerful to be resisted any longer. Moreover, Gordon was chosen for the mission despite his reputation for "unsteadiness," a reputation confirmed in the early months of his mission when he grossly underestimated the power of the Mahdist movement (he claimed at one point that he could wipe out the Mahdi with 500 well-trained troops). When he subsequently recommended that the most notorious Sudanese slave trader of his day be removed from prison in Cairo and be installed in Khartoum as the Khedive's personal representative – a sort of anti-Mahdi – his about-face caused dismay among his abolitionist supporters in Britain.

The story of the storming of Khartoum in January of 1885 by the Mahdi's troops and the subsequent beheading of Gordon, events which occurred as a British expeditionary force under the "Modern Major General" Sir Garnet Wolseley were attempting to force their way down the Nile River to rescue him, would become one of the most well-known stories of imperial sacrifice circulating in late-Victorian Britain. While Kitchener would ultimately reverse the political outcome of the story in 1898 with his victory at Omdurman, the dramatic tale of Gordon's undoing in 1885, repeated in dozens of popular hagiographies published at the time and amplified by Gordon's own voice from beyond the grave when his *Khartoum Journal* was smuggled out of the Sudan in the 1890s, contains all the elements of both public tragedy and bureaucratic farce.[1] From a bureaucratic point of view, it was the most public and dramatic failure of "the responsibility system" in action in the nineteenth century. It also brought together in a complicated and contentious working relationship the two men who represented the opposite extremes of imperial theory: the idiosyncratic and obsessive charismatic hero General Charles "Chinese" Gordon, Britain's man in the Sudan, and the consummate imperial bureaucrat, Sir Evelyn Baring (later Lord Cromer), the advisor to the Egyptian Khedive who was responsible for "supervising" Gordon's mission from Cairo by telegraph.[2] The most important scenes of this dramatically public failure of British imperial policy thus juxtapose the most visible imperial hero of the day with the self-effacing bureaucratic higher-up who would become the most effective exponent of invisible indirect rule.

The "responsibility system" is based, at least in theory, on the premise that the "man on the ground" is the one best equipped to judge what needs to be done. He is therefore given great leeway to improvise a way of accomplishing the ends of imperial administration by circumventing the rigidities of bureaucratic process. In the event he is invested with symbolic powers far beyond those of mortal men – a carefully nurtured prestige – and charged with duties ordinarily felt to be beyond the scope of individual action. As Tidrick argues, the "responsibility system" values swift and decisive action and, its necessary corollary, "the autonomy of the junior officer."[3] In that sense, the "responsibility system" calls upon ordinary Britons to take extraordinary risks under circumstances which are unfavorable to the use of large-scale force. Gordon's own success in leading the imperial Chinese army against the rebellious Taipings in the 1860s seemed to have demonstrated that he possessed extraordinary powers of "personal influence" over non-European people. Interestingly, though, it would be the British who would come to believe more fervently in the power of Gordon's charisma than virtually any of the followers of the Mahdi. His "mystical qualities of character," supposedly validated by his success in China, would subject first W. T. Stead, then the English reading public, then, finally, the old anti-imperialist Gladstone himself, before being exposed as completely ineffective in the Sudan against the Mahdi's superior power of personality.

Cromer's painfully evenhanded account of his dealings with Gordon in *Modern Egypt* makes for interesting reading, if for no other reason than that Cromer's account of Gordon is so symptomatically inconsistent. Speaking loud and clear through Cromer's account is the ideology of professional service in all its inconsistency: willing to acknowledge, on the one hand, the occasional necessity for the use of personal power, but, in the end, dismissing it as ultimately anachronistic and inefficient. Aware on the one hand of the necessity of charismatic instruments for the accomplishment of imperial goals, Cromer is nonetheless suspicious of the methods of personal influence and of the policy of relying on the man rather than on the system. Thus, having twice rejected the Gladstone government's request to "use" Gordon in Khartoum, Cromer eventually bows to pressure on the third request, while extracting the concession that the mission be strictly limited to the evacuation of Khartoum. However, Cromer subsequently complains to his higher-ups about the very idea of being asked to supervise a man chosen because he eschews supervision. As he says in a letter to Lord Granville in January of 1884: "It is as well that Gordon should be under my orders, but a man who habitually consults the Prophet Isaiah when he is in a difficulty is not apt to obey the orders of anyone." Unlike a well-trained and reliable charismatic figure such as T. E. Lawrence (discussed in Chapter 5), Gordon, Cromer fears, is too independent and unsteady for accomplishing the objectives of a policy which is, in any event, incoherent.

When Gordon finally arrives in Khartoum and begins sending telegraph messages back to Cairo, Cromer laments the necessity of having to translate Gordon's inconsistent stream-of-consciousness musings into a consistent plan to be sent on to Lord Granville in London. However, the note that sounds most insistently through his estimate of Gordon's accomplishments is the note of the dismissive bureaucrat with his carefully measured contempt for an instrument whose positive qualities are undermined in practice because exercised in so "public" a fashion. Thus, Cromer inventories Gordon's qualities of character:

In fact, except personal courage, great fertility in military resource, a lively though sometimes ill-directed repugnance to injustice, oppression, and meanness of every description, and a considerable power of acquiring influence over those, necessarily limited in numbers, with whom he was brought in personal contact, General Gordon does not appear to have possessed any of the qualities which would have fitted him to undertake the difficult task he had in hand.[4]

The astonishing feature of this passage is the fact that Cromer here prefaces his condemnation of Gordon with such a long list of Gordon's positive attributes. While Cromer, to be sure, is evenhanded enough to realize that the Sudan policy failed for reasons that had less to do with Gordon's personal shortcomings than with Gladstone's incoherent policy, his summary judgment on the subject implies that individual character is finally irrelevant:

Looking back [he is writing in 1908] at what occurred after a space of many years, two points are to my mind clear. The first is that no Englishman should have been sent to Khartoum. The second is that, if any one had to be sent, General Gordon was not the right man to send.[5]

The emergent ideology of professional class "expertise" saturates this judgment, occasionally even bringing the class issues involved directly to the surface. It is a telling moment when Cromer's usually "reasonable" discourse yields to a direct expression of professional class resentment of Gordon for having appealed directly to the British reading public by "pouring forth the vials of his wrath on the official classes."[6] It is rare in Cromer that professional class resentment finds such direct expression in "proconsular" distaste.

Necessarily this leads to the other important theme in *Modern Egypt*'s account of Gordon: the critique of a "newspaper-led" foreign policy, driven not by the sober calculations of national interest which Foreign Office experts are paid to make, but by the emotion-laden summary judgments of influential editors like Stead, fed copy directly by Gordon himself, who benefit financially from whipping public opinion to a frenzy in favor of ill-considered African adventures. In his discussion of this theme, it is the "proconsular" voice which speaks once again, as Cromer knits the professional class ideology of expertise to an explicit invocation of an older, Tory resentment of the role the great unwashed now insist on taking in public affairs through their surrogates, the newspapers:

It was, I think, Lord Beaconsfield who said that the English were the most emotional people in Europe, and Lord Beaconsfield was a keen observer of human nature. Lord Salisbury once wrote to me: "It is easier to combat with the rinderpest or the cholera than with a popular sentiment."[7]

When all is said and done, however, *Modern Egypt* returns to an oddly positive evaluation of Gordon, one which is based in an acknowledgment of what one might call the decorative function of charisma. The Sudan tragedy may have been ill-considered policy marred by faulty recruitment but it was still high tragedy: a theatrical staging of self-sacrificial heroism that Cromer finally understands as an anomalously successful failure: "I have dwelt on the defects of character which unsuited him [Gordon] for the conduct of political affairs. But, when all this has been said, how grandly the character of the man comes out in the final scene of the Soudan tragedy."[8]

The disaster at Khartoum can be recovered as a moment of revelation of "character." In lauding Gordon for staging his own self-sacrifice, Cromer attempts a complicated bridging of a gap which his own professional ideology would widen: the gap between an expert and a public vision of imperial history, between history conceived as the story of systemic agency and history conceived as the story of heroic individuals. Capable on the one hand of deploring the baneful influence of abolitionist sentiment in Britain on the Gladstone government's decision to send Gordon to Khartoum in the first place, Cromer nonetheless recognizes what one might call the "systemic" function of the spectacle of individual heroism which ultimately guaranteed the dead Gordon a lasting place in the pantheon of heroes of the British Empire. By losing his head in Khartoum, Gordon comes to stand for those features of British "character" – "pluck," rigid adherence to high principle, devotion to duty in the face of severe danger and public misunderstanding – which Cromer's own essays on imperial service will celebrate as the unsung qualities of imperial bureaucrats. As we have already seen, Cromer celebrates these qualities of personality as both the character traits which a properly organized colonial service seeks to instill in its servants and – impossibly – the preexistent qualities of a more general "British character." The latter claim, of course, can then do effective service as justification, through its assumption of British moral superiority, for Britain's right to rule "subject races." Even if the heroic character mucks up "History," he makes spectacular and politically useful "history."

In a remarkable way, Cromer's account of Gordon in *Modern Egypt* is also a kind of parable of the complex relationship between agency and instrumentality in the imperial field. Much like Conrad's *Heart of Darkness*, which we will discuss below, *Modern Egypt* tells the story of the agent reduced to the position of instrument, Cromer the supervisor become the victim of Gordon the manipulative – and dangerously autonomous – figure he ostensibly supervises. While *Modern Egypt*'s account of Gordon seems ultimately to serve the purpose of channeling Gordon's anarchic energy into the service of systemic goals retrospectively, of making Gordon a hero whose beheading will one day do service to justify efficient retaliation, Cromer nonetheless insists that Gordon represent all that is wrong with sending individuals to do jobs only large, well-supervised organizations can accomplish. Gordon, in short, is domesticated by Cromer, made to stand as exemplar both of all that is fine about individual British character and of all that is wrong with ill-conceived imperial policy driven by the desire to appease public sentiment. Published six years after *Heart of Darkness*, *Modern Egypt* unconsciously recapitulates some of Marlow's attitude toward Kurtz without Marlow's devastating irony.

In fact, the parallels with Conrad, the British/Polish novelist best known for his treatment of the relationship between bureaucratic forms of social organization and history, imperialism as adventure tale and imperialism as the central fact of modern history, are even more intriguing because of Conrad's preoccupation with the theme of instrumentality and agency. Through the fictional creation of a series of memorably "unsteady" characters in positions of leadership including Kurtz, Lord Jim, and Nostromo, Conrad examines the way in which the kind of agency on which Weber bestowed the name "charisma" comes to be exercised in the imperial field. Moreover, Conrad is preoccupied with the dangers that the autonomy of the charismatic figure poses for bureaucratic objectives, and thus, his novels train their focus ultimately on a disciplinary project, on the way in which such autonomy is curbed and finally channeled into the service of bureaucratic ends.

As we discussed in Chapter 1, the colonial bureaucrat's subjectivity inhabits a space which is difficult to stipulate along the "god–thing" axis: conceiving himself the puppet of an imperial destiny which it is the goal of the bureaucracy he controls to manufacture, he is simultaneously puppet and puppeteer, instrument through which Britain realizes its imperial destiny and initiating agent who conceptualizes that destiny for Britain. The implicit "doubleness" of the figures most directly involved in carrying out imperial projects stems both from the ideological need to pledge allegiance to larger historical metanarratives which invest his work with meaning (at the price of making him simply the pawn of larger forces at work in the world) and from the practical need to take charge of history himself.

With this in mind, we can see Conrad as the most important European literary figure before Kafka to take an interest in exploring this political irony in his fiction and the one who supplies the names for the colonial bureaucrat's two "romantic" faces: Kurtz and Nostromo, "his own man" and "our man," source of value and purpose and incomparable instrument for the accomplishment of anyone's purpose. Conrad not only identifies the poles between which bureaucratic identity oscillates, but he explores the dynamics of a particular process of substitution – of deferral, ultimately – which characterizes the operation of bureaucratic logic and, ultimately, supplies its impossibly refined sources of satisfaction. The ideal colonial administrator of Cromer's imagination, who would derive his chief satisfactions from the rather refined pleasure of not being recognized for his own accomplishments (who would, to put it baldly, take the lack of public appreciation of his work as the supreme token of appreciation, who would, in short, eschew the "publicity" of the *Pall Mall Gazette* in favor of anonymous service by telegraph and dispatch box), finds his fictional analogue in Marlow's self-effacing megalomania in *Heart of Darkness* (1899) and *Lord Jim* (1900) and in Decoud, Charles Gould, and Dr. Monygham in *Nostromo* (1904).

Conrad's use of bureaucratic figures bespeaks his interest in these historically new forms of social organization, increasingly characteristic of life under monopoly capitalism, according to his contemporary Max Weber, and suggests the extent to which Conrad was fascinated by this new form of socio-political organization which could be held, in large measure, responsible for the rapid political and economic expansion of Europe in the nineteenth century. Moreover, Conrad explores the "psychological" complexities inherent in the bureaucratic problematization of intention and purpose, a problem raised for Conrad's generation by – above all – Darwin's *Origin of Species*.[9] What is often taken by contemporary critics as Conrad's "proto-existentialist" thematic, rather than being discussed in relation to his *fin de siècle* or *fin du globe* sensibility, can and should rather be situated in relation to the question of bureaucracy and the problematic of intentionality to which it is joined in turn-of-the-century Europe.

2

That the depiction of Kurtz in *Heart of Darkness* was inspired by the adventures of both Livingstone and Stanley and that the book offers a critique of Stanley's (and Leopold's) inhumane system in the Congo

Free State has been remarked before.[10] While Kurtz's role as "rogue-bureaucrat" has been addressed in a very persuasive recent article by Michael Levenson, the degree to which Marlow's presentation of Kurtz is shaped by the exigencies of Marlow's own bureaucratic position (his role as functionary of the Company) has generally evaded critical scrutiny, although it has much to do with conditioning his construction of Kurtz and, finally, undermining his narrative authority, or, at least, his political "innocence."[11] The Kurtz presented to us by Marlow is the company's man's dream of autonomous agency, a projection of a company operative so independent of bureaucratic control that he fulfills the prime function of the company – making profit – from a position of almost miraculous independence of its authority. Like the independence displayed by the rogue-heroes of Kipling's "disciplinary" imagination (Stalky and Kim above all), Kurtz's autonomy is enabled by his always already having been disciplined, by his always already having been the best agent the company has. While remaining healthily skeptical about the ultimate worth of the new economic and social order the Company is imposing in the Congo (at least in Part I), Marlow nevertheless enters with enthusiasm upon his duties as functionary of the Company. Moreover, by assuming the role of central narrator, he insures that the "failure" of Kurtz the rogue-agent will be read as a "tragic" cautionary tale: a dramatization of the kind of "failure" that inevitably befalls those who attend too closely to the unknowable sources of their own motives, the unknowable determinations of their own actions. Chained within the carefully designed universe of Marlow, we readers are given the instrument's romantic view of the agent.

The frame narrative of *Heart of Darkness* begins by evoking a Chaucerian English social microcosm with the Director of Companies playing the Host: a genial deity presiding over a universe pared down to competing "companies" organized according to a familiar specialization of function. Marlow is the only member of this group identified by a name; the others are given only bureaucratic titles. Moreover, Conrad's assignment of role in the frame narrative is duplicated in Marlow's tale: Marlow tells us of his interactions in Africa with "the Chief Accountant," the "fork-bearded agent," and the "Manager" – all of them distinguished by titles instead of proper names. Marlow also describes how, when he arrived in Africa, he "stepped into the shoes" of a man named Fresleven, a European who attained an unwonted notoriety when he was killed by initially intimidated natives who took offense at his beating their chief (*Heart of Darkness*, p. 12).[12] The purpose of this narrative episode seems to be to insinuate that the "shoes make the man" rather than the other way around: the role places the individual in a position which causes him to suspend or to lose sight of his everyday humanity, a lesson which we as readers must – despite Marlow's self-protective, self-justifying irony, which proleptically enforces our attention onto Kurtz – apply to Marlow, given the shoes he chooses to wear.

Marlow's characterization of his own motives in undertaking the river captain's job evokes the convention of initiatory innocent autonomy so common in adventure literature. He tells us his curiosity is piqued by the white spaces on the map of Africa; he is growing restless and dissatisfied with the civilized life of the metropolis. The motive which drives adventure is no motive at all; the European adventurer does not go to Africa under the compulsion of "lack." Despite Marlow's attempt to coerce his listeners into granting his political innocence, however, *Heart of Darkness* clearly suggests that Marlow is well aware of the political implications of joining the company, as his ironical treatment of the Company's "civilizing mission" implies. Marlow's pose as the inside outsider is the counterpart of his ideological bad faith. The "singleness of intention" which he applauds in the Russian's book on sailing returns ironically to haunt the reader, who begins to sense that Marlow himself, despite his use of critical irony, may be unable to achieve singleness of intention: that is, be unable finally to decontaminate the meaning of his activities on the river, to free them from service to the economic ends of the company whose employee he is (Marlow, in fact, neatly displaces attention from his own "duality" by developing the tragic theme of Kurtz's "duality" – godlike and demonic – of intention).[13]

Marlow's much-discussed "gospel of work" is thus his way of anchoring himself by veiling certain questions of intention and purpose. In fact, Marlow never explicitly asks for what purpose he works, instead preferring to treat his job as simply a fact which conditions his sanity and enables him to avoid falling into a self-referential abyss (the abyss into which Kurtz, he insists, has fallen). In speaking of the steamboat to which he has dedicated so many loving hours of labor, for instance, he says,

she was nothing so solid in make, and rather less pretty in shape, but I had expended enough hard work on her to make me love her. No influential friend would have served me better. She had given me a chance to come out a bit – to find out what I could do. No. I don't like work. I had rather laze about and think of all the fine things that can be done. I don't like work – no man does – but I like what is in the work – the chance to find yourself. Your own reality – for yourself – not for others – what no other man can ever know. They can only see the mere show, and never can tell what it really means. (*Heart of Darkness*, p. 31)

Not only does this episode show us Marlow congratulating himself for having avoided solipsism, in Hegelian fashion, by embodying his subjectivity in an object, but it does so by insinuating that an individual can wholly own the meaning of his own gestures, can control the process of semiosis to such an extent as to insure that words mean only what the speaker intends them to mean. Beyond implying a highly dubious, Humpty Dumpty-like theory of language here, this passage suggests that Marlow can only assert his own mastery over the imperial enterprise in which he is engaged by claiming to be disengaged from its discreditable objectives. Ironically, however, despite his breezy claim to mastery of his "own reality," Marlow is a character whose power is severely limited. He does not even have the authority to rein in the reckless "Pilgrims" while they are aboard the ship, we eventually discover. When it suits his purposes, Marlow deliberately disguises his role as bureaucratic functionary in this novel in favor of an articulation of the mystique of independent agency. Yet it is precisely this role as functionary which – to Conrad's credit – the story itself does not allow its readers to lose sight of. Marlow would have us believe, on the one hand, that he is an autonomous moral agent carefully constructing important moral distinctions between the tragically noble/demonic Kurtz and all those "lesser" beings – the Company functionaries who despise Kurtz for his success and his onetime possession of "moral ideas of a sort," who despise Kurtz, in effect, for embodying a reproach to their own narrowly "material" aspirations. If one reads Marlow's adventure up the river as the relatively efficient dispatch of a job, on the other hand, the moral distinctions which Marlow tries to construct between himself and Kurtz (as well as between himself and the Manager) become, finally, evanescent.

While the transferential relationship between the two main characters has been remarked before, and while other readers of this book have noticed the way Conrad tends to ironize and subvert most of the differences between Marlow and Kurtz in the act of allowing Marlow to assert them, the implications of this interchangeability have not been thoroughly explored in relation to the thematic of bureaucratic motivation.[14] Kurtz's suspect "charismatic methods" make him the best collector of ivory the Company has. Marlow's piloting ability renders him indispensable for the job of removing Kurtz. Kurtz's "moral" motivations and original connections with European missionary groups are the kind of job training which provide him with the ability to understand the hidden reality of "belief," endowing him with the ability to probe beneath the surface of custom in order to install himself as the all-too-human object of veneration (or so Marlow would have us believe). Not accidentally, this allows him to become the best ivory collector in the Company while also, at least initially, helping to shore up the "moral" prestige of the Company's work in Leopold's Congo among misguided but influential missionary groups back in Europe. Likewise, Marlow's shipboard training allows him to infer from surface ripples the existence of hidden snags, thus keeping his steamboat afloat on the journey up- and downriver while preserving his European identity (i.e. his bureaucratic loyalty to the Company reinforced, ironically, by his carefully reiterated claims of estrangement from the Company's objectives in Africa) from the dangers of deracination to which Kurtz seems to him to have succumbed.[15] It goes without saying, moreover, that Kurtz's power of "words – of burning noble words" – is symmetrical with Marlow's ability to spin a conspicuously ambiguous yarn, as the frame narrative and Marlow himself remind us more than once.[16]

In short, Marlow constructs the myth of Kurtz the charismatic rogue-agent to serve as a cautionary tale about the dangers of abandoning Company discipline, but he does so while ostensibly distancing himself from the Company men who accompany him upriver and from the discipline of the profit motive which controls the Company. The psychological irony here is not unknown to careerists, especially to those who reach the top in large business organizations: the best way to express one's contempt for the values of small-minded materialism is to do one's job, not merely well, but spectacularly well. Grandiosity of ambition combined with an ironic detachment from what are popularly taken to be the very concrete goals of business is what marks the difference between the "captain of industry" and the petty materialist.

The implications of his distancing strategy are interesting. Marlow's representation of Kurtz has to be seen as tainted by Marlow's own need for expiation and self-justification. Marlow constructs Kurtz as a tragic hero or suffering god in order to deflect attention from his own implication in the Company's business – the indispensable "capataz" who protects white officialdom by quietly accomplishing its objectives while claiming to have pledged allegiance to the rogue Kurtz's "nightmare" over the Company's. In working to protect his own reputation by constructing a particular one for Kurtz, Marlow suggests that moral choice and economic or bureaucratic necessity are radically disjunct. He privileges the "moral" for the reader of the book (or the hearer of his tale) while relegating the "economic" or "material" to background, thereby constructing a deceptive moral hierarchy on which he and Kurtz are implicitly assigned a privileged place defined by its difference from the space occupied by the Manager, who is consigned to the lowly status of vulgarly racist (and inefficient) materialist. Marlow situates himself as Kurtz's "heir," deflecting his listeners' attention from the question of who he works for and onto his representation, in the final pages, of how diligently he worked to enhance the reputation of the man whose career he was instrumental in destroying.

Even Marlow's "gospel of work" participates in this hierarchization, identifying the humble Marlow with "lesser men" (the Hegelian "proletariat" who realize their self-integration, not by mastering others but by infusing inert matter with their own subjectivity – through work for others) by paying tribute to Kurtz's Frankensteinian tragic grandeur, evidenced in his "soul's" struggling against itself in the impossible, godlike predicament of failing while attempting to decree limits to its own aspirations. Marlow is thus engaging in ironic self-revelation in characterizing his choice of Kurtz as a choice of "nightmares." Kurtz is Marlow's "dream": the company functionary constructs the myth of the independent and tragically heroic individual agent so that he can pledge public allegiance to a failed god who once possessed "moral ideas of a sort" (which here reduce ultimately to "possessing independent moral agency": the "gift" ostensibly denied the bureaucrat but attributed to the "charismatic" figure). In claiming some affinity with this product of his own projections, Marlow insinuates a difference between the Marlow-who-acts (and thus does his job) and the Marlow-who-narrates (and thus constructs the tragic myth of Kurtz). He decontaminates himself ideologically, in effect, extracts himself from the dirty mess of commercial imperialism, at the cost of splitting himself. As he says on the death of Kurtz:

"However, as you see, I did not go to join Kurtz there and then. I did not. I remained to dream the nightmare out to the end and to show my loyalty to Kurtz once more. Destiny. My destiny! Droll thing life is – that mysterious arrangement of merciless logic for a futile purpose. The most you can hope from it is some knowledge of yourself – that comes too late – a crop of inextinguishable regrets." (*Heart of Darkness*, p. 69)

Marlow's claim about the inevitable belatedness of self-knowledge, the only boon which the tragic hero wins for himself and his audience in classical tragedy, can be read ironically as an inadvertently personal confession of political capitulation. Marlow the "idol" is really Marlow the "idolator," finally, as the "moral" project of pledging allegiance to a Kurtz rehabilitated in Marlow's narrative works to usher behind the curtain the economic ends of the Company (so evident in Part I) which, nevertheless, retain their determinative prominence behind the scenes. Conrad presents a narrator tainted by his own inability or unwillingness to scrutinize his own bureaucratic position, and presents European commercial imperialism as a highly effective ideological system whose power effects can be seen both in its capacity to generate the appearance of its own critique and in its capacity to occlude questions of ultimate responsibility: questions which can never be allowed to emerge unambiguously from the vivid shipboard stories one tells one's boss.[17]

## 3

*Lord Jim*, which Conrad was finishing about the same time that he was writing *Heart of Darkness*, assigns the narrator Marlow a somewhat different role. No longer a younger man locked in an oedipal struggle with an older figure whom he delivers up to death while treating as tragically holy, *Lord Jim*'s Marlow plays the role of paternal sponsor of a younger man whose rule-observing rebelliousness fascinates him. If *Heart of Darkness*'s Marlow peddles a suspect notion of agency, designed to dismiss from our minds the idea that commercial imperialism might operate systematically, *Lord Jim*'s Marlow is rather different. This Marlow seems to be trying to understand the determinations of individual agency – defined implicitly here in terms of the heroic ideal of fidelity to an exacting ideal of self-sacrifice. He poses for us what seems the central question of character in terms that the text itself calls "psychological": how can a timid parson's son who has already failed to live up to his high ideals once find redemption in Patusan? *Lord Jim* is a meditation of sorts on the work which is rule, on the character which the ruler must portray to accomplish his job successfully. Unlike *Heart of Darkness*, however, *Lord Jim* presents us readers with charismatic rule staged not as recklessly selfish tyranny (à la Kurtz) but as selfless fidelity to a "higher" code of conduct metaphorically identical with the marine officer's code.[18] Thus, the novel is implicitly about initiation into the powers and responsibilities of those who uphold the "white man's code" – about how initially unpromising Englishmen can be groomed to fit the role of "one of us" – and thus about the recruitment and training of leaders.

Because Marlow treats Jim as a mystery to be plumbed, the novel has usually been read as a book about the mysteries of what the Victorians liked to call "character."[19] Indeed it is precisely the book's focus on the problematic determinants of individual action that caused an earlier generation of critics to applaud the book's "Modernist" aesthetics. A newer critical generation, on the other hand, finds this focus to be alternatively a serious political limitation to the novel or a moment which opens impressive self-deconstructing possibilities regardless of its discreditable assumptions.[20]

But the central question the book raises is: is Jim truly a mystery worth solving? It may well be that the novel foregrounds Marlow's treatment of the mystery of individual being precisely to challenge "commonsense" notions of individual subjectivity. Marlow's attempt to plumb the mystery of Jim may well be a sign of just how desperately he – Marlow – needs to discover an individual in the machine which fails to follow the rules. We may pose the issue thus: while *Heart of Darkness*'s Marlow curbs Kurtz's dangerous autonomy by interpreting him in terms of Faustian tragedy, *Lord Jim*'s Marlow is determined to insure that Jim, by the end, has bound himself to a determinate code of noble behavior, has become "one of us" (signified, above all, by the discovery near the end of the book that Jim's life on Patusan has the predictable structure of romance and that Jim has played his assigned role admirably well). What Morse Peckham says of the goals of behaviorist psychology (which he claims is a prescriptive science bound to reducing the randomness of human response) applies to Marlow's "experiment" to insure that Jim becomes "one of us": "The aim of behaviorist psychology is to make behavior more predictable and less free."[21]

Making the main character's actions predictable: isn't this what all *Bildungsromanen* do? Certainly the novel of initiation often seems to present the adult world as having a somewhat rigid – or static – structure to which the initiate must learn to adapt himself. Another way of putting this point is to say that Jim is a character in search of a leading role in the right play. The play is found for him in Patusan, in the final part of the novel, for Patusan gives Jim the opportunity to stage his own fidelity to an external code – the imperial code of the risk-taking white leader of a non-European people. Paradoxically, it is only when that play is found for him, when he is driven to devote himself wholly to the conventional role of "white leader" in an imperial romance, that we readers are rewarded with a satisfactory sense of closure to his novelistic "character": by the end of the novel, easily recovered as the necessary reparation for his cowardice in the *Patna* episode. The paradox then would be that Jim seems to have lived a satisfactorily complete novelistic life for us only when his novelistic subjectivity has been evacuated of its depth – of, in short, its unpredictability. Jim behaves like "the romantic" Stein calls him only when he binds himself to play the rigidly responsible role of "the romantic."

The novel's chief metaphor is, not surprisingly, the "inquiry" (likewise, the novel suggests not only that ship and island are metaphorically equivalent, but that an analogous equivalence holds between the rules meant to govern white behavior in both places – the marine officer's code and the code of the "white leader"). The main inquiry (the official examination of the *Patna* incident by a panel of figures including Brierly) is duplicated by Marlow's own "inquiry" into Jim's character at Charley's Restaurant. This, in turn, is replayed between Marlow and a succession of new bosses each time Jim flees another job at the first hint that his *Patna* disgrace may come to light. The final "inquiry" occurs near the end of the novel, as, in the aftermath of Jim's death, Jewel seeks to understand from Marlow whether Jim was "false" to her in going to Doramin to take personal responsibility for the death of Dain Waris. With all this inquiring going on, one might well get the impression that the novel is intent on resolving the mystery of Jim's character. However, none of the inquiries produces an adequate account of its object. Thus, while questioning Jim at Charley's Restaurant, Marlow simply reproduces Jim's exasperation with the official inquiry board's questions while – seemingly – endorsing Jim's skepticism: "They wanted facts. Facts! They demanded facts from him, as if facts could explain anything!"[22] While Marlow seems to share Jim's skepticism here, we might well begin to suspect that "extenuating facts" are just what Marlow is seeking to find "in Jim" through his own inquisition:

Why I longed to go grubbing into the deplorable details of an occurrence which, after all, concerned me no more than as a member of an obscure body of men held together by a community of inglorious toil and by fidelity to a certain standard of conduct, I can't explain. You may call it an unhealthy curiosity if you like; but I have a distinct notion I wished to find something. Perhaps, unconsciously, I hoped I would find that something, some profound and redeeming cause, some merciful explanation, some convincing shadow of an excuse. (*LJ*, p. 43)

Thus, Marlow confesses that he cannot explain his own motives in going after Jim's at the restaurant which bears his name. Secrecy is given double play here, as the inquisitor withholds the secret determinations of his own behavior – by professing ignorance – in the act of trying to expose the other's secrets. Yet, as inquisitorial "putting of the question" tends to produce "truths" of a sort, so "inquiry" in *Lord Jim* will nonetheless produce what we might call the effect of a locked space in which secrets are held, the effect of psychological interiority.

Read this way, the novel seems to be about irreconcilable potentials in Marlow's design for Jim. The "character" is born only in transgression of the very laws held to be the foundation of social – read, professional – order; obedience, by contrast, eliminates the effect of "character" defined in terms of "individuality," the sense of something withheld from public view, of behavior governed by unknowable determinations. According to this latter model, to be a mystery to others is to possess a "character." Precisely when Jim has ceased to resist, has willingly taken the stage in a conventional imperial role by binding himself to a predictably tragic plot ("to the destructive element submit yourself"), he is, ironically, evacuated of the "depth" which his failure on the *Patna* suggested he possessed. Yet in the first half of the novel, Marlow seems to want to know why Jim was unable to follow the rules on the *Patna*. He is puzzled by what "in Jim" kept him from fidelity to the code while at sea. The various inquiries in the text thus serve a policing function ultimately: conspicuously failing to describe the "truth" of Jim's character, but producing prescriptions for Jim's future reparative behavior in the form of descriptions of his character. Moreover, that policing function is exercised both over Jim by Marlow and over us by the text. By constructing the Jim of the first half of the novel as that-which-resists-the-rules, Marlow's narrative invests him with the metaphysical interiority conventionally known as "the mind," in Peckham's words that seem appropriate to *Lord Jim*: 'merely . . . the abyss of ignorance that lies between stimulus and response."[23]

That Marlow's rhetoric is responsible for constructing this illusion can be gleaned from the fact that Jim never confesses any guilt, and indeed, appears anything but conventionally repentant when he retells the story of his fall/jump from the *Patna* to Marlow at Charley's. His brief summary – "I had jumped . . . It seems" (*LJ*, p. 87) – is, if anything, a blunt refusal to accept culpability, by failing to account for the very thing that is at issue. His response suggests that his decision to jump was a random event, impossible to account for in terms of causal logic.

What's more, Marlow even seems to accept Jim's own arrogant refusal of responsibility as a sign of his superiority, a sign that he acknowledges the binding authority of the code that "we" all must follow. Playing Marlow to Marlow, we might say that Marlow seems to believe that Jim ought to feel sorry but that he ought not to act sorry. These two inquiries – Marlow's and the official one – thus put Jim in a double bind by attempting to produce evidence of personal feelings that cannot be publicly aired without violating the code itself, whose central requirement is heroically stoical reticence.

The reasons for the requirement of reticence, although not discussed openly by Conrad, are not hard to find. If Jim were to try to account for his behavior as determined by a quite natural fear of death, he would be simply owning up to the same banal feelings that the code is designed to make it impossible for marine officers to admit publicly. There are rules prohibiting the expression of fear because everyone is afraid. As the French lieutenant says to Marlow, the fear "is always there" (*LJ*, p. 111). The fear of death, in other words, cannot adequately account for the cowardice of the *Patna*'s crew because it does not distinguish them from the crew of any other ship floundering at sea. One does not die "of being afraid."

On the other hand, this rule of reticence has an imperial justification as well, for the code of marine officer behavior while aboard ship serves a function which is identical to the "white man's code" on land (both in India or Aden – we are not explicitly told where the official inquiry takes place – and in Patusan). Because the code requires the white man to stage his own indifference to death before the Other, no public inquiry into the case of white men who failed to do so could proceed very far without risking grave political embarrassment. Indeed, it is a telling moment when Jim admits to Marlow that the Malay helmsmen on board the *Patna* were initially incredulous at the thought that the *Patna*'s white officers might be abandoning ship (*LJ*, p. 78).

The implication is that Jim's decision to face the inquiry board can be seen in two, ultimately incompatible, lights: 1) as an act of bravery, a proof that he is of the "right sort," a reparation for his cowardice on the *Patna* (the light in which Marlow prefers to take it), or, ironically, 2) as a grave act of disobedience threatening to expose the whole system of white rule on both land and sea before the eyes of the colonized (Marlow inadvertently brings this issue to the fore by trying with some visible strain to steer his readers away from it). Thus, Jim's failure to disclose privately to Marlow is matched by the inquiry board's failure to disclose publicly, and the board's failure, the novel implies, is predetermined by its own structural unwillingness to uncover the truth:

> How the *Patna* came by her hurt it was impossible to find out; the court did not expect to find out; and in the whole audience there was not a man who cared. Yet, as I've told you, all the sailors in the port attended, and the waterside business was fully represented. Whether they knew it or not, the interest that drew them there was purely psychological – the expectation of some essential disclosure as to the strength, the power, the horror, of human emotions. Naturally nothing of the kind could be disclosed. The examination of the only man able and willing to face it was beating futilely round the well-known fact, and the play of questions upon it was as instructive as the tapping with a hammer on an iron box, were the object to find out what's inside. (*LJ*, p. 47)

In brief, the truth cannot be found out 1) because the truth is banal and thus already "known" (the crew feared death and thus abandoned ship to save their hides); 2) because that banality cannot be uttered in a public forum without embarrassing the "confraternity" of whites (who are, as Marlow admits, held together by nothing more than the requirement to obey the dictates of the code, but who, out of political necessity, stage themselves as a confraternity of heroic characters not simply as a group of obedient actors); and 3) because "the psychological" itself is nothing but a placeholder for those determinations of behavior that by definition cannot be known. The novel thus suggests that the true determinants of individual behavior lie "outside," in the political culture of empire, but that Marlow, for reasons of his own, will attempt to deflect us onto the mysterious territory of the "inside," precisely because such a territory is unknowable and thus will readily accept authoritative inscriptions from the pen of a grand inquisitor.

Marlow's subsequent "adoption" of Jim should then be understood not in descriptive but in prescriptive terms: Marlow takes on the job of prescribing Jim's behavior – binding him to a reparative narrative – under the guise of trying to explain him. Moreover, the narrative Jim comes to live will necessarily have the repetitive/reparative structure of a Victorian *Bildungsroman*. Marlow will take Jim out of his self-conceived despair, out of his belief that his life is a series of unique events ("These things happen only once to a man . . ." [*LJ*, p. 72]), and bind him to a narrative with the metaphorical structure of repetition-with-difference: take him out of, in short, an "unintended" plot-life of accident and interpellate him into a structure of "intentionalized" teleological process culminating in the experience of rule (perhaps "leadership" is a better word than "rule" here, for Jim behaves like a *condottiere* on Patusan).

For this reason, Conrad designs the *Patna* affair to defy logical prediction. The ship which should have sunk did not. The bulkhead which should not have held did. The "unimaginable" panic of the pilgrims which should have occurred did not. All of this suggests that what panics Marlow in listening to Jim's account is both the randomness of the events Jim lived through and the randomness of Jim's response to them, a response which – presumably – should not have been made by "one of us." What worries Marlow, in short, is the indeterminate nature of Jim's behavior. Moreover, the project for making Jim a man by binding him to a predictable plot which can function as reparation for the "failure" on the *Patna* is a strategy designed, at least in part, to insulate Marlow from troubling reflections on the fact that his own behavior might be similarly "unintended"[24].

> He was of the right sort; he was one of us. He talked soberly, with a sort of composed unreserve, and with a quiet bearing that might have been the outcome of manly self-control, of impudence, of callousness, of a colossal unconsciousness, of a gigantic deception. Who can tell! From our tone we might have been discussing a third person, a football match, last year's weather. (*LJ*, p. 63)

While he recognizes in Jim the outward signs of a member in good standing of the ruling class ("quiet bearing," "manly self-control"), Marlow is nonetheless troubled by the thought that those features may well be determined by – "Who can tell!" – despicable sources ("impudence," "callousness," "deception"). If one gives this episode a "Darwinian" or "Freudian" reading, then Marlow is assigning a determination to Jim's behavior that can be glossed in terms that post-Darwinian culture associates with "unconscious" causes: "evolutionary egoism" – the brute instinct of self-preservation. Certainly, the novel allows us, if we wish, to read Brierly's excessive uprightness as an expression of deep-seated egoism, and thus, to read his suicide as an ambivalent act, betokening both his despair (brought on by his inquiry into Jim and his implicit realization that his own "difference" is nothing but "sameness" – obedience) and his desire to stage his superiority to those other lesser beings who cannot master, as he can, the slavish instinct to live. Indeed, the text does not seek to close off psychological inferences of this sort but to cause them to proliferate, and thus to implicate us readers in the very politically dubious process of inquiry which it dramatizes through Marlow.[25] Thus, as even Marlow admits, "Who can tell!" Our suspicions about what Marlow seems to fear have been awakened: does he fear the possibility that acting "one of us" is all there is to being "one of us"?; that fidelity to the professional code (rather than, say, possession of the "right character") is all that qualifies one for membership in the exalted profession?

The unease which Jim's account of the *Patna* incident inspires in other seamen can be accounted for by its random and consequently maddeningly indeterminate nature. After all, before (in narrative time) Conrad depicts Marlow interrogating Jim at Charley's Restaurant, Marlow tells us that Brierly committed suicide after having presided over the *Patna* inquiry. This reversal of the temporality of the story is done to prepare us for situating Marlow's own "inquiry" into Jim. Marlow's comment on Brierly ("he was probably holding silent inquiry into his own case" [*LJ*, p. 48]) directs us, proleptically, to the significance we are to assign to Marlow's inquiry. The indeterminacy of the *Patna* affair and the unknowability of Jim's motives are precisely what force the inquisitors to judge themselves inadvertently. Brierly goes so far as to pass judgment on the guilty party and carry out the sentence of execution: in his case, the discovery of hidden depths, hidden wishes, is equivalent to the discovery of transgressive desires which deserve punishment. Unlike Brierly, though, Marlow remains determined not to judge himself but to exonerate himself by judging Jim and condemning him to a reparative plot. Marlow's job remains a disciplinary one throughout. Under the guise of a search for the hidden determinations of Jim's behavior, he prescribes those determinations, and thus interpellates Jim within a narrative of reparation that largely absolves Marlow of the need for true self-inspection. Thus Brierly's plaintive question, "why are we tormenting that young chap?," reveals that Brierly at least does not get the point of the "torment": it is not to "find" a preexistent guilt but to produce the effect of guilt by inscribing penance on the wax tablet that is the young subject.

The two-part structure of Jim's plot-life suggests an homology between the ship's crew and passengers and the island's leaders and people. In fact, this homology is reinforced in the novel by Conrad's having Jim serve as mate on a ship filled with Muslim pilgrims (as well as by having Jim improvise a "capstan" on Patusan to use in hauling artillery up a mountain). This homology, in turn, implies a relationship between the seaman's code and the code governing white behavior in the non-European world, and the novel reinforces that suggestion by staging what can only be called the "imperial anxiety" of white officials at the inquiry. When Marlow mentions that the "whole waterside" is talking of the *Patna* affair, he clearly implies that what the "whole waterside" is talking about is the cowardice of whites. The *Patna* incident threatens the carefully nurtured prestige of an imperial order founded on the carefully peddled illusion that whites are more than they seem (Orwell would call this the "pukka sahib code"). Thus, when Marlow first spots Jim at the inquiry, he is looking forward to seeing him squirm on the witness stand:

I waited to see him overwhelmed, confounded, pierced through and through, squirming like an impaled beetle – and I was half afraid to see it too – if you understand what I mean. Nothing more awful than to watch a man who has been found out, not in a crime but in a more than criminal weakness. (*LJ*, p. 37)

The double meaning of abjection is clearly at work in this passage, as Marlow envisions Jim as both abject insect about to be impaled and, by metonymy, Christ about to be sacrificed. What seems otherwise to be an unambiguous moment in which Marlow licks his chops in anticipation of Jim's public humiliation turns out to be a moment which ambiguously raises by lowering Jim in our estimation.

Yet the mention of "more than criminal weakness" tells us something else about the code by which Jim is going to be judged. How can, we might ask, "weakness" be considered "more than criminal"? Weakness usually extenuates crime. Only beings who exist on rather a high plane – gods perhaps – might consider weakness "more than criminal" since only they don't have to worry about bodily weakness. In holding Jim to these impossibly high standards, Marlow simultaneously conjures a special professional fraternity into existence (those judged by impossibly high standards – their own), pronounces Jim excluded from this fraternity by virtue of his weakness, and then smuggles his body in the back door as the sacred sacrificial victim of rules too harsh for anyone to live by. The paradox that runs through Marlow's reiteration of the professional bond – "one of us" – is that even the charter members have not earned the right to belong to this exalted club. Through Marlow, the novel constructs the paradigmatic Modernist experience of self-exile.[26]

Thus, Jim's geographic "exile" to Patusan in the final third of the novel marks his membership in the professional fraternity rather than his exile from it; it is the realization of the process of *Bildung* to which Marlow has submitted him. It is his job. It is that which makes him a figure of legend, and, as Marlow says, allows him to approach "greatness as genuine as any man ever achieved" (*LJ*, p. 183) – a comment which, when read in an equivocal light, anticipates *Nostromo*'s ironic insinuation that heroism is only achievable by the dead who have been reduced to characters in heroic narratives.

The Patusan episode of *Lord Jim* is self-consciously conventional in a Western literary sense, a combination of Stevensonian boys' novel and island romance tacked onto the end of a piece of Conradian psychological fiction (the pirates of *Treasure Island* invade *The Beach of Falesá*). Pathak, Sengupta, and Purkayastha have summarized the fabular features of the Patusan narrative succinctly: "talismanic rings are conferred, and save; rajahs are decadent and lecherous; coffee is poisoned; clocks have stopped."[27] Patusan is even haunted by a snake in the garden (Cornelius) who is given to "creeping" about the island and who, Marlow tells us, "taints" the story. We readers know the rules which govern this kind of fiction, and thus recognize that the conventional codes of literary romance are being made to converge here with the conventions of the "white man's code." But by having his narrator Marlow remind us that he is telling us a romance ("Remember [he says at one point] this is a love story I am telling you" [*LJ*, p. 221]), Conrad makes the conventionality of this type of heroism and this kind of love the point of the episode (as Marlow says of Jewel's love for Jim: it is "idyllic" and "true" [*LJ*, p. 224]). The Patusan episode is thus not simply about what Marlow wants us to believe it is about (Jim's redemption through heroic risk-taking and assumption of responsibility for "his" people and "his" love). It is about the conditions under which behavior can assume predictable – and thus meaningful – form. It is the story of Marlow's determination of Jim's story, and thus, a highly tendentious tale whose contradictoriness nonetheless allows it to escape Marlow's control in the end.

Marlow cannot control its meaning completely because he is a character in the idyll as well as its narrator. His double role is underlined in his entanglement with Jewel at the end of his stay on the island. While Jewel's motives in speaking to Marlow are comfortably understood in conventional terms – the anxiety of a lover to understand her beloved's unclassifiable autonomy ("They always leave us" [*LJ*, p. 230]) – Marlow's reponses are the self-interested claims of a rival in a love triangle as much as they are attempts by Marlow to fix Jim's behavior as penance. While Jewel's question – "Do you want him?" (*LJ*, p. 235) – poses the issue of Jim's ultimate allegiances (while insinuating that the competition is fundamentally sexual), Marlow's rationalization for not "wanting" Jim ("Because he is not good enough") restates the judgment the professional confraternity make of themselves as if it were a uniquely individual judgment applicable only to Jim. Moreover, Marlow tells the story of his taking final leave of Jim in terms that seem to sexualize their bond (Jim: "I shall be faithful." Marlow: "I turned my burning face away." [*LJ*, p. 248]). The "confraternity" has become a homosocial one, and Marlow's leavetaking a conventional novelistic renunciation: "And, suddenly, I lost him . . ." The idyll Marlow has been telling not only stages a conflict between professional duty and personal love and thus creates the impression of a subject with an interior torn by conflicting desires (a conflict displaced and dramatized at the end when Jim himself renounces Jewel to go to Doramin and accept his fate), but also manages to eroticize Marlow's tie to Jim, and consequently places Marlow in a compromising position within the idyll as an interested party attempting to narrate it as if he stood safely outside.

The love story swallows up the story of professional duty by offering the terms in which professionalism is to be discussed. By situating desire at the center, the idyll constructs Jim as a desiring subject, torn between his erotic allegiance to Jewel and an analogous homosocial allegiance to the professional fraternity Marlow represents. By staging his departure as a conventional renunciation, Marlow gives the impression that Jim has been abandoned by white society, that he is engaged in work which has value only as psychological reparation for him, that he is no longer doing his job.

Jim's failure to fight Gentleman Brown at the end ironically testifies to the success of Marlow's project for him. Like Jim, Brown is an exile, and thus seems in this superficial sense to be "one of us." But, in playing Marlow to Brown, in giving Brown a "second chance," Jim reveals the debilitating weakness imposed by a code which creates the impression of a confraternity of men who are alike only in the negative sense that they cannot be at home anywhere. But Brown is Jim's moral antithesis, and thus Jim's failure is rather anxiously recovered by Marlow at the end as a success of sorts: a successful sacrifice which reinscribes the moral boundaries between those who acknowledge responsibility and suffer and those who cannot.

4

The problem of agency and the relationship between subjectivity and narrative is rendered in even more complex form in *Nostromo* (1904), a novel published during the year when Panama proclaimed its independence from Colombia after a revolution engineered at least in part by a

US government eager to find a convenient route for building an inter-oceanic canal. In this novel, the figure of Nostromo ("our man"), the "indispensable capataz de cargadores," seems to represent the very opposite of Kurtz: Nostromo is the consummate instrument. He works for "the Europeans" for reasons that Marlow would have understood, since they ultimately boil down to Marlow's reasons: work for others can be rationalized as offering relief from the burden of self-consciousness and self-constructed ends – ironically because it encourages the illusion of individual agency. Either one can work for others or one can choose to work for others: this is one way of summing up this choice which is really no choice. When Nostromo finally comes to realize his "worth" after his adventure in the gulf with Decoud (i.e., that, as Teresa Viola had warned him, he was not adequately compensated for his own self-expenditure, that "worth" itself can be defined as the excess for which one has never been compensated), he is reborn as a split charac-ter, thereafter capable of deceit, and no longer controllable by the public currency of his "reputation."[28]

*Nostromo* is Conrad's most searching excursion into the question of value, and the main character's self-undoing reveals, finally, a problem-atic of value created by the impossibility of the individual's bearing complete responsibility for assigning it to his own activity. Modern capitalism creates the preconditions for the discrediting of inherited historical metanarratives which have traditionally assigned a place and a worth to certain kinds of human activity, while, nevertheless, requiring the recirculation and reinterpretation of these discredited metanar-ratives for the accomplishment of economic rationalization as a world-wide project (although even this way of formulating the expansive tendencies of capitalism "overintentionalizes" what can only be seen as systematic in retrospect).[29] Captain Mitchell's narration of the counter-revolution in Sulaco late in the book is symptomatic of this dual necessity at work. Mitchell tells the story of Sulacan independence in terms of the conventional categories of individual heroism and unitary intentionality, despite the fact that Conrad's novel has already, by this point, worked hard to discredit "Whiggish" readings of precisely this sort. The stark contrast between the way history happens in the book and the way Captain Mitchell says it happened implicitly discredits all narratives which rest in the soft sand of romantic heroism and unitary intentionality.

The problem of the relationship between value and narrative "ends" is established from the beginning. The story of the "gringo" ghosts who haunt Azuera, waiting to prey on unsuspecting fortune hunters, establishes, not simply the insatiability of material appetite, but the grounding of all appetite in the material. Thus, the "gringo" ghosts become the model for desiring in the novel. Every main character, from Decoud to Dr. Monygham to Charles Gould to Nostromo to Fr. Corbelan, affixes conventionally material ends to their own desiring activity. Yet fixing one's desire on material goals neither makes the "idea" of "matter" more "concrete" here nor makes one's ambitions more achievable. In fact, the singleminded pursuit of material goals is identified by the novel as an "ideal" and thus inevitably obsessive pursuit carried on in opposition to the "pleasure principle" (accounting also for the self-sacrificial ethos which governs the behavior of most of the main characters). Not surprisingly, it is represented, *ad absurdum*, in *Nostromo* by the "gringo" ghosts who somehow undergo great physical suffering for a post-mortem obsession: "They are now rich and hungry and thirsty – a strange theory of tenacious gringo ghosts suffering in their starved and parched flesh of defiant heretics, where a Christian would have renounced and been released."[30]

This episode of the gringo ghosts points to a problem for the conceptualization of the goals of desire here: what is required for the object of desire to achieve the status of sublimation? The gringo ghosts are frozen in a state of "thwarted sublimation," denied interpellation in the conventional narratives of spiritual redemption because their narrative lives were controlled by ends which had never transcended the status of the material. For them, the pursuit of wealth is still firmly mired in an unsublimated "excremental vision." The sublimatory process, which, working ideally through the alchemy of human culture, ought to transform excrement into pure value itself, cannot work without widespread agreement about its trajectory. In other words, the silver of the San Tomé mine can never completely achieve the status of socially approved object of value in the novel because it can never free itself of its "debased" materiality in the absence of a social consensus on what are the legitimate goals of human life in Sulaco, what are the ends of the narratives of life in a culture where inherited Christianity's myth of self-transcendence is in the process of being discredited – for the educated classes as well as for working-class liberals such as Viola.

Thus, *Nostromo* posits a plethora of different, and competing, "goals" for human desire, many of which achieve a specious concreteness (and a unitary appearance which disguises their heterogeneity) in the image of the San Tomé silver. The silver itself provides a classic Conradian instance of substitution of means for end. To Charles Gould, it acquires a metaphorical status as paternal prohibition: it comes to orient his desiring activity precisely when his father, broken psychologically by his struggle against Costaguanan history, urges him to give it up. In fact, Conrad's narrator describes Charles' decision to return to Costaguana to get the mine working once again in terms that reveal that he adopts this project deliberately as substitute compensative object:

Action is consolatory. It is the enemy of thought and the friend of flattering illusions. Only in the conduct of our action can we find the sense of mastery over the Fates. For his action, the mine was obviously the only field. It was imperative sometimes to know how to disobey the solemn wishes of the dead. He resolved firmly to make his disobedience as thorough (by way of atonement) as it well could be. The mine had been the cause of an absurd moral disaster; its working must be made a serious and moral success. (*Nostromo*, p. 48)

If an "absurd moral disaster" can be transformed into "a serious and moral success," then surely disobedience can be sublimated into a "higher" obedience. While oedipal "disobedience-as-atonement" has a long history in the bourgeois novel (from at least the opening pages of *Robinson Crusoe* on), it is striking that the silver achieves a privilege as end here precisely because it is a substitute. Gould's later rationale for his obsession with the mine logically follows from this:

I pin my faith to material interests. Only let the material interests once get a firm footing, and they are bound to impose the conditions on which alone they can continue to exist. That's how your money-making is justified here in the face of lawlessness and disorder. (*Nostromo*, p. 60)

Not only does this passage render a strikingly Marxist-flavored conception of history as determined, "in the last instance," by relations of production, but it also represents a concession to the contradictory idea that mastery of history is achieved by setting up substitute instrumental goals which, once established, impose their own rule. Gould, in other words, articulates a Marlow-like philosophy of "idolatry": the instrument, once invested with privileged status as *telos*, becomes the god and imposes its own law. The ostensibly independent agent – Gould – who argues for the restoration of the mine should then, subsequently and retrospectively, be seen not as "god" but as "prophet" for divining the trajectory of history's narrative, for foretelling the future as determined by the material. The "prophet" is, in other words, a "Gian' Battista, Nostromo": not the manufacturer of his own truth but rather the "one who comes before" and through which a "higher authority" articulates its "Truth." The liminal space of prophecy on the agent/instrument continuum is the liminal space of the Cromeresque bureaucrat who works for other goals than his own but whose work of articulating those goals is "indispensable" to establishing their primacy. Moreover, Marlow's words on imperial idolatry come back to haunt Gould's claim that the material productive forces determine history: in implicitly offering this idea as "something you can set up, and bow down before, and offer a sacrifice to . . ." Gould denies a cosmic role to an anthropomorphic force yet substitutes in its place an "idea" which, as Dr. Monygham will later remind us, is "inhuman . . . [and] without rectitude."

In effect, all of the main characters in this novel behave like "nostruomini": bureaucratic functionaries operating at the behest of others at one time or another, or as the agents of an idea – a plan – which, once articulated, assumes the status of *telos*. Even the American financier Holroyd, puppeteer par excellence, finds it necessary to present himself as the puppet of forces much larger than himself, forces which are variously identified here with both missionary Protestantism and economic modernization. Nevertheless, the fact that Conrad has Captain Mitchell narrate his history of the separation of Sulaco from Costaguana late in the book insures that Conrad's readers will not mistake this act of fictionalizing of the past for anything other than what it is: a familiarly "Whiggish" recuperation of the past as a providential plot organized around a unitary intention – Decoud's "plan" – realized by Nostromo's courageous "ride" which, finally, enables Barrios' military victory over the Monteristas. Captain Mitchell's "history" (and, Conrad implies, every "history") constructs a projective fiction of the past as the working out of an originary intention realized by design, not accident. In fact, one might go so far as to argue that Conrad sees this as an absolute requirement under which the past becomes "tellable" and consequently meaningful. "Value" and "purpose" (not to mention, "courage") are aftereffects of teleological narrativization, and as such are imposed over against the story of mere coincidence and accident – pure contiguity, pure successivity – which the book posits as the structure of the actual – history before it has been "humanized."[31] Indeed, this is precisely what Cromer's *Modern Egypt* does with the "unsteady" Gordon once he is safely dead.

By obviously ironizing Mitchell's history, though, the book also raises subterranean questions about the status of Gould's metanarrative which posits that history is determined by material production. And the novel does this by carefully interweaving Gould's plot with Nostromo's (and consequently discrediting narrativization itself). Gould bears a name which inevitably associates him with the earthly substance which, in the late nineteenth-century economies of Europe and the US, carries the ambiguous signification of both absolute standard of value and token of relative value, simple "currency" – an empty cipher – capable of taking on whatever value it is assigned within an economic order at a particular moment in history. Nostromo – not surprisingly – who arguably functions as the "currency" of Sulaco, is also celebrated by the "blancos" in the novel for being both a store or source of value and an empty indicator. Because he seems to embody all the heroic virtues associated with courageous action and selfless fidelity, he is treated as a "source," the charismatic man of action admired by all. But because he seems to possess these inherent qualities required for heroic action, he is also treated as indispensable currency and lent out to others as needed: in these cases, his value is not inherent but rather bestowed on him by the occasion in which he makes himself "indispensable" (his value, in other words, is identical with his exchange value). Moreover, as Gould's name suggests that his pursuit of the "silver" of San Tomé is the pursuit of a debased substitute for "the real thing," Nostromo's name suggests a man whose work will always be for others: a signifier gesturing toward value residing, necessarily, elsewhere. Finally, where Gould grows gradually more and more inarticulate as the Monterist revolution unfolds, finally assuming the lumpish status of inert matter himself, Nostromo gradually "descends" over the course of the novel from "capataz" to "thief" (a parallel reinforced by Conrad's complex narrative strategy, which effectively diminishes Gould's role in the narrative action after [in "story" time] the Sulacan revolution, while giving pride of place, in the final pages, to Nostromo's untimely and operatic demise). Identifying Conrad as a "complex materialist," Jeremy Hawthorn argues:

Conrad's significant insight in *Nostromo* is to have seen that although, fundamentally, it is material interests not ideas that effect historical change, material interests effect this change through ideas. A comparable paradox is the fact that although it is men like Holroyd and Gould who are the tools of material interests, they are themselves the most idealistic of men, like Keats's two brothers in "Isabella," at least half-ignorant of their true motives or of what they are doing.[32]

Implicit in Hawthorn's claim is the idea that value is established through the perlocutionary effect of its articulation: precisely what Gould grows less capable of accomplishing as he grows less capable of speech.

If Gould represents here the necessity of erecting an absolute standard of value (however questionable) for the sake of any standard, then it is the cynical boulevardier Decoud who is given the task of puncturing pretenses, of articulating a reductive philosophy of "de-sublimatory" questioning which represents a strong challenge to Gould's ideological fantasy of a reparative or regenerative trajectory to history. In fact, Decoud explicitly defends his plan for "separation" (by which we might read the necessity of an infinite regress of "separations" brought on by the inherently atomistic tendencies of a politico-economic order founded on the large-scale production of private wealth for the few) by arguing that it is the only plan that is realizable in view of the constant temptation the mine will always pose for the venal "Indios" across the mountains. Moreover, he offers it because the very cynicism of its assumptions is the repressed subtext of heroic romance, thus helping guarantee its appeal to indispensable "sentimentalists" such as Gould and Holroyd. As he says to a shocked Mrs. Gould:

Well, there would be some poetical retribution in that man [Hernandez] arising to crush the evils which had driven an honest ranchero into a life of crime. A fine idea of retribution in that, isn't there? (*Nostromo*, p. 155)

Decoud's plan will work because it presupposes a widespread human need to transform dirt into silver, criminality into heroism, History into narrative; it will work because Decoud sees through the pretense of "sentimentality" into the truth that most humans need to cast themselves in prominent roles in "sentimental" narratives. Decoud steps out of the sentimental only to the extent that he recognizes the widespread need for sentimental narrativization.

However, Decoud himself cannot escape the sentimental simply through consciousness of it. In fact, his prime motive in conceiving the revolution – his love for Antonia Avellanos – is avowedly sentimental. Beyond that, however, lies a too-comforting assumption about the whole notion of "the plan": in *Nostromo*, "plan" has no projective function; it is the name one assigns only retrospectively to a series of plausibly contiguous events once one has ordered them teleologically after the fact. Even to say Decoud's plan "works" is to misread the incoherent chronicle of accident, unforeseeable consequence, and indeterminate chaos that is the "story" of the struggle for Sulacan independence as – somehow – the coherent narrative working out of Decoud's intention. That is, to say Decoud's plan "works" is to render the story of Sulacan independence in a way that is suspiciously similar to the

Whiggish fairy tale told by Captain Mitchell in the latter part of the book. Instead, Conrad has Decoud commit suicide because even he has no faith that his plan will be carried out, and in doing so, Conrad denies Decoud's "plan" a role as originary intention. Decoud's plan only "works" retrospectively.

If the investment of value requires a sublimated object, then the assertion of value presupposes the establishment of a hierarchy which fixes the relationship of "high" to "low." Unfortunately for Decoud, his greatest attribute is his greatest flaw: his clear-sighted ability to penetrate the disguises of value, to see gold or silver as, essentially, excrement or dirt, means he cannot also believe in silver or gold or love or anything else which acquires value only through the process of spiritualization, through becoming an "idea." Thus, when Nostromo leaves him on Great Isabel Island in charge of the silver, it is Decoud who is blessed with the penetration to see that Nostromo has unselfconsciously turned the trick of giving his own "monstrous vanity" the appearance of "all virtues" (*Nostromo*, p. 214). Nostromo's desire for adulation is symmetrical with Gould's more private desire to vindicate his family and attach himself to a worthwhile cause (which, not accidentally, serves his own economic interest). Yet it is this observation which disempowers Decoud. Because he sees this, Decoud is rendered incapable of believing in any of the values which Nostromo seems to represent (especially the value of fidelity, a classic Conradian second-order virtue which can only be celebrated as such if one suspends discussion of what end one ought to be faithful to). Decoud's lack of faith is dramatized in his despairing suicide. He ultimately kills himself because he has no faith in the efficacy of his own plan. As Kurtz discovered, the "god" or "designer" can "worship" or "sentimentalize" himself only at the cost of abandoning the very traits of character – demystified clarity of vision – which allowed him to install himself in the place of god to begin with. God, in other words, is the first atheist, the first to recognize fully what it takes to play the role of god.

The dramatic center of the novel – the turning point in Nostromo's career – occurs when he meets Dr. Monygham. While Gould gradually comes to feel "debased" by his contact with the criminality of Costaguanan life (the "lawlessness of the land") because his self-conceived narrative trajectory requires the "misty-eyed" triumph over the base material, Monygham is Decoud-like in his inability and unwillingness to lose sight of the grounding of all value in the base and the material. He demonstrates his courage by manipulating both Sotillo and Nostromo.

The latter he manipulates by convincing him that he is indispensable; in fact, that the public assumption that he is dead makes him absolutely necessary for undertaking the ride to Cayta. When Nostromo responds to his request with the retort "I am nothing," Monygham follows with a rejoinder that is simultaneously a flatteringly cynical form of manipulation and a perfectly appropriate statement of the paradox of value here: "you are everything" (*Nostromo*, p. 328). The point is complex: nothing is everything because of the illusory nature of all value; but also, nothing which lies outside of narrative (i.e. is "dead") can have value because value is conferred only through narrativization and thus always performs its tricks retrospectively. And this paradox is ultimately related to the racial, economic, and class themes in the book. While the cynical Monygham's disingenuous act of persuasion is an indispensably heroic act from a certain point of view (that is to say, it is an efficient cause of the success of the Sulacan revolution), Nostromo is necessary to the whole enterprise because the lower classes are necessary to accomplish any work at all, or, as the novel puts it: Nostromo is valuable because the "passionate, clear-minded" Southern mentality is indispensable to accomplish the purposes of the "misty-eyed" Northern "idealists" (*Nostromo*, p. 239). In bureaucratic terms, the instrument is indispensable to the agent in the bureaucratic hierarchy which this novel proposes as a metaphor for life in an industrial world governed by the desacralized ethos of capitalism. Given the fact that the novel itself relentlessly questions the goals and motives of those Northern "idealists," this "racial" typology has the status – finally – of a deliberately fictional claim asserted simply for the sake of establishing ground rules for the sake of ground rules. To Conrad, shit does not cease to be shit simply because treating it as silver gives people something worth doing, something worth striving for.

Thus, Conrad has Dr. Monygham articulate a final, chillingly disturbing vision of the dominance of material productive forces, a vision which manages to raise questions about the ends of production itself once they are embodied in the bureaucratic order of modern capitalism. In response to Mrs. Gould's plaintive plea "Will there be no rest?," Monygham responds:

"No!" interrupted the doctor. "There is no peace and no rest in the development of material interests. They have their law, and their justice. But it is founded on expediency, and is inhuman; it is without rectitude, without the continuity and the force that can be found only in a moral principle. Mrs. Gould, the time approaches when all that the Gould Concession stands for shall weigh as heavily upon the people as the barbarism, cruelty, and misrule of a few years back." (*Nostromo*, p. 366)

And this result is perfectly consonant with the assumption which governs the whole novel. Originating outside narrative in the land of the dead, the "material" can potentially be inserted within a variety of historical metanarratives, as the Monteristas' cynical political use of the Gould Concession earlier in the novel has already shown. The paradox is that even the human is inhuman until inscribed in a narrative order which assigns it purposes which seem to serve supra-human ends, but which, unfortunately for us "moderns," have already been discredited as "all too human."

# CHAPTER 5

# T. E. Lawrence and the erotics of imperial discipline

Consequently the relation of master and man in Arabia was at once more free and more subject than I had experienced elsewhere. Servants were afraid of the sword of justice and of the steward's whip, not because the one might put an arbitrary term to their existence, and the other print red rivers of pain about their sides, but because these were the symbols and the means to which their obedience was vowed. They had a gladness of abasement, a freedom of consent to yield to their master the last service and degree of their flesh and blood, because their spirits were equal with his and the contract voluntary.     T. E. Lawrence, *Seven Pillars of Wisdom*

With the coming of World War I, the first general European war since early in the industrial age, one begins to glimpse the appearance, for the first time, of the recognizably modern bureaucratic military state: one featuring universal conscription and the deliberate reorientation of domestic productive capacity to the manufacture of war materiel on a vast scale. When the war was over and its cost, measured in masses of slaughtered young men, was weighed against the relatively minor adjustment of the European balance of power that the Versailles Treaty imposed, many Europeans concluded that the mechanized slaughter of modern warfare rendered obsolete all previous ways of measuring the efficacy of individual agency and the glory of battle. Modern history would seem, to the immediate post-war generation, to be careering out of control, driven by the engine of conscripted armies marching to their own doom.

The horrors of World War I, and especially the ghastly carnage produced by trench warfare on the Western Front, encouraged a cultural reaction in Europe in the 1920s which attempted to discredit, not only war profiteers, incompetent generals, and imperialists, but the very apparatus of the bureaucratic state itself. Now the very giving of orders was itself become suspect, along with the goals of the project for which orders are issued. By the 1920s, what was left of the faith in individual efficacy and personal heroism – the Victorian faith in individual historical agency – had few heroes to focus on: a few gentlemanly pilots who had engaged in dogfights high above the senseless slaughter of the Western Front, perhaps; a few battlefield heroes noted, mainly, for exceptional feats of self-sacrifice. While the World War saw the first appearance of modern state-directed propaganda efforts, the very nature of the war itself almost guaranteed that it would be much harder to identify individual heroes than to demonize the enemy as "Hun" or "Visigoth."[1]

One notable exception to this generalization was T. E. Lawrence, who began to be extolled immediately after the war, mainly through the popular lectures of Lowell Thomas, as its one certifiable hero, the unacknowledged "King of Arabia." One need not search far to find a reason why Lawrence the military leader was lionized: he led an outnumbered band in an extraordinarily successful guerrilla campaign against an enemy armed with all the machinery of the modern industrial state; he achieved enormous success with a minimum of casualties; he took front stage in the only campaign of World War I which pitted an underarmed colonized people against the forces of a reactionary empire. More astonishing to many Europeans and Americans than even the success of Lawrence's underarmed band was the spectacle of the world's largest empire – the British Empire – committing advisors and troops to an avowedly "anti-imperial" cause. In pledging itself to defeat imperial Turkey in Arabia, the British government seemed to have authorized the eventual independence of the Arab people. However suspect actual British motives in the Arab Revolt appear in retrospect, the appearance of a major imperial power fighting ostensibly for the independence of a colonized people appealed to the only popular idealistic impulses to survive the War: the impulses fired by Woodrow Wilson's pledge, in his Fourteen Points, to replace *Realpolitik* with the ideal of national self-determination as the chief structuring principle of the post-war world order. It was in this atmosphere that the Lawrence of popular repute, "Lawrence of Arabia," came to be widely celebrated as the apostle of something that might be called "Indirect War," the only type of war the weak can wage against the strong.

For all his authentic feats of heroism and for all the public adulation showered upon him, Lawrence is remembered chiefly now as the author of a book, *Seven Pillars of Wisdom*, which is almost unique in the annals of military memoirs. *Seven Pillars* is a remarkable adventure narrative whose protagonist manages to combine an extraordinary degree of self-promotion with an almost masochistic self-denigration. It is a narrative that, while clearly given the diachronic narrative structure of a journal of a successful military campaign, also testifies to the steep personal cost of deferred recognition and bureaucratized consciousness. Lawrence lived in his own life what was merely tendentious moralism in Cromer, and his account of the Arab Revolt is both a revealing complaint about the political and psychological limitations of indirect authority and an anguished examination of the limitations and erotic compensations of subaltern status. In fact, the publishing history of the book could stand as a metaphor for one of its chief lessons. Although written in the early 1920s, it was only privately printed in 1926. A full edition of the work was withheld until the 1930s. This history suggests that Lawrence was reluctant to submit to the eyes of the world this account of his war work, and this "Victorian" reluctance has, for those who have read the book, recognizable sources – political, bureaucratic, and personal/sexual – indirectly acknowledged in its pages.

Whatever his motives, Lawrence's reluctance to publish *Seven Pillars*, nevertheless, effectively fed his mythic reputation by denying the public access to a first-hand corrective to the hagiographic distortions confected by Lowell Thomas. Reticence can easily be recuperated by the reading public as heroic modesty; certainly, as we have already seen, this is what happened to David Livingstone's reputation in the Victorian age. Whether Lawrence was deliberately encouraging his own mythologization by refusing to speak out is subject to some doubt, however. His motives in withholding his account for so long probably range across the spectrum running from laudable personal modesty to deplorable Victorian prudishness. Yet one motive was undoubtedly his allegiance to the bureaucratic code of silence. Although hardly an "old hand" of the Cromer school and personally a bit too eccentric to fade into the background with the rest of Cromer's bureaucrats, Lawrence nonetheless seems to have imbibed the unforgiving professional lesson Cromer taught: he seems to have subscribed to the professional code which forbids the public vaunting of accomplishments whose true worth can only be properly gauged and appreciated by knowledgeable and credentialed higher-ups within the military and Foreign Office bureaucracies.[2] A junior grade officer who, early in the Middle East campaign, rather quickly found himself with political and military responsibilities appropriate only to a general, Lawrence both made effective use of the advantages of subaltern status and indirect command, and suffered from the limitations. The complicated effects subaltern status has on Lawrence's exercise of authority are thus among the most important preoccupations of *Seven Pillars*, and, ironically, the chief – if inadvertent – reasons its main protagonist was able to assume mythic status in European culture.

Despite subscribing in some ways to the bureaucratic code of self-effacement, Lawrence also seems to have secretly enjoyed his public visibility in Europe and America as figure of myth. Moreover, the very public celebration of Lawrence in Europe and America in the immediate post-war period had an important, and double, ideological impact on the movement for Arab independence for which he fought. While inadvertently teaching the lesson to the world that the Arab Revolt could not have succeeded without being designed by British officers, and thus seeming to give the lie to the carefully crafted illusion of an indigenously led revolt, the celebration of Lawrence the myth also invested Lawrence the man with independent popular authority which he seems to have hoped to put in the service of Arab interests at post-war peace conferences.[3] Lawrence's public visibility, like his very visible entry into Damascus with Arab troops in October of 1918, was eventually put in the service of larger political ends, however controversial they were and and remain to this day.[4] There can be little doubt that his reputation enhanced the standing of the Arab delegation among the Great Powers assembled to redraw the map of the world at, first, the Versailles Conference (where he was chief advisor to Prince Feisal) and, later, the Cairo Conference of 1921 (where he worked for Churchill's Foreign Office to establish the sons of Hussein as rulers of the newly created Arab states of Iraq and Transjordan, "supervised" under British mandate until after World War II).[5] In a complicated fashion, Lawrence himself remains true to the Cromer ethic in a personal sense; violates its central requirements by encouraging his own sanctification as war hero; plays a notably ambiguous, but highly visible, political role in redrawing Middle Eastern boundaries in the aftermath of World War I; and then retreats to self-enforced obscurity in later life when he adopts the personae of, first, "Aircorpsman Ross" and, then, "Private Shaw."[6]

Although *Seven Pillars of Wisdom* contains many passages in which Lawrence avers that his role in the Revolt was chiefly that of instrument of an awakening Arab nationalism, it is also clear that Lawrence was a much more active "manager" of the Arab figures involved in the Revolt than he sometimes found convenient to acknowledge. Indeed, in post-war governing circles he was seen as the most flamboyant exponent of a very active form of Indirect Rule: a singularly charismatic figure bound to a thoroughly bureaucratic array of duties.[7] His "active" strategy in dealing with Britain's Arab allies was perhaps most baldly revealed in his "Twenty-seven Articles," which appeared in the *Arab Bulletin* in August 1917, before his role in organizing the Revolt was widely known. In these guidelines, Lawrence clearly casts himself in the role of chief agent of the Revolt, while deploying a "Cromeresque" logic to justify the strategy of acting through the façade of Arab authority:

Your ideal role is when you are present and not noticed. Do not be too intimate, too prominent, or too earnest. Avoid being identified too long or too often with any tribal sheikh, even if C.O. of the expedition. To do your work you must be above jealousies, and you lose prestige if you are associated with a tribe or clan, and its inevitable feuds. Sherifs are above all blood-Arabs. Let your name therefore be coupled always with a Sherif's, and share his attitude towards the tribes. When the moment comes for action put yourself publicly under his orders. The Bedu will then follow suit . . .[8]

While there can be little doubt that these guidelines are structured in accordance with the conventions of War Office memoranda on strategy, and thus conform to the bureaucratic requirement that agents in the field justify their activities to the military bureaucracy as the active pursuit, by indirect means, of ultimately British objectives (a requirement under which Lawrence often chafed, as he tells us again and again in *Seven Pillars*), the role Lawrence constructs for himself here also conforms to an important theme of his own self-presentation in the book. For *Seven Pillars* is a compelling narrative largely because it centers itself on the world-historical activities of its originally obscure archaeologist-hero whose birth is shrouded in mystery (is he an orphan? illegitimate?), and whose activities on behalf of, alternately, British war and imperial objectives and the ideal of Arab nationhood (which only served British objectives until the movement threatened to become dangerously successful) eventually placed him at the center of the most triumphant feats of a war which had seemed, by the Spring of 1918, to have sealed for all time the coffin of individual heroism.

Moreover, Lawrence's dual role as hero/bureaucrat is related in a complicated fashion to his double role as author and protagonist. Lawrence the protagonist of *Seven Pillars* manages the double game of claiming authorship of the historical narrative in which he emerges with a central role while also standing back from that role, regarding it as if it had been written for him by forces beyond his control.[9] Both active and passive simultaneously, he epitomizes the self-division of the imperial bureaucrat and demonstrates the degree to which his subjectivity is constituted through a renunciation which eroticizes it. Unlike the Victorian heroines studied by Kucich, whose withdrawal into silence leads to an eroticized expansion of interiorized experience in a novelistic world structured by withdrawal and outward silence, though, Lawrence's self-containment is imposed upon him by the demands of his role as both agent and instrument of British geopolitical objectives in the very sphere of the globe – the Middle East – which Cromer had already done so much thirty years earlier to annex to Britain's "sphere of interest." Few did more than Lieutenant Lawrence to deliberately remake the political structure of the Arabian peninsula in the aftermath of the Great War, yet the post-war world of Arabia is by no means a wholly "Lawrentian" construct. Indeed, Lawrence's own subaltern status, something of a convenience during wartime, had much to do with his post-war political failures also. To his regret, many Arab leaders came to rely on him to design satisfactory terms of independence which, as a low-ranking officer, he found himself ultimately powerless to confect.

As he tells us in *Seven Pillars*, Lawrence was torn between incompatible nationalist and bureaucratic imperatives long before the war was even over. As Arab successes in the guerrilla war against Turkey mount in 1918, his insistence that Prince Feisal take Damascus to forestall British and French attempts to enforce the terms of the Sykes–Picot agreement (the details of which he revealed early on to Feisal) becomes the overt goal of his campaign, at least according to his account in *Seven Pillars*. Yet General Allenby's successful advance through Palestine in late 1918 occasions his many musings on the possibility of seeing his own success across the Jordan as deriving its significance from his role simply as Allenby's "right flank" – a consideration made necessary in any case by his official British military role as Allenby's subordinate. This alternating allegiance to British and Arab objectives in the war (objectives which would become clearly antithetical with the sudden collapse of Turkish power and the accelerating demands by England's ally France for a say in the post-war order of the Middle East, ultimately forcing a political choice, as Lawrence himself saw it, between two antithetical historical metanarratives – one imperial and one nationalist) does not demarcate the only axis of his self-division. Indeed, as the latter half of *Seven Pillars* reveals, Lawrence is torn by the demands of competing self-conceptions: he comes to see himself, alternately, as an active agent of revolt and theorist of a new kind of war – guerrilla war – and a passive instrument of larger historical forces which would inevitably give birth to Arab nationhood in any case – "the new Asia which time was inexorably bringing upon us" (*SP*, p. 661).

I will examine here, first, the erotics of submission as Lawrence has described it and, secondly, the political implications of this erotic experience for the antithetical political and military goals toward which Lawrence was working. For reasons that I hope to clarify, a true understanding of Lawrence requires one to accept an aporetic logic of motive: to contemplate how the victim's victimization secures his mastery, to understand how those who issue orders can derive the authority to do so only from an authority not themselves, to comprehend how pain can become a kind of refined pleasure and how the abject subject becomes holy when he discards his bodily form to enter into the pure textuality of nationalist narrative.


2


Both Lawrence's erotics of submission and his idea of Arab nationhood are complexly tied to his imagination and experience of the desert. One of a long line of British travelers and commentators powerfully drawn to the Arabian desert for motives as much erotic as political and religious, Lawrence himself represents the culmination of this long tradition of British travel writing, for he ushers out the old era of politically "innocent" fascination with a culturally alien but historically rich area of the globe and ushers in a new era of actual and extensive British rule in Arabia (the final major territorial expansion of the British Empire, in fact). Many of his Victorian predecessors seem quaint dilettantes by comparison. They include the rigidly ethnocentric Eliot Warburton and Benjamin Disraeli, both infected, in their own ways, with a late Romantic, and rather abstract, affection for the Arabian desert as the cradle of Western religious ideals; the Victorian explorer and cultural rebel Sir Richard Burton, who made the Pilgrimage to Mecca in disguise in the early 1850s; and, above all, Charles Doughty, whose *Travels in Arabia Deserta* (1885) was reprinted in a new edition in the 1920s at Lawrence's request and with Lawrence's contributing an Introduction. In fact, many of the ideas on Arab culture which Lawrence discusses in this Introduction were actually recirculated later in the Introduction to *Seven Pillars of Wisdom*.

Like both Doughty and Burton, Lawrence took great sensual delight in the seemingly spare experience of the desert, and like both, he adopted Arab dress to smooth his passage through Arabia.[10] As in the case of many European travelers in the Middle East, his delight in the sensual richness of what would otherwise seem barren experience is accompanied by a familiar form of European primitivist romanticism: the celebration of the Bedouin for embodying precisely those cultural values that modern European civilization seems to have abandoned. To Lawrence, the Bedouin Arabs "had no half-tones in their register of vision." In contrast with European self-doubt and indulgence of ambiguity, Arabians,

were a people of primary colours, or rather of black and white, who saw the world always in contour. They were a dogmatic people, despising doubt, our modern crown of thorns. They did not understand our metaphysical difficulties, our introspective questionings. They knew only truth and untruth, belief and unbelief, without our hesitating retinue of finer shades. (*SP*, p. 38)

The ethnocentrism that undergirds this form of Western "primitivism" has been much discussed, and, in any case, is not strictly relevant here.[11] What is relevant here, though, is Lawrence's motive in celebrating a vision of reduced experience as a cure for the ills that afflict Western consciousness: above all, the ills of self-consciousness and self-doubt. He celebrates "the Arab" precisely for reducing the complexity of given experience in favor of a "purer," or "cleaner" vision of reality, stripped of ambiguities. Not surprisingly, the all-purpose valorizing adjective "clean" is applied over and over again to Arab and, especially, Bedouin, peoples in this book.

This issue has ironic resonance in *Seven Pillars*, itself in many ways one of the greatest (and, to use Lawrence's terms, "dirtiest") dramatizations of the tortures of self-doubt and moral and political ambiguity ever written. The "clean" Arab of the desert, emancipated from the doubts that so afflict Englishmen like Lawrence, is also, by virtue of these virtues, capable of taking decisive action against the oppression of the Turk. Essentially a martial people, the Arabs can be counted on to accomplish the nasty work of warfare without any messy second thoughts. Taken in its extreme form, this view might be called a theory of the enabling power of narrowed experience: history can be made more forthrightly by those who are not paralyzed by thought. The irony lies in the fact that the self-doubting Lawrence makes himself so central to the success of the very mission he credits to the unselfconscious Arabs. If unselfconscious martial vigor is the key to success in rebellion, then what is one to make of Lawrence's own example? How can the excess-

ively self-conscious European become the center of a war only successfully waged by the unselfconscious? And what, then, is the status, finally,
of Lawrence's own theory of guerrilla war? These questions are never
answered directly in *Seven Pillars*, although Lawrence does devote a great
deal of fretful attention to his own dubious claims to legitimacy as the
field commander of the Arab Army.

Part of the appeal of the desert to Lawrence lay in its inability to be
domesticated, its refusal to answer to human needs and wishes. The
desert Arab Lawrence celebrates is aware of the disciplining effect of an
environment which cannot even be conceived as "hostile" to human
desires without anthropomorphization: "My Arabs were turning their
backs on perfumes and luxuries to choose the things in which mankind
had had no share or part" (*SP*, p. 40). Implacable without providing the
comfort of active hostility, the desert is the fit place for conceiving a
transcendent god who is "not anthropomorphic, not tangible, not moral
nor ethical, not concerned with the world or with him [the Arab], not
natural" (*SP*, p. 40). A god, in short, who wields power over the
individual but will brook no appeal is a fitting inspiration to the "Semitic
creeds" which lay "a stress on the emptiness of the world and the fullness
of God" (*SP*, p. 41). Moreover, this unforgiving creed was the "faith of
the desert . . . impossible in the towns" (*SP*, p. 41).

While Lawrence identifies this submission as the "faith of the desert,"
one cannot ignore the relevance of this view of the desert Arab to
Lawrence's own position as agent of a distant and demanding British
government. Not only was the issue of submission to implacable authority of direct relevance to Lawrence in the desert, but the authority to
which he did submit would often seem remarkably "not anthropomorphic" to him. Divining the deliberately obscure and ambiguous "intentions" of a government which was playing a double game in the Middle
East created many difficulties for Lawrence. The British government
was responsible both for the so-called 1915 "McMahon Letters" to
King Hussein (which clearly held out a promise of support from the
British government for an independent Arab nation should King Hussein choose, as he eventually did, to launch a rebellion against Turkish
rule in the Hejaz) and for the machinations of Sir Mark Sykes (who
negotiated the secret 1916 accord with France which came to be known
as the "Sykes–Picot" agreement, pledging British cooperation in restoring French hegemony in Syria in the aftermath of the war). Which
position represented, finally, British "intentions"? Historians disagree
because, of course, governments, especially governments at war, so

seldom display unitary intentions. Both the McMahon Letters and the Sykes-Picot accord served British war interests in different ways: the former by encouraging the Arabs to open up an Arabian front; the latter by pacifying Britain's chief ally on the Western Front in Europe. Yet, for Lawrence, Britain's chief agent in the field, Sykes' pledge to restore Syria to France after the war created major tensions with the Arab leaders, requiring him over and over again to dance gingerly about the question of just what those intentions were.

Although the constraints of warfare and desert existence deny one the leisure to examine the finer shades of difference, according to Lawrence, they do enable other possibilities for "clean" or "pure" experience: most notably, erotic possibilities that constitute an important subtext to this book. Sex between men, or between men and boys, apparently quite frequent during the campaign, is described by Lawrence as a "cold convenience" nonetheless rendered "pure" in the homosocial atmosphere of guerrilla warfare:

The public women of the rare settlements we encountered in our months of wandering would have been nothing to our numbers, even had their raddled meat been palatable to a man of healthy parts. In horror of such sordid commerce our youths began indifferently to slake one another's few needs in their own clean bodies – a cold convenience that, by comparison, seemed sexless and even pure. Later, some began to justify this sterile process, and swore that friends quivering together in the yielding sand with intimate hot limbs in supreme embrace, found there hidden in the darkness a sensual coefficient of the mental passion which was welding our souls and spirits in one flaming effort. Several, thirsting to punish appetites they could not wholly prevent, took a savage pride in degrading the body, and offered themselves fiercely in any habit which promised physical pain or filth. (*SP*, p. 30)

Not only does this passage associate sterility with homoerotic experience (and consequently with the transvalued "cleanliness" of Bedouin life), but it also clearly imagines a peculiar ascetic sublimation, whereby the sensual is somehow transmuted into a "mental passion" which, working in the service of the de-individuating experience of warfare, ultimately promotes the high ideal of nationhood (the "flaming effort"). Moreover, the "savage pride" which Lawrence attributes to those who refuse sex in the field manifests itself in "degrading the body": an experience which is invested with double meaning here as both refusal of sexual pleasure and substitute realization or displacement of it, a self-punishing endorsement of the ultimate goal of sublimation and an autotelic experience of bodily pleasure. As Kaja Silverman has argued, *Seven Pillars of Wisdom* indicates "both the conditions under which masochism can sustain an aspiration to mastery, and those under which it can lead elsewhere."[12] Over and over again in *Seven Pillars*, the reduction of possibilities is represented as enabling rather than limiting, fostering ingenious adaptations which the text describes in terms of "cleanliness." Lawrence not only credits homosexual experience with being "cleaner" than the unavailable heterosexual variety, but also argues that it promotes rather than undermines *esprit de corps*. If one traces the ironic logic of the latter in the military theme of the text, one notices a parallel. *Seven Pillars* converts the ungenerous British and French supply policies toward the Arabs, policies of which Lawrence was critical at the time, into an inadvertent advantage: by limiting Arab military potential in conventional warfare, Allied supply policies predetermined guerrilla warfare "revolt" rather than "war" – as the Arab Army's only, and ultimately successful, mode of operation.[13]

Ironically, even the self-punishing refusal of some (including, it seems, Lawrence himself) to have sexual relations with other men prepares them for the grander self-punishment that is warfare. Even they serve who refuse to indulge in the "cold convenience" of homosexual sex for, if nothing else, in refusing sex out of guilt, they are simply teaching themselves potentially valuable military lessons about the limits of personal endurance and strength. If an army on the march is conceived of as a homosocial system, then whether one does or does not actually engage in homosexual sex, one is serving, Lawrence seems to be claiming, the larger goal of raising corps morale: either by forging close personal bonds through sexual relations with other troops or by steeling oneself for sacrifices to come by learning to take pleasure in denying oneself pleasure.[14] The refusal to have sex, in short, is itself erotically charged. One can abjure the sex act itself to procure the even more refined erotic pleasure of denial. Lawrence is theorizing war as a closed erotic system in which both self-indulgence and self-denial have become one.

This recognizably "Victorian" paradox of lust experienced as self-punishment and self-denial as richly erotic self-indulgence is then projected by Lawrence back into the history of Arabian religions. The conventional difference between asceticism and worldliness collapses, as Lawrence sees both experiences as forms of obsessive expenditure:

The disciples, in the endeavour to strip themselves and their neighbours of all things according to the Master's word, stumbled over human weaknesses and failed. To live, the villager or townsman must fill himself each day with the pleasures of acquisition and accumulation, and by rebound off circumstance become the grossest and most material of men. The shining contempt of life which led others into the barest asceticism drove him to despair. He squandered himself heedlessly, as a spendthrift: ran through his inheritance of flesh in hasty longing for the end. The Jew in the Metropole at Brighton, the miser, the worshipper of Adonis, the lecher in the stews of Damascus were alike signs of the Semitic capacity for enjoyment, and expressions of the same nerve which gave us at the other pole the self-denial of the Essenes, or the early Christians, or the first Khalifas, finding the way to heaven fairest for the poor in spirit. The Semite hovered between lust and self-denial. (*SP*, p. 42)

Like St. Augustine, Lawrence refuses to disjoin "lust" and "self-denial," but, for all that, neither does he connect the two in anything like Augustine's recognizably Christian narrative sequence of "sin" and "error" preceding and conditioning a later orgy of "repentance" and "moral righteousness." Rather he identifies both as expressions of one undifferentiated desire for self-negation or self-expenditure that underlies, as well, the personal risk-taking of war. If overindulgence in sensual experience testifies to the presence of ultimately ascetic impulses, this book argues, then surely the practice of self-denial can nonetheless liberate a great variety of imaginative possibilities for erotic play.[15]

The celebration of the desert Bedouin, then, masks a political thesis underwritten by a complicated and contradictory erotics, and so, not surprisingly, the collapse of "lust" into "self-denial" portends an analogous collapse of some of the other main ethnographic oppositions here. To put one example into the form of a proposition which, admittedly, Lawrence does not formulate in any explicit form: if asceticism is a variant form of lust, then surely town life can be seen as just another form of nomadic existence, regardless of the fact that the difference between the Bedouin and the cultivated Arab of Damascus, otherwise so important to Lawrence because of the opposite cultural values each represents, is thereby rendered ephemeral. In a surprising way, what is at stake for Lawrence in folding "lust" into "self-denial" is, among other things, the viability of a political and ethnographic category of identity – the "Semitic body" – which is designed to contain the oppositional categories "Bedouin" and "town Arab," an opposition which threatens the coherence of Arab national identity.

Unlike Victorian predecessors such as Disraeli and Burton, whose ethnographic categories were shaped by the relatively rigid essentialist category of "race" (associated, at least in the early nineteenth century, with Comparative Philology's notion of the "language family" as well as with inherited European aristocratic notions of lineage), Lawrence is at least willing to acknowledge that "nationality" is not a matter of mysterious essences. He admits outright, in fact, that the only answer to the question "What are Arabs?" is that they are a "manufactured people" (*SP*, p. 33).[16] Nor does he spare himself criticism for helping to manufacture the Arab people in order to achieve the political aims of the revolt. Yet, unlike earlier Romantic predecessors whose attempts to comprehend "the Arab" were conditioned by contemporary notions of a *Volksgeist* or *Volkstimme*, Lawrence here proffers a more fluid organic metaphor – "the Semitic body" – as an alternative to the essentialist rigidity of inherited Victorian notions of "the Semite." Although still something of an essentialist notion, Lawrence's metaphor of the "Semitic body" offers the benefits of a single organic image capturing the historical flux of displacement, wandering, and alternating urban and desert habitation which is the history of Arabia. It holds in tension the contradictions he uncovers in Arab identity:

> The tribes found themselves driven to the very edge of cultivation in Syria or Mesopotamia. Opportunity and their bellies persuaded them of the advantages of possessing goats, and then of possessing sheep; and lastly they began to sow, if only a little barley for their animals. They were now no longer Bedouin, and began to suffer like the villagers from the ravages of the nomads behind. Insensibly, they made common cause with the peasants already on the soil, and found out that they, too, were peasantry. So we see clans, born in the highlands of Yemen, thrust by stronger clans into the desert, where, unwillingly, they became nomads to keep themselves alive. We see them wandering, every year moving a little further north or a little further east as chance has sent them down one or other of the well-roads of the wilderness, till finally this pressure drives them from the desert again into the town, with the like unwillingness of their first shrinking experiment in nomad life. This was the circulation which kept vigour in the Semitic body. There were few, if indeed there was a single northern Semite, whose ancestors had not at some dark age passed through the desert. The mark of nomadism, that most deep and biting social discipline, was on each of them in his degree. (*SP*, p. 37)

The last line is especially significant, for Lawrence returns again and again to his claim that the "Arab," finally, is he who is "disciplined" by the desert, whether immediately in the present (the Bedouin) or only in the relatively recent past (the town Arab).[17] Where a European Social Darwinist would read the alternating periods of Arab history and the constant movement of its people as a sign of "unprogressive" movement

punctuated by periods of clear cultural "regression," Lawrence's outlook guarantees that he will see the periods of return to the desert as a
"disciplinary" moment devoutly to be wished and ultimately regenerative to the Semitic body. The Lawrence who subjected his own body
to long periods of thirst in the hot sun of the desert while traversing as
much as eighty miles per day on the back of a camel (and who even
walked barefoot across many miles of the frozen Jordan valley once
during the particularly harsh winter of 1917–1918) is here identifying
analogous forms of self-punishment as the key to the "vigour" of the
"Semitic body."

## 3

Lawrence's disciplinary imagination thus issues in a thesis about the
Arab people which is, to say the least, notably if inadvertently self-
revealing. It goes without saying that the man who was known to his
Arab troops for exemplary acts of self-denial – extraordinary even by
the standards of the desert Bedouin – and who would, in later life, beg
his Army friends to flagellate him for what now seem the most trivial of
transgressions, has constructed a thesis about the disciplining of a people
which suggests that discipline is for him far from a purely negative
experience. For Lawrence, discipline and submission have assumed a
powerfully attractive erotic charge connected with an erotics of self-
negation.[18] Brute physical punishment, especially, seems to have provided a powerful stimulus to his imaginative experience of de-individuation: in a personal sense, providing him with a brief holiday from the
political and moral difficulties of playing the role of "Lawrence of
Arabia," and, in the social sense (through warfare, for instance) helping
him to forge a nation out of a group of tribes inhabiting the same desert.

*Seven Pillars*, then, is a book which celebrates the dissolution of individuality – fusion – in the socially acceptable form of nation-building and
military *esprit de corps*, and in the less-than-acceptable form of an authoritarian celebration of self-submission – "happy slavery" and penitential
punishment, not to mention self-extinction.

The role played by actual bodily punishment – indeed, torture and
rape – in this text comes to light in Lawrence's narration of the Deraa
episode. Entering Deraa one day in 1918 to reconnoiter the Turkish
positions, Lawrence adopts the disguise of a Circassian because it
comports well with his fair skin and blue eyes. Oddly, he remarks on
how the pain of a broken toe, acquired in an earlier train-mining

incident, adds to his accessory sense of deceitfulness, not toward the Turks his enemy, but toward his Arab allies – a theme which becomes increasingly prominent in the second half of the book as the Allied armies draw nearer to Damascus. And he does so through the familiar metaphor of guilt as "weight":

I was in Halim's wet things, with a torn Hurani jacket, and was yet limping from the broken foot acquired when we blew up Jemal's train. The slippery track made walking difficult, unless we spread out our toes widely and took hold of the ground with them: and doing this for mile after mile was exquisitely painful to me. Because pain hurt me so, I would not lay weight always on my pains in our revolt: yet hardly one day in Arabia passed without a physical ache to increase the corroding sense of my accessory deceitfulness towards the Arabs, and the legitimate fatigue of responsible command. (*SP*, p. 441)

The dual connotation that the "weight" metaphor is given here (literal body "weight" and the metaphorical "weight" of the burden of guilt) is perhaps overdone in this spasm of "Lawrentian" rhetoric, but it is nonetheless interesting that Lawrence connects here, with the deliberation of reconstructive memory, his guilt over his dual role with the pain produced by a broken toe. Moreover, he devotes much space in the second half of *Seven Pillars* to self-recrimination of precisely this sort. One suspects not only that a process of reinterpretation is going on here (not surprising in the least, given Lawrence's difficult position as the agent of British imperial interests disguised as a project to produce Arab independence) but that what Lawrence calls "guilt," and which he will enlist to authorize pain-as-punishment, is – experientially – rather aftereffect than cause. To put it bluntly: in Lawrence, "guilt" is typically conjured up and retrospectively assigned as cause to legitimize – after the fact – experiences of pain and disciplinary punishment that have their own, autotelic, and erotic, function in his libidinal economy. The excessive emphasis which *Seven Pillars* places on Lawrence's political guilt at being forced to serve two masters, which has often been remarked by critics, a guilt seemingly disproportionate in light of Lawrence's clearly difficult political and bureaucratic circumstances, can be seen rather as a rhetorical "cause" assigned only retrospectively to experiential "effect" – punishment, torture, physical pain. His motive (conscious, unconscious, or some combination of both) would then be double: to impose on painful experience in the past a kind of sequential and logical order it lacked at the time of experience, and to legitimize, to make acceptable for his readers, experiences of bodily pain which Lawrence himself seems to have recognized as guilty pleasures. Indeed, one might go further in a direction mapped out, in a different context, by Geoffrey Galt Harpham: that "guilt" here constructs the illusion of self-presence retrospectively by allowing the subject to assume a place in a narrative order at the price of a complete bodily ascesis, and entry into pure textuality. The ultimate horizon of self-punishment, the horizon of both pleasure and pain in fact, is self-negation, the destruction of the body to achieve a complete interpellation in language.

Not surprisingly, then, the horrific torture and rape in Deraa, recounted in one of the most discussed passages in *Seven Pillars*, seems to have left Lawrence with feelings of guilt – "stained" is his oft-used word – seemingly out of all proportion to his actual culpability (if indeed he could legitimately be considered culpable at all). The impression given is that of a man intent on disguising painful pleasure – or heightening it – by insinuating that he somehow deserved his ill-treatment, that Deraa was an expiatory experience for him because only the language of expiation renders guilty pleasure publicly admissible. No doubt the double discourse of abjection is at work here as well: intense suffering raises the abject one above the rest of us who are, by comparison, unsanctified by similar intense suffering; yet it does so by seeming to reduce him beneath us – to nothing but unpalatable meat. The duality of this subject's position – heroic sufferer and pathetic victim – is reinforced both by his elevation through recognition by a superior (the Bey) and by his reduction to a beaten, broken, and undesirable body. Thus, when he is initially captured by the Turks in Deraa, Lawrence finds himself, like Christ, a special object, desired immediately at the highest levels: "The Bey wants you" (*SP*, p. 442). And this special status is reconfirmed in the Bey's bedroom where, after having spurned the Bey's advances and then hurt him by jerking his knee into his groin, Lawrence is, in order: beaten with a slipper, kissed, and then given a shallow knife wound in the ribs which bleeds in the manner of the suffering Christ. Moreover, his special/abject status is confirmed here even more starkly by the indeterminate nature of the Bey's words of recognition:

In my despair I spoke. His face changed and he stood still, then controlled his voice with an effort, to say significantly, "You must understand that I know: and it will be easier if you do as I wish." I was dumbfounded, and we stared silently at one another, while the men who felt an inner meaning beyond their experience, shifted uncomfortably. But it was evidently a chance shot, by which he himself did not, or would not, mean what I feared. (*SP*, p. 445)

Although Lawrence asserts that the Bey is only pretending he knows that Lawrence is not a Circassian, the very indeterminacy of the Bey's claim to "know" ("know" what? that he is an Arab? that he is English? that he is "Lawrence"?) produces a strange orientation to language in the beaten and humiliated Lawrence. The Bey is treated by Lawrence, at least momentarily, as the Lacanian "subject-presumed-to-know" here. Not only does Lawrence assume that the Bey has turned him inside out, exposing in the process his inner being, but that the Bey is exercising power over him by refusing unambiguously to reveal precisely what knowledge he has of Lawrence's inner being. The Other who knows the self but won't reveal what he knows in an unambiguous way exercises an absolute form of power and enforces an absolute subjection. Moreover, this type of imaginary surrender to the other is also typical of Lawrence in *Seven Pillars*. As Silverman says of Lawrence's use of Arab dress, his "corporeal envelopes": "Within *Seven Pillars*, they also bear luminous witness to the extraordinary porousness of Lawrence's subjectivity – to the ease with which he was able to discover himself within the Other."[19]

The very possibility that the Bey might have "known" him as "Lawrence," rather than simply as an Arab passing for a Circassian, has occasioned interpretations of this passage which emphasize this as an important recognition scene in the heroic narrative – Lawrence here dramatically unmasked by the Turks as "Lawrence of Arabia"; just as Odysseus, disguised as an old warrior when he arrives in Ithaka, becomes dramatically self-identical with "Odysseus" the wandering hero upon stringing his bow.[20] In heroic epic, of course, the recognition scene, the moment when the disguised and etiolated hero steps into the place of his legendary self, is a moment in which the hero conventionally resumes his powers, a resumption signified, usually, by heroic magic: the actual man stepping into the armor of the hero of legend and thereby putting on the hero's powers with his armor. But here the Bey's attempt at both literal and figurative "penetration" eventually proves futile when, after having Lawrence whipped by his underlings, he finally rejects him as too gruesome to rape (*SP*, p. 445), leaving Lawrence to be raped finally by the same Turkish soldiers who had just beaten and tortured him. The recognition scene here is an ironic one in which the hero's powers can only be assumed to be proportional to the degree of his abjection.[21]

The equation of sexual "knowledge" and personal "knowledge" in the Deraa rape scene is startling, but even more startling is Lawrence's abject willingness to accept that the other "knows" him, a willingness revealed in his summary comment: "the citadel of my integrity was irretrievably lost" (*SP*, 447). Lawrence conflates sexual intactness and political honesty in this comment (he may well have been a virgin until this moment), condemns himself retrospectively as "raddled meat," and cites, as confirmation of his own low opinion of himself, the Bey's disgust with the body he himself ordered tortured. So intent is Lawrence on convincing his readers that his Deraa rape was a form of penance richly deserved that, as a reader, one almost loses sight of the villainy of the Turks committing the torture. While feelings of complicity are quite common among the victims of both rape and torture, they remain unanalyzed as such here. The passage instead suggests either that Lawrence still felt complicitous at the time he wrote *Seven Pillars* or that he was intent on conveying the full erotic experience of his torture and rape, and thus, intent on admitting to his readers that to experience rape and torture as "sexual" one must, on some level, desire them: that one's experience involves an extreme degree of self-distantiation enabling one to see with the perpetrator's eyes, desire oneself with the perpetrator's desires.[22] This latter interpretation finds some confirmation in his description of being kicked repeatedly by the Turkish corporal wearing a nailed boot: "I remember smiling idly at him, for a delicious warmth, probably sexual, was swelling through me . . ." (*SP*, p. 445). Lawrence's feeling of self-imposed guilt is thus a defensive gesture which serves the purpose of self-estrangement and self-punishment: the Turk who punishes Lawrence implicitly acts on behalf of Lawrence. If it is right that Lawrence be kicked, then the Turk is doing what Lawrence desires and Lawrence assumes some small degree of mastery of an experience – even if not at the moment of experience but only later, during the writing of *Seven Pillars* – over which he had no actual control. Thus, the role of victim can be made to serve the function of mastery, provided the victim of torture can project himself into the place of the torturer.[23] This irony is duplicated on the political level when the pose of subaltern status, under Indirect Rule, is presented as a guarantee of control: "Wave a Sherif in front of you like a banner and hide your own mind and person" is Lawrence's most famous formulation of how self-effacement can function as a strategy of control.

Consistent with the outward "Victorian" reserve of the man himself but unusually – indeed, deplorably – graphic by earlier Victorian standards of representation, Lawrence's account of his physical abuse by the Turks manages to accumulate multiple meanings. On the one hand, Lawrence's "rape" by the Turks sutures him into the role of the colonized as emblematic victim of Turkish injustice, thus helping to justify – through a metaphorical reenactment of Arab victimization – a rebellion that might otherwise seem contrived mainly to serve the global ambitions of a European power. Moreover, the scene is a psychologically striking representation of the ambivalence of the torture victim in his own right, converting pain into a peculiar form of pleasure as a psychological defense strategy. If war itself is conceived as a form of torture, then surely this psychological strategy has an important practical function for a book subtitled "A Triumph."

On the other hand, the scene accumulates other meanings that cannot easily be squared with these. For one, Lawrence's guilt, even if retrospectively imposed, arrives at the scene at a rather awkward moment. To construe torture and rape as deserved punishment is to at least imply that rebels deserve punishment like this. Moreover, however much the scene in Deraa serves an obvious ideological function – staging through displacement the metaphorical Turkish "rape" and "torture" of Arabia with Lawrence sutured into the place of "the Arab" trapped in the city; an obvious and vivid contrast with earlier scenes of "clean" homosexual eroticism among Arabs in the desert that involve no compulsion and certainly no physical torture and which fuse the Arabs into an effective fighting force (Eros in the Aristophanic sense: the power which brings divided beings together) – Lawrence cannot suppress the evident feelings of erotic delight which bubble to the surface here in his recounting of an episode in which he plays the role of victim but sees with the eyes of the victimizer. At least in the Deraa episode, Lawrence's protean ability to occupy both sadistic and masochistic positions, to identify both with the brutal Bey and with his Arab victims, raises disturbing questions about his commitment to the very cause for which he suffered. To read the scene this way commits one to question the degree of his commitment to the Arab cause (a commitment which, in any event, he cannot make for bureaucratic reasons). Of course, as agent of the British government, he repeatedly accuses himself of being a traitor to the Arab cause he helped to make, and he uses this self-abasing posture to justify his claim to have set out to undermine British and French plans for a post-war order in the Middle East. Yet the pleasure which self-abasement yields for him makes the issue of his ultimate allegiances undecidable.

The unresolved ambivalence of his stance here has wider implications, as the "erotic excess" of his unmasterable experience in Deraa

spills over to shape other aspects of his retrospect. The political implications of this erotics for the political and military project of Arab Revolt
requires fuller discussion, for Lawrence's erotic theme is subtly worked
into the political theme that dominates the second half of the book.

4

While there can be little question that Lawrence originally joined the
war effort and undertook the mission to Feisal in order to further British
objectives in the war against Turkey and her ally Germany, once he
meets Prince Feisal he is quite impressed with what he sees as Feisal's
conscious mastery of the situation (in true Orientalist fashion, Lawrence
describes himself discovering in Feisal "the prophet" to give form to the
idea behind the Arab revolt [*SP*, p. 70]). Yet Lawrence identifies himself
as the originator of the theory of guerrilla war. At one point, while
confined to his tent for ten days with a painful bout of dysentery,
Lawrence finds the time to actually ruminate on a new theory of warfare
which departs radically from Foch's theory of "absolute war," the then
accepted standard strategic theory for military leaders on the Western
Front. From his dysentery-induced ruminations evolves a new belief,
announced in portentous Lawrentian prose, that the Arab revolt must
take the tack of "rebellion" rather than "war." This decision then
dictates the eventually successful strategy detailed in the rest of the book
– the mining of the Hejaz Railway, the taking of Akaba by its unde-
fended side, the stepped-up campaign of slow attrition against the
Turkish army throughout the Arabian peninsula – "indirect war," one
might term it, for it becomes the military equivalent of Indirect Rule. By
avoiding pitched battles against well-armed, massed forces, Feisal and
Lawrence construct a new standard for measuring success in an historically new kind of warfare.

Thus, Lawrence borrows the authority of Feisal to take effective
command of the Arab Army in its campaign against the Turks, as he
borrowed the authority of the British Army in making an arrangement
with Feisal. While there can be no doubt that it was precisely this insight
that guaranteed the ultimate practical success of the revolt (for the
British – and especially their French allies – were reluctant to provide
the Arabs with modern weapons in enough quantity to make Feisal's
army a truly formidable force in pitched battles with the Turkish Army),
one cannot help reading out of Lawrence's characterization of the
campaign as "rebellion" a hesitance on his part to go all out. "Rebel-

lion" pays implicit tribute to the power of the adversary: it is the only type of war the weak, of necessity, can wage against the strong. In *Seven Pillars* it develops further politically complex connotations, forecasting the possibility that the Arab Revolt would eventually turn into a rebellion against British and French imperial power, as it threatened to do in the final days of the campaign to take Damascus.

It would appear that Lawrence wrote *Seven Pillars* to counter the widespread belief in the immediate post-war era that the Arab Revolt was staged merely to defeat Turkey and give Britain and France an opportunity to divide up the Middle East. Although Lawrence's narrative attempts – somewhat desperately – to balance the irreconcilable objectives of Feisal's Arab Revolt and British Middle Eastern policy, represented in the two figures Lawrence deployed to personalise his self-division – Allenby and Feisal – there is no question that the final pages also dramatize a problematic political situation in which all Lawrence's efforts on behalf of the Arab cause ironically serve Allied geopolitical objectives quite well. Thus, Lawrence's pose as rebellious subordinate to Allenby, racing ahead of Allied troops to take Damascus first, turns out to be quite a useful way to accomplish British objectives in the war. Moreover, Lawrence's own tendency to pleasure himself through the assumption of masochistic guilt makes it difficult to know whether or not to credit his stated intention of founding an independent Arab state.

Undoubtedly, the "professional" circle of British "experts" assembled by Clayton in Cairo at the beginning of the campaign constitutes just such a structure, and Lawrence would become its chief ornament by 1918. Moreover, Lawrence's tribute to Clayton, who was chief of British Intelligence in Egypt, given in the early part of *Seven Pillars*, is saturated with a cloyingly Kiplinguesque appreciation of the special abilities of an elite corps of dedicated professionals – "wild men such as we" – guided by a charismatic figure (much like Kipling's "Head"), himself necessarily something of a rebel in relation to the command structure of the British Army, and who is described by Lawrence in the extravagant terms appropriate only to God or Kurtz: "It was not possible to say where Clayton was and was not and how much really belonged to him" (*SP*, p. 57). The celebration of Clayton's professional expertise and autonomy constitutes him as a self-consciously "charismatic" figure, capable of surmounting the restraints imposed on other bureaucrats. Yet this kind of excessive praise from an underling is also conventional professional gesturing: praise is hollow when it comes from below, from those who can benefit by praising higher-ups, and it cannot come from above either, for reasons that Cromer stipulates. But the terms in which Lawrence celebrates Clayton reveal that he, at any rate, shares the professional conceit, so common to Intelligence officers in general, that they are secretly powerful individuals involved in a complicated act of rebellion against a cumbersome military hierarchy which will never adequately recognize their important contributions to the cause: thus, the importance of recognition by other, similarly "knowing," professionals. The terms of Lawrence's tribute to Clayton, then, cast in the metaphors ("wild men") common to elites who believe themselves to be writing their own rules, is an anticipatory appreciation of his own greater accomplishments as "irregular" leader of an even "wilder" band of men. Lawrence, in short, stages his own self-congratulation within the pages of his book, and appropriates the language of rebellion for the intelligence operation within which he was an important cog.

No doubt some of this self-congratulation was richly merited. There is no question but that Lawrence himself was a great military strategist. In fact, one of his strengths was his ability to appreciate the differences between "rebellion" and "war," and especially, the difference between military success on the ground for its own sake and the semiotic function of military success – what, in other words, a certain kind of success (or failure, for that matter) communicates to the enemy. Moreover, this difference between what a military maneuver "does" and what it "says" was not something which was easily grasped by more conventional military men, and not only because they had been miseducated in Clausewitz and Foch. Lawrence enjoyed an inadvertent advantage over conventional military men in being forced to direct a "rebellion" without being given materiel adequate to accomplish the task along conventional military lines. The theory of guerrilla war he propounds is the invention of the "weak" who must make do in a struggle against the "strong."

Thus, Lawrence's troops undertake the mining campaign against the Hejaz Railway initially to cut off Turkish troops at Medinah. However, Lawrence quickly realizes that, although the Arab Army probably could achieve a complete and permanent severing of the rail link between Maan and Medinah, the result of that conventional "victory" might be ultimate defeat, if the Turks abandoned Medinah and re-garrisoned the north with these newly-freed troops. Lawrence's solution to this problem is a highly unconventional, half-hearted dynamiting campaign which disrupts rail operations but does not sever them: a campaign which gives the Turks ample reason both to underestimate the power of the Arab Revolt and to continue to tie down 25,000 badly needed troops in Medinah until the end of the war. In fact, the official British military history of the war gives an impressive numerical summary of the importance of Lawrence's operation in aiding Allenby. Allenby, it seems, was able to carry out his successful offensive in the Fall of 1918 with 250,000 troops because 200,000 of the 250,000 Turkish troops in the area were preoccupied with Lawrence and his relatively small Arab Army of 30,000.[24]

On the level of ideological warfare, the equivalent to this military strategy was Lawrence's discovery that Feisal's "preaching was victory, the fighting a delusion." Thus, Lawrence's famous paradox – "To the clear-sighted failure was the only goal" (*SP*, p. 412) – becomes understandable as a necessary ideological tactic for recruiting reluctant desert tribes into the movement, for suturing the Bedouins into a nationalist narrative. Guerrilla war of this sort is preeminently a kind of novelistic war, driven by the preaching of "rebellion" and the celebration of "privation," and requiring, as a dramatic necessity of ultimate success, initial failures. Thus, "rebellion" must "fail" initially, for reasons that parallel the reasons why 'privation' can be seen as 'satisfaction.' The logic of nationalist rebellion is also a narratological one based in bodily ascesis in the interests of textual or narrative teleology. Indeed, no sooner is this narrative formulated – quite early in the book, in fact – than its ultimate goal is revealed by Lawrence in a passage which reveals a striking – if not playfully absurd – ambitiousness:

The conjunction of Semites, an idea, and an armed prophet held illimitable possibilities; in skilled hands it would have been, not Damascus, but Constantinople which was reached in 1918. (*SP*, p. 145)

Like many of Lawrence's political fantasies, this is not a modest one. Not only does he fantasize an awakened Arab power with ambitions of conquest that extend far beyond the goal of seizing Damascus, but he projects a nationalist project become imperialist in turn, an Arab Army threatening the conquest of not just the Turkish capital of Istanbul, but the ancient Byzantine capital of Constantinople (ironically, conquered in 1453 by the non-Semitic Turks). The conflation of late-medieval fantasy with twentieth-century military goals is another sign of the "already-textualized" nature of the narratives Lawrence is attempting to write, and the shift of allegiances here – from Crusader Europe to Saracen Arabia – testifies again to the protean nature of Lawrence's identifications. When Lawrence decides that the Arabs can be organized into a nation because of their common language (although some do not share the Muslim faith, some originate in diverse locales, and many nurse ancient grudges against one another), the linguistic/ascetic nature of the idea of Arab nationhood is made clear: "The master-key of opinion lay in the common language: where also, lay the key of imagination" (*SP*, p. 336).

As a strategist and theorist of guerrilla war, Lawrence displays ample mastery. Yet his passivity is a crucial component as well. The complex attitude of "Lawrence" the character in the final days of the revolt, detailed through the constructed intimacy of the journal form, is underwritten by his complexly eroticized consciousness. Although his self-reproaches increase late in the book as he gradually grows disenchanted with his double political role, these self-reproaches are complexly over-determined. In fact, he steps up his insistence that the Arabs must take Damascus before the Allies do while also paying marked (and rhetorically excessive) tribute to Allenby as the latter's military successes in Palestine multiply in the final months of the campaign. His pose as the rebellious subordinate, carefully devising his own strategy, his own war aims and post-war political aims, contrasts strikingly with the almost cloying emotionality and dependent passivity of his celebration of Allenby's "mastery." This reaches a peak after the capture of Damascus, in fact, when he welcomes relief from the responsibility of ruling the unruly city thus: "I might let my limbs relax in this dreamlike confidence and decision and kindness which were Allenby" (*SP*, p. 659). Given the fact that he is quite aware at this late date of British and French intentions to divide up the Middle East into their own – dramatically expanded – spheres of influence, his "surrender" to Allenby at this point suggests an inability to reconcile conflicting political demands undergirded by a powerfully eroticized urge to "serve" his original masters and retreat into the security of privatized experience.[25]

Lawrence's celebration of the Arab tradition of "voluntary slavery," then, must be understood in the context of his professional dilemma: the imperial bureaucrat, torn by multiple and irreconcilable allegiances, embraces a theory which seems to offer a utopian, bodily, compensation for the sacrifice of self-surrender, a reconciliation between pain and pleasure, self-negation and self-transcendence. Thus, he says,

Servitude, like other conduct, was profoundly modified to Eastern minds by their obsession with the antithesis between flesh and spirit. These lads took pleasure in subordination; in degrading the body: so as to throw into greater relief their freedom in equality of mind: almost they preferred servitude as richer in experience than authority, and less binding in daily care. Consequently the relation of master and man in Arabia was at once more free and more subject than I had experienced elsewhere. Servants were afraid of the sword of justice and of the steward's whip, not because the one might put an arbitrary term to their existence, and the other print red rivers of pain about their sides, but because these were the symbols and the means to which their obedience was vowed. They had a gladness of abasement, a freedom of consent to yield to their master the last service and degree of their flesh and blood, because their spirits were equal with his and the contract voluntary. Such boundless engagement precluded humiliation, repining and regret. (*SP*, p. 466)

The claim that this type of "contract" is "voluntary" is pure mystification, especially in light of what we have already seen of Lawrence's tendency to reconceive obedience to necessity as voluntarily chosen service. Mastery, to Lawrence, chiefly involves obedience reconstructed as an intentional act of an autonomous subject. If one connects these sentiments on Arab "servitude" with Lawrence's own political/bureaucratic predicament, for which it serves as metaphor, though, one can observe that Lawrence seeks a release from the unbearable tensions of his political/bureaucratic dilemma by imagining the condition of "voluntary slavery": for "voluntary slavery" transvalues servitude as freedom, pain as pleasure, and instrumentality as agency. As the main characters in *Nostromo* reinscribe senseless accidents in a narrative order which assigns them purpose and meaning, Lawrence constructs servitude as a voluntary, contractual arrangement and, in the process, constructs the illusion of historical agency and individual efficacy. The "slave" of history becomes, thereby, the "master" of history. In this sense, Lawrence offers the most dramatic narration of the very psychological conditions which enable Cromer's theory of bureaucratic/imperial service to function, while inserting himself into a central, if ambiguous, place in two mutually exclusive historical narratives: one imperialist and one nationalist.

# CHAPTER 6

# Resurrecting individualism: the interwar novel of imperial manners

You are a creature of the despotism, a pukka sahib, tied tighter than a monk or a savage by an unbreakable system of tabus.

George Orwell, *Burmese Days*

The political leaders most impressed with T. E. Lawrence's deeds of valor – Lord Curzon and Winston Churchill – sought to reconceive the British imperial mission in the aftermath of World War I, and their reconceptualization would place greater emphasis not only on the indirect exercise of power but on a new (at least public) commitment to the eventual independence of the lands Britain ruled. The Commonwealth idea, which benefited from Lawrence's public support, was one new idea which seemed to offer a chance for the British government to retain its colonial empire while making fine adjustments in the way colonialism was portrayed to the public. In the immediate postwar era, as Kathryn Tidrick has said, "The Commonwealth became to politicians and men of affairs what Indirect Rule was to the DO – a chance to display those qualities which justified them in the possession of an empire, and thereby ensure its perpetuation."[1]

Another new idea was "mandate" rule. Lord Cromer's view of imperial service as a moral duty the conqueror performs for the conquered seems to have finally become official policy in this period, with the acceptance by the British government of League of Nations' "mandates" to rule a number of territories said to be "on the road" to independence. However powerless the League ultimately turned out to be, it did require that the imperial powers of Europe at least pay lip service to the goal of eventual – if far off – decolonization. In accepting mandates, Britain tacitly accepted the logic of mandate rule along with its dubious goal: self-cancelling power.

The idea of "mandate rule" had less to do with actual decolonization than it did with the way the British and French governments wished to portray imperialism to the rest of the world. Nevertheless, it did require dramatic changes in the discourse about empire, as many formerly unapologetic imperialists found themselves forced to pay at least token attention to the ultimate goal of decolonization and eventual democratic independence for the colonies. These adjustments are illustrated in the career of Frederick Lugard.

At the end of the nineteenth century, Lugard gave the appearance of a typical African adventurer from the period of the "Scramble" (if there was such a creature). While courting the favor of Joseph Chamberlain who eventually became Colonial Secretary under Salisbury, he also forged an alliance of convenience with Sir George Goldie, the director of the Royal Niger Company, who had grand plans to turn the Company into an African version of the East India Company. After making a series of false treaties with Niger tribes on behalf of Goldie's company in 1894 and 95 (when the local king in the town of Nikki refused to cooperate, he secured the signature of the local imam and butcher and then claimed that the treaty had been signed by the king), Lugard managed to impress Chamberlain, who eventually appointed him to the post of high commissioner for Northern Nigeria in 1900. From this position, Lugard, spoiling for a pretext to attack and conquer the northern Fulani Emirates, sent back to Britain a series of lurid and highly exaggerated reports on what he claimed was widespread slave-raiding which threatened to leave the northern areas of the Niger "depopulated."[2] Lugard's manipulation of a reluctant Colonial Office continued right through to the end of the Boer War at the beginning of 1903 when, describing the towns of Kano and Sokot as towns "ruled by an alien race who buy and sell the people of the country in large public slave markets," he attacked the towns with a large military force, finally subjecting them by April of 1903, and thereby demonstrating the futility of the "responsibility system" when responsibility is left in the hands of an irresponsible person.[3]

Oddly, in light of his later verbal commitment to "mandate" rule and the ideal of eventual colonial self-governance, Lugard, in power in Nigeria from 1900 to 1906 and then from 1912 to 1919, actually behaved in a way calculated to destroy local sovereignty and to exalt his own autocratic position. Not only did he crush the Fulani Emirates militarily and then subordinate the emirs to British rule from Lagos, but he then attempted to impose a neofeudal type of emirate rule upon the areas of southern Nigeria which had become largely Christianized and connected to the European trading system. When he was replaced in 1919 by

Hugh Clifford, the proconsul-novelist, he left a colony in administrative chaos, reduced to that state in large part by his own unwillingness to delegate the authority he wished to see devolve upon Nigerians.[4]

In retirement from colonial service in the 1920s, however, Lugard seems to have quickly evolved into an articulate spokesman for imperial reform. His previous practice as an administrator seems to have fixed the idea of Indirect Rule as a "conservative practice, hostile to the ambitions of educated Africans and those influenced by Christian missionaries, to urban growth, to the spread of the money economy, and to the vision that new African nations were in the making."[5] Yet Lugard's work after retirement and his later writing committed him to a view of Africa which, for all its conservative suspicion of educated Africans, was nonetheless strongly opposed to the overtly racist and confiscatory policies which were being actively put into place in the white settler domains of South Africa, Kenya, and Rhodesia.[6] Lugard's "dual mandate" was hostile to "alienation of African land, forced or manipulative labor arrangements, the destruction of African culture and chiefly authority, and the neglect of education," all of which were to become prominent features of those other white settler-dominated societies.[7] The enlightened colonial administrator celebrated by Margery Perham in the interwar period was this newly refurbished Lugard: the author of *The Dual Mandate*, an attempt to turn ambivalence about conquest into enlightened policy in an era when conquest had lost its public aura.

Needless to say, the benevolent conception of imperial service set forth in *The Dual Mandate* neither reflected actual colonial practice very well nor resolved the contradictory tensions implicit in a project of "supervising" in order to foster habits of independence. Nevertheless, in emphasizing the duty to foster habits in the colonized that would serve them well under eventual independence, Lugard's vision of colonial service conforms rather neatly to the ideology of Indirect Rule, which requires the European administrator to present himself in a self-effacing manner, as merely an "advisor" to local leaders. While British resolve to continue its direct rule over the colony of India was never actually relaxed in the interwar period, its commitment to mandate rule elsewhere in the globe would make its intransigent attitude toward Gandhi and the Indian independence movement increasingly difficult and embarrassing to defend.[8] In a sense, British imperial rule generally during this interwar period was undertaken in a "bad faith" which was deepened by the growing incompatibility between the desire to be powerful and the desire to seem noble.

Three important interwar novels – E. M. Forster's *Passage to India*, Joyce Cary's *Mr. Johnson*, and George Orwell's *Burmese Days* – dramatize this "bad faith" of the post-war Empire particularly well, and all are written by novelists who were deeply involved in promoting what can now be seen as a recognizably twentieth-century attitude toward bureaucracy. All three conceive the Empire as a bureaucratic jugger-naut crushing indifferently beneath its wheels both the colonized and those English officials employed in its service. Moreover, all three see the behavior of British officials in the interwar period as an exercise of power to accomplish goals in which some of the officials themselves seem to have lost faith. All three writers, in other words, to a greater or lesser extent, conceive of the Empire as a bureaucratic system which has escaped individual control, and all three were implicated in the con-struction of a recognizably Modernist ideology of individualism as a counterweight to the ideology of bureaucratic efficiency and "modern-izing" benevolence which buttressed official attitudes. If it was becom-ing increasingly embarrassing by the 1920s and 30s for Britain to celebrate its rule over millions of dark-skinned people for the sheer delight in conquest for its own sake, these writers sought to expose the hypocrisy of "supervisory" rule as well.

Strongly impressed by Forster's *Passage to India*, which was first pub-lished in 1924, both Orwell and Cary sought to portray the Empire as a system of manners anchored in social/bureaucratic codes coming under increasing stress during the interwar period, and for both writers the imperialist's language becomes the chief symptom of what is wrong with colonialism. For all three novelists, in fact, the "surface" of social life is identified with its essence; the meaning characters attach to events (or "non-events") acquiring much more importance than the events them-selves. What actually happened to Adela Quested in the Marabar Caves, to take the best example, is beside the point to Forster; what various characters in the novel believe happened – what interpretations they offer of that politically fraught moment – is central to the drama of *A Passage to India*. As the dramatization of the arbitrariness of power in Kipling tends to draw our attention as readers to the structure of power, so the focus on the surface of social existence – to the coded nature of English life in the colonies and to the consequent failure of British rules to compass adequately the reality of life for Britain's colonized subjects – tends to make the inadequacies of official codes the ironic center of the drama. This distances the Modernist novel from the now-discredited values of adventure fiction in a way that Kipling and Conrad were never completely willing to do. By implicitly detaching what Kipling called the "law" from its embedding in either the cosmos or Darwinian natural order, and rooting it instead in the increasingly insupportable and historically contingent conditions of a certain model of imperial rule, Forster, Cary, and Orwell are able to dramatize material which carries the potential for tragedy while never completely escaping banality, and consequently, irony. Thus, all three writers see the Empire as an increasingly insupportable bureaucratic system, relying less on the overt exercise of power than on a set of indefensible coded prescriptions for behavior, and threatened less by revolutionary restiveness within the colonized population than by seemingly marginal disasters precipitated, more often than not, by other Europeans.

Although *A Passage to India* was an important text for both Orwell and Cary, it is also, of the three under discussion here, the one least conscious of the connection between English colonial manners and the official system of bureaucratic rule, possibly because Forster did not have the first-hand experience of imperial service that Orwell and Cary both did. I will discuss Forster briefly first before treating the disenchantment of the able Nigerian District Officer Joyce Cary. Orwell, whose *Burmese Days* was written almost a decade before Cary's *Mr. Johnson*, will be discussed last. The reason for this has to do with tone: *Burmese Days* is the most savagely satirical treatment of British rule of the three novels under discussion, one which will have no truck with either Forster's civil, if utopian, yearning for transcultural personal friendship between individuals or with Cary's "Kiplinguesque" – and consequently equivocal – appreciation of the value of imperial work such as road-building. The reasons for that may well have a biographical root: *Burmese Days* was written by a man who knew what it was like to do the dirty work demanded of those at the bottom of the official hierarchy, for Eric Blair spent a number of years as a policeman in colonial Burma during the 1920s.[9] *Burmese Days* is a novel of imperial manners converging on apocalyptic satire, the angry work of a writer all-too-familiar with the direct and brutal exercise of power over other individuals. More so than the other writers under discussion, Orwell sets out to demystify the ideology of the self-sacrificing bureaucrat.

2

In identifying "civilization" with "conversation," Forster's *Passage to India* (1924) highlights the interpenetration of language and politics.

Thus, the end of the novel, which sees Fielding and Aziz trying but failing to establish the kind of "conversation" for which the author seems to yearn, centralizes the issue of language. For what is finally at stake for Forster in *A Passage to India* is the very possibility of a signifying system (a language of "explanation" rather than simply of "utterance," we might call it) that will enable speakers to understand one another, for misunderstanding seems to be the order of the day in colonial India. In short, the characters in *A Passage to India* do not speak the same "language," despite the fact that they all call what they are speaking "English." The question Forster implicitly poses over and over again is: is there a language of meaning – a conceptual metalanguage, it might be called – which could insure that English and Indians "mean" the same thing when they use the same verbal expressions? Can Englishman and Indian share signifieds rather than simply verbal signifiers? Can there be, in Homi Bhabha's words, a "civil discourse" which is somehow free of the distorting effects of imperial politics and which somehow enables people from alien traditions to communicate with one another, to establish contact between different minds?[10] Of course, to pose the issue of understanding in this extreme way is to suggest just how utopian such a goal is, viewed philosophically. As Wittgenstein, Derrida, and others have suggested, the very possibility of "contact between minds" rests on a complex metaphysical foundation which may not bear up under close scrutiny: to believe in such "contact" is to assume that there are "minds" which harbor "signifieds" that are not simply reducible to other "signifiers" in need of explication themselves, and that one can infer individual "intentions" which are somehow accessible through inference despite the distortion produced by actual utterances.

While *A Passage to India* does not focus overmuch on the colonial official, it does characterize the language of officialdom, and it devotes some attention to dramatizing the coercive nature of the "official" mastercode, which, for the colonial official at any rate, offers the bureaucratically necessary, psychologically comforting, illusion of an India already overwritten with readily decodable meanings. If Ronny Heaslop's speech is representative, the codes by which British officials live seem to consist chiefly of tautological axioms which resist revision by evidence from beyond the limited experience represented in these axioms. Heaslop not only accepts the logic of conventional Anglo-Indian racism (by insisting, for instance, that Aziz reveals his "impudence" in talking with Mrs. Moore in the mosque early in the novel, Heaslop has implicitly written the sphere of the personal out of existence), but he also is chained within a recognizable system of official "oriental" knowledge. Thus he devotes time to scrutinizing the dress of Dr. Aziz for signs that will simply confirm the conventional rules by which the governing class exercises power. Unaware, for example, that Aziz has lent a collar stud to the Englishman Fielding in a gesture of friendship early in the novel, Heaslop calls Adela's attention to the fact that Aziz is missing this stud. To Heaslop, the missing stud comes to signify "the essential slackness that reveals the race."[11] Bound to the closed signifying system of official-dom which identifies being Indian with being "slack," Heaslop is simply peddling a tautology: Indianness implies slackness; slackness is the sign of Indianness. To read a character's language in Forster is often to gauge the limits of his world, and the world of a colonial official like Heaslop is a notably narrow one.

Moreover, there seems to be no exit possible for Heaslop from this closed semiotic space. It is difficult to imagine how Aziz's behavior could ever fail to confirm the "knowledge" of the Anglo-Indian official about "the Indian." Like the "echoing walls" of the Battacharyas' civility which prevent Adela Quested from grasping "India" at the Turtons' "bridge party" early in the novel, differentials of power bedevil all attempts at transcultural knowledge in this novel. Like so many dra-matic moments in this text, the "bridge party" dramatizes a political and cultural problematic in the form of a problem of language and manners. For the "conversation" that is "civilization" to take place, the partners in the conversation must "mean" the same thing when they speak the same words. Yet, since "meaning" and "intention" are invisible entities that can only be inferred but never observed directly, how would one ever be sure about what two different minds intend in the absence of additional cues or a preexisting mastercode, the authority of which is accepted by both parties, and which establishes the rules for decoding? Moreover, how could such a "meeting of the minds" ever occur among people who do not consider each other equals and who do not share certain cultural presuppositions? Even if there were something like the "international civilization" that a writer like V. S. Naipaul now celebrates, would such a thing guarantee translatability without co-ercion in the absence of political and cultural equality? Discursive incommensurability is not merely a problem characterizing encounters in the imperial field, of course. Differentials of power (say, for example, class differences) can produce misunderstandings stemming from the fact that two parties to a conversation live by different codes. To take a "domestic" example: is the unctuous civility of the English butler to his employer's guests a sign of friendly intentions? hostile mimicry? or the simple performance of duty? In the absence of other cues or of a mastercode which assigns determinate meaning to such utterances, can one ever know for sure?

The "echoing walls" of the Battacharyas' civility provide a good example of the problematic involved. Forster says of Mrs. Battacharya and her sister Mrs. Das: "There was a curious uncertainty about their gestures, as if they sought for a new formula which neither East nor West could provide" (Forster, p. 43). Forster's "as if" is a significant qualification here, suggesting both that the characters will not find a "bridge" language (for no such language can exist in an atmosphere of political inequality) and that there ought to be such a language (this is the utopian promise that implicitly shadows all interactions among Britons and Indians in the novel: the impossible-to-realize promise of Mrs. Moore, one might call it). Thus, when Mrs. Moore proposes that she and Adela visit them at their home, Mrs. Battacharya welcomes them any day. The latter's seemingly generous gesture has a different meaning for her than it has for Mrs. Moore and Adela, we are led to infer. Mrs. Battacharya's "echoing" civility seems to be an improvised gesture, a return for Mrs. Moore's polite attempt to "bridge," but not at all intended as an actual invitation. It has a meaning analogous to the meaning of the conventional countersign "How are you?" which, among most middle-class Americans, is simply a gesture intended to initiate conversation, not an explicit query about the state of one's health (as anyone knows who has breached this rule of politeness by responding to such a question with an impolitely detailed list of physical and mental annoyances). As Mrs. Moore and Adela discover later, the appearance of "conversation" at this point in the novel disguises an incommensurability of meanings: a truth which they discover only after they pay an awkward visit to the Battacharyas and realize that they were never expected.[12]

While Forster satirizes the pretensions to knowledge of the Anglo-Indian ruling elite, it is through the aggressively impolite naïveté of Adela Quested – whose name suggests a questioner on a quest – that he dramatizes the "truth" which Heaslop speaks to his mother early on: that there is no "private" sphere in India. A land under surveillance by an increasingly incompetent group of imperial officials, the India which is just beginning to stir with revolutionary ferment cannot be "known" by British officialdom for reasons that parallel why Adela cannot infer the "intentions" behind others' discourse. The official mastercode does not adequately account for discrepant meanings. Moreover, if an adequate mastercode could in fact be found, it would have to be discovered only by those outside the official bureaucracy of rule, figures whose thoughts are not chained within the limitations of the bureaucratic need to reconfirm official wisdom, figures – perhaps – such as Fielding and Aziz. Yet because official policy assigns all Indians by definition to the category of imperial subject, none can ever be completely independent of the power game of ruler and ruled, master and subject. No Indian, in other words, can fail to confirm by his behavior one or another aspect of the mastercode which has been carefully constructed by British officialdom in the interest of maintaining power. In short, British officialdom insists on employing a mastercode here, but the coercive nature of this code makes interactions between British officials and Indians anything but "civil" in the sense of that term that Forster would find acceptable. The rules of "civil discourse" have been imposed by British officialdom on a subject population in order to write off all discrepant meanings as signs of political subversion.

Once having posed the issue in such stark and uncompromising terms, Forster can only close his novel with a pathetic lament for the "friendship" between Fielding and Aziz that, alas, can never be – or, at least, "not yet." The vaguely utopian unfulfilled promise of the close of the book reflects the extent to which a Bloomsbury ideology of the personal is being resurrected in this text as the very model for an anti-bureaucratic, anti-imperial wish. The dream of the end of imperial hegemony, an hegemony which inflects and contaminates all personal relations within the novel, is accompanied by the utopian wish for a "human" or "personal" relationship, a "meeting of minds," that can somehow occur outside the constraints and distortions imposed by the need to rule and its coded prescriptions for behaving and interpreting others' behavior. Yet this can only be realized in fact through another dream: a dream of the end of the power to compel meaning. The utopian promise of the possibility of actual conversation is undercut, not only by the political fact that Aziz and Fielding can never have such a conversation until India is no longer a dependency of Great Britain, but by the fact that, as the novel implicitly concedes, all "conversations" are effects of the operation of the system of British rule over India. *A Passage to India* collapses into a final, defining incoherence: Forster demonstrates that translatability – indeed "civility" – is only enabled by a certain form of "incivility" – the power to compel shared meaning. Yet he tempts his readers at the end of the book with the failed dream of meaning which might – somehow – be shared outside the realm of official power, in the individually negotiated semiotic space of the "personal."

For a writer who accords greater agency to the individual utterance in reshaping or displacing the structure of meaning, though, we must turn to Joyce Cary.

3

Cary's career in the Nigerian Political Service during the war years not only gave him the time to teach himself how to write but left him with valuable firsthand insights into the actual operation of a system of Indirect Rule.[13] Although initially an enthusiastic supporter of Lugard's policies in Nigeria, Cary gradually grew disenchanted with them, eventually denouncing both the dual mandate and Indirect Rule in his non-fiction book *A Case for African Freedom*, which was published in 1941.[14] On the evidence of the essays he wrote in the 1950s as Britain was preparing to grant independence to its African colonies, however, Cary seems to have evolved a more ambivalent attitude toward Indirect Rule and the dual mandate policy near the end of his life. In these essays his attitude combines a gently ironic skepticism about the worth of the imperial *mission civilisatrice* with an implicit willingness to acknowledge the worth of Britain's "civilizing" function.[15] Like Conrad, Cary seems to have been able simultaneously to applaud "good" imperial work like road-building and the imposition of English legal structures and to acknowledge that these things bring dramatic changes to Nigerian society: some of them welcome (because they undermine the authority of traditional tribal organizations and corrupt emirs) and some of them quite unwelcome (because they usher in an ethic of anomic personal acquisitiveness that finds its ultimate expression in criminality).

How did Cary, himself a very able Assistant District Officer who possessed the organizational qualities and fluency in Hausa that Lugard required of British administrators in the Fulani Emirates, reach the point of rejecting Indirect Rule as policy? How did he come to see the contradictions implicit in the project of fostering independence through paternalistic supervision? The answers to these questions will provide us with important insights, not only into *Mr. Johnson*, the best of Cary's four "African" novels, but into the problem of Indirect Rule, for which Cary's Nigeria was the most important test case. *Mr. Johnson* presents its readers with a central character who stands in more than one place: as a clerk to the British Assistant District Officer, he is used to satirize the paternalism of Indirect Rule; as a colonized Nigerian himself, he is treated as the somewhat absurd product of the system outlined by Lugard and Margery Perham – the grotesque result of mimicry rewarded by the imperial bureaucracy; yet, as the ultimate organizer of the road-building project and the victim of absurd British justice in the end, Mr. Johnson also comes to stand for a new Nigeria in the process of construction – the martyred hero of an emerging postcolonial consciousness with which even Cary cannot fully come to terms; in short, the mimic whose mimicry is productive not of repetition but of discrepant or unassimilable meanings. Two models of language – of manners, in effect – are in conflict in *Mr. Johnson*: in one, language acquires meaning by virtue of a preexistent signifying system – a *langue*; in the other, meaning is capable of being altered by the production of novel individual utterances.[16] The fact that Johnson can be read as both parodic figure and epic hero underscores the profoundly undecidable tone of the novel, an undecidability that is a direct result of Cary's masterful dramatization of incommensurable cultural meanings. To decide how to read "Mr. Johnson," one must choose an interpretive context from among the mutually exclusive cultural (and ultimately political) alternatives offered by the book – British "official," Nigerian nationalist, or Nigerian "tribal." To decide how to read *Mr. Johnson*, one must choose between mutually exclusive ironic and epic readings. The novel thus locates itself in a space between ironic and epic readings, offering to resolve its ambiguities only to the reader who has made a preemptive commitment to a particular political framework for reading it.

Consequently, the Johnson to whom we are introduced in the beginning of the novel is a figure of contradictions – and he remains one throughout the book. A stranger to Fada, he is presumably a missionary-trained Igbo from the South arriving in Fada in search of a wife among the bush pagans. When he spots his future wife Bamu, he courts her with the promise of marrying an important clerk with the impressive annual salary of £15. This episode establishes Johnson as the novel's serio-comic mediator between the world of English officialdom (the world of his job, and, most importantly to him, his rank) and the non-Muslim, non-English world of the bush pagans. Johnson's idea of marriage, "a compound of romantic sentiment and embroidered underclothes," renders his interest in the pagan Bamu, needless to say, unaccountable, for Bamu seems anything but congenial. Instead, Cary depicts Bamu as a character who attaches no value whatsoever to the type of self-transformation to which Johnson has bound himself, a woman fatalistically resigned to her family's design to sell her into marriage – presumably the common fate of most of the women of her tribe.[17] When Johnson comes on the scene making inexplicable promises of raising Bamu up out of the world of her tribe, he nonetheless finds that he has to capitulate to tribal convention to the extent of negotiating the bridal price with Bamu's brother Aliu. Anything but a "noble savage" himself, Aliu is characterized by Cary as a shrewd bazaar bargainer willing to sell Bamu at the highest price he can extract from Johnson, for Aliu knows that there is nothing else to do with "strangers" but "fleece" them if they inexplicably offer themselves to be fleeced (*MJ*, p. 17).

The bargain Johnson strikes with Bamu's family, thus, highlights the disjunction in modes of understanding which is being dramatized in the novel. In asking Bamu directly if she will marry him, he shocks her by breaching her rules of etiquette, and Bamu expresses her displeasure in what seems to her to be an acceptable manner: by refusing to speak with him directly but instead abusing him to her brother in Johnson's presence (*MJ*, pp. 27–28). Despite abundant evidence that Bamu has absolutely no interest in him, Johnson presses on with his suit, intent, he claims, on making Bamu into a "civilized" lady whether she wants to be "civilized" or not. Then, after a day of tortured negotiations with Bamu's family, Johnson finally strikes a bargain with Aliu and returns to his station to proclaim his love for Bamu to his friend and fellow clerk Mr. Benjamin:

"Oh, but, Mister Benjamin, my Bamu is mos' beautiful, clever girl you can tink. First time she sees me, she says, 'Mister Johnson, I 'gree for you, I don't like dese savage men – I like civilized man. Mister Johnson,' she says, 'You good nice government man, me government lady. I love you with all my heart – we live happy, loving couple all time everyday.'" (*MJ*, p. 31)

Everything Johnson says here is a lie, of course, but "lie" may be an inaccurate term for what is going on here. Johnson is a character for whom language is not so much referential as projective: like Beowulf or Achilles (or, perhaps more appropriately here, Don Quixote), Johnson often uses language to commit himself publicly to heroic action in a prospective glorious future rather than to register or record a fact in the present. Cary constructs Johnson as a man of plausibly heroic – and ultimately generous – impulses while, simultaneously, undercutting these impulses with irony by suggesting that Johnson may serve merely to parody Lugard's *mission civilisatrice* for Nigeria. By having his hero attempt to "civilize" Bamu, Cary, who was himself initially enthusiastic about Lugard's ideas, raises serious questions about the assumptions behind the grand project sketched out in *The Dual Mandate*. Among the chief imperial assumptions implicitly challenged here are that somehow Nigerians will – eventually – come to desire European "civilization" and that Nigeria is already a potential "nation" in the western European sense rather than, as Cary depicts it, a geographical congeries of disparate people alien from one another in language, culture, and religion, linked together only by imperial administrative fiat.[18] Through his main character, Cary suggests that Lugard's paternalistic nation-building project is, in the final analysis, a quixotic one. The impossibility of Johnson metaphorizes the impossibility of Lugard's grand project.

"Quixotic," perhaps, but not in the everyday sense of "foolishly idealistic," which is now the commonly accepted meaning that the term "quixotic" has acquired. Rather, Cary's Johnson is depicted as a Quixote without a Sancho Panza, and thus, a protean figure whose final meaning cannot be simply read ironically, a figure who exists in an indeterminate space, whose meaning remains to be articulated within a range of antithetical possibilities.

Consider, for example, Johnson's improvised songs. When he returns to his station delighted with having succeeded in arranging his marriage and pleased with his luck in having the English ADO Rudbeck to "worship," Johnson leads a half dozen townspeople in a rendition of the patriotic tune "England is my country," embroidering the song along the way in a West African tradition of improvisation. Although the song begins on a seemingly celebratory note,

> Oh, England, my home, away der on de big water.
> England is my country, dat King of England is my King.
> His heart is big for his children –
> Room for everybody.

it quickly becomes more ambiguous in tone:

> I say hallo, I act de fool.
> I spit on de carpet of his great big heart.

Indeed, these last two lines imply a contempt for the King's authority which, nevertheless, is simultaneously undercut by the implication that the King's "big heart" may be "big" enough to take the young man's acting the fool and spitting on the carpet as signs of affection. The unruly child, in other words, may well be paying implicit tribute to the benevolence of the father by deliberately exercising his license to play the unruly child. Much of Johnson's "rebellious" behavior in this novel, whether it be his behavior toward white authorities such as his boss Rudbeck or toward the Emir and his agent the Waziri, falls into the ambiguous space between the extremes of true rebelliousness and a playful rebelliousness which actually confirms rather than undercuts the legitimacy of authority. In a more complex way than Kipling ever attempted, Cary dramatizes a rebelliousness which asserts the subject's bond to a figure of "higher" authority (this theme can be read either in Kiplinguesque terms or as a dramatization of the "dependency complex" perhaps best discussed by Mannoni).[19] Like Kipling's *Stalky and Co.*, which interposes the discreditable housemaster between the noble "Head" and the rebellious Stalky, so Cary's novel has Johnson introduce a contemptible intermediate figure – the "Pramminister" (whose title ironically infantilizes him: the "prime minister" who is pushed around in a "pram") – into his narrative song:

> De Pramminister he come running from his clerk-office.
> He shout out to de King, Up on top; you majesty, I see um,
> I see um like lil black ting no more big than stink bug.
> He drunk, he play de fool, he black trash,
> He no care for nobody. He bad dirty boy,
> He spit all over de carpet of you great big heart.
> All right, you majesty, I go catch him now,
> I go trow him right out right over de top of Pallamentright
> In de river Thames, kerplash.
> De King, he say, oh no, Mr. Pramminister, don't do so,
> I know dat Johnson from Fada, he my faithful clerk from Fada,
> He drunk for me, he drunk for love of his royal King,
> He drunk becas he come here, he doanno how to be so happy,
> He got no practice in dem great big happiness,
> Why, what he do now, he laught. Poot, what's de good to laugh.
> He dance. Poot. What's de good to dance.
> He walk on his han's.                                    (*MJ*, p. 37)

By offering a different interpretation of the clerk's spitting, the King reminds his "underling" the "Pramminister" of the bond which his clerk's "drunken" transgressiveness reinforces rather than disrupts. The novel poses the issue of conflict and obedience in undecidable terms: is it about the so-called "dependency complex" of colonized people, about Kiplinguesque conflictual bonding among imperial bureaucrats (what one might be tempted to call the "dependency complex" of imperial bureaucrats), or actual anti-imperial subversiveness which, for politic reasons, can only take the form of a pledge of allegiance to a higher – but abstract – authority? The issue is important here because of the conventional European insistence on the difference between European "autonomy," structured through fidelity to an internalized but not concrete and immediately observable authority, and African "dependence," believed by some Europeans to be an effect of fidelity to a material and consequently visible authority (among Mannoni's Malagasy for instance, the dead ancestor, whose body assumes the central place in the cult of the dead). Yet, as *Heart of Darkness* masterfully demonstrates and as Fanon argued more than thirty years ago, this distinction Europeans are apt to insist on – between the "African," who is governed by a concrete authority representing itself to him in its material immediacy, and the "Oedipal European," who has internalized authority strictures psychologically and thus appears to Africans to behave with seemingly godlike autonomy – is finally discreditable, for the same reason that the conventional English Protestant belief that "idolatry" characterizes the belief practices of pagan Africans but not of sophisticated European megalomaniacs like Kurtz or Stanley is questionable. "Dependence" is finally a psychologistic name assigned by Europeans to the actuality of political "inferiority" which they have imposed by force (Fanon); "autonomy" is the flattering self-description assumed by those European rulers who imagine themselves living in the "night of the first ages" with nary a policeman about them (Conrad). In fact, as our discussion of Conrad has already pointed out, "autonomy" in this psychological sense is the chief illusion to which the European bureaucratic subject is prey.

Mr. Johnson personalizes his relationship to this more abstract authority of the king here through his relationship to Rudbeck the ADO: his "worship" of Rudbeck metaphorizes his imagined relation to George V. Unlike Aliu who expects extra-tribal authority to be "dangerous, selfish, inexplicable," Johnson expects all authority to acknowledge a duty to those it supervises, a paternal duty that goes well beyond the purely formal tie of bureaucratic relationship to express "personal" affection. Thus, when Johnson is first reunited with Rudbeck early in the novel, the latter greets him with a "Good morning" which Johnson immediately misunderstands as a sign that just such a paternalistic bond holds between them:

Rudbeck, new to the service, has treated Johnson, his first clerk, with the ordinary politeness which would be given to a butler or footman at home. He has wished him "Good morning," hoped that he enjoyed his holiday, sent him a bottle of gin for the new year and complimented him once or twice on a neat piece of work. Johnson therefore worships Rudbeck and would willingly die for him. He thinks him the wisest, noblest and most beautiful of beings. The very look of him now on the stoop gives him such a shock of joy and relief that he bursts into tears. Johnson, after all, is only seventeen and completely alone. He falters, "Oh, Mr. Rudbeck, may God bless you – I pray for you all time." (*MJ*, p. 23)

Through the bureaucratic relationship between Johnson and Rudbeck, Cary condenses a complex set of relations: that between the colonizer and the colonized, the English official and the "civilized" (i.e. now rootless by virtue of his job) Nigerian, and, perhaps most importantly, the bureaucratic official and his underling in a system of Indirect Rule (which Rudbeck experiences unconsciously as a difference in social class). In establishing a personalized dependency relationship between Rudbeck and Johnson which Rudbeck then betrays late in the novel, Cary examines metaphorically the relationship between colonized Nigeria and imperial England. Yet the personal relationship between the two here is constructed less by the empty-headed Rudbeck (who, trained to see himself in a self-effacing role, pays little attention to the fact that his Nigerian underlings invest him with imaginary powers), than it is imagined by Johnson himself. While British rule is anything but neutral in its effects on Nigerian society (indeed, the completion of Rudbeck's road inaugurates a revolutionary transformation of Nigerian social and political life the beginning stages of which are dramatized in the pages of the novel), Cary nonetheless represents all his British administrators as careerists conceiving themselves as neutral "supervisors" of an order evolving somehow independently of them rather than active ideologists of *mission civilisatrice*: bureaucrats, in other words, rather than feudal lords or charismatic rulers. Indirect Rule, according to this model, is not "rule" in the classic sense, and Cary's English officials, although finding themselves in positions of authority, are presented as largely incapable of articulating a compelling vision of the purposes for which they work, let alone guiding the colonized in an intentionally benevolent way along a path to "civilization," as the script of Indirect Rule requires.

For this reason, ADO Rudbeck is represented as the figure of reticence in the novel. Yet his very speechlessness, far from signifying a laudable reserve of politic wisdom, becomes the means for Cary to satirize this bureaucratic code of behavior. Rudbeck fails to speak, we gradually discover, not out of a sense of politic delicacy, but because he doesn't perceive and hasn't the faintest idea why he does what he does. Contrast him with Johnson in this respect, a man whose overflowing rhetoric is a symptom of his engagement with life in all its multiplicity. Despite his role as the figure of colonial mimicry, it is Johnson, not Rudbeck, who becomes the chief figure of agency in the book – even if by default. It is Johnson who encourages Rudbeck to pursue his road-building scheme despite the obstacles to the road's completion; Johnson who articulates the value of roads in bringing the "civilization" which, he claims, "all men" desire (*MJ*, p. 86). It is Johnson who ultimately devises the ingenious method of embezzlement which will provide Rudbeck with the funds to pay for the completion of the road. More-over, it is Johnson who is able to identify his own desires in the moment of their articulation; Rudbeck, Cary makes clear, is blind to his own motives. In other words, Johnson uses language to create relationships that others cannot see because they have never thought of putting things together in precisely the way he has. Johnson, in short, improvises, and his improvised rationalizations become the novel's chief means of expo-sing to criticism the British imperial system as an ad hoc system – an ill-conceived experiment in human social engineering on a massive scale; of constructing a plausible notion of "civilization" as an *ex post facto* goal which justifies, in retrospect, the means of imperial work; and of parodying the official instrumentalist language of justification that ap-pears over and over again in the writing of Cromer and Lugard. Rudbeck, therefore, who has no idea why he likes to build roads, will find, in Johnson, a useful instrument capable of producing for him a rhetorically compelling justification for what it is he likes to spend his time doing. The very language of justification is thereby pried free of any referential function in this novel, and the ostensible public goal of imperial rule – "civilization" – comes to stand as an unanalyzable figure of ideological authority – the answer to all ultimate questions that begin with "why?" In short, a British fetish.

For this reason, then, the novel presents the contrast between Rud-beck and his dour predecessor Blore as a contrast between two conflict-ing notions of the value of imperial work, both of them rooted in unanalyzed personal preferences, "hobby horses":

Just as Blore is particular about tax assessment and is always collecting statistics, so Rudbeck, even as a junior, as soon as he comes to a station, sends for the chief and complains about the roads. He spends his afternoons riding or driving about the country inspecting bridges; and he loves to make maps and draw on them, in dotted lines of red ink, new trade routes.

In this he has no sympathy from Blore, who considers motor roads to be the ruin of Africa, bringing swindlers, thieves and whores, disease, vice and corruption, and the vulgarities of trade, among decent, unspoilt tribesmen. (*MJ*, p. 46)

Not only does the "responsibility system" of British colonial rule actually give assistant district officers the freedom to choose what work they will invest most effort in, but, as Cary indicates here, it makes the ADO responsible for designating the value of his own work – and thus, in the process, invests him with the power to redefine radically, if he chooses to, the meaning of the "civilization" which British rule is imposing on Africa. Moreover, as the novel will make clear and as this passage hints, the justification which is produced is typically nothing but a high-minded rationalization of personal preference designed to promote individual bureaucratic ambition. Consequently, Cary's novel ultimately equivocates about the value of the imperial system itself: *Mr. Johnson* manages both to endorse Blore's "custodial" fear (the building of Rudbeck's road does, we discover, increase crime, as not only Blore but also the Emir predict) *and* to treat that fear with irony.[20] The central irony of the novel is that the British administrators are presiding over a project of vast social transformation the dimensions of which they cannot comprehend, yet are incapable of crafting a language capable of representing it and justifying it fully. The imperial project in *Mr. Johnson* is represented as an "unintended" event, an irresponsible exercise of the power to transform Africa for the sake of something to do.[21]

The authority of what Mr. Johnson calls "civilization" here is thus seriously undermined. When "civilization" devolves into nothing but personal preference, it necessarily loses any claim it may have otherwise had to loftier sanction. When Blore is ADO, "civilization" implicitly involves adjudicating local disputes and pretending to preserve local ways of life; when Tring is ADO, "civilization" involves the teaching of a rather strict adherence to written rules; when Rudbeck is ADO, "civilization" involves the building of a road which radically transforms the social and material basis of Nigerian life.

The effects of this emptying of "civilization" of all but purely instrumental content can be seen in Mr. Johnson's service to Rudbeck on his road project. Johnson not only manages to improvise a means for funding the project as well as a strategy for motivating bush pagans to work on the road, but he becomes the most articulate spokesman in the book for a desperately naïve theory of the value of road-building – the instrument become the agent of historical change. Moreover, Cary suggests both that the road is a novel unifying force in Nigerian life and that it is the bringer of an unwelcome feature of European modernity – criminality. This is why Cary can represent Johnson as a classic representative of the colonized consciousness, both the chief author of colonialist ideology, the spokesman for the ideal of *mission civilisatrice*, and the embodiment of what is usually represented as its antithesis – the criminal.[22] As a stranger to Fada, Johnson projects a grand vision of new Nigerian society by taking his clues from the clueless British imperial administration on which he is dependent. In taking on the role of chief ideologist for *mission civilisatrice,* Johnson tries to sell the idea to the Emir's chief advisor thus:

"The Emir is an old savage fool – he has no idea of civilized things. Roads are a most civilized thing. When this road is opened, Waziri, you will be surprised." Johnson waves his hand. A feeling, more than a vision, of satisfied desires floats through his experience. "The markets will be full every day of every kind of thing – there will be heaps of money for everybody, all you in Fada will be rich –"

"I won't be surprised," Waziri says. "I know what your road will do – I've seen it before – everything turned upside down, and all for nothing."

Johnson laughs at this pessimism. "You are not civilized, Waziri. You don't understand that people must have roads for motors."

"Why, lord Johnson?"

"Because it is civilized. Soon everyone will be civilized."

"Why so, lord Johnson?"

"Of course, they must be – they like to be," Johnson says. "You will see how they like it. All men like to be civilized." (*MJ*, p. 86)

The novel ratifies Johnson's predictions in certain respects (the completion of the road brings an enormous increase in trade, and thus, among other benefits, a dramatic increase in tax revenue flowing to the British colonial administration), while it also realizes the Waziri's dire predictions (crime increases dramatically; strangers arrive sowing the seeds of discontent with the Emir's reactionary rule). But what this passage dramatizes above all is the impossibility of locating the authority of "civilization" beyond the name itself. Johnson's justification amounts to a tautology: when the Waziri asks him to explain why the people must have roads, he responds with the claim that they must have roads to carry the "motors" (automobiles). But what warrants the need for "motors" is the simple "fact" that "motors" are "civilized." The argument in favor of "civilization" must seek its warrant in presupposing the very "civilization" it sets out to justify. As we have already seen in our discussion of Stanley, when *mission civilisatrice* is identified with "modernization" in the economic sense, it cannot find a justificatory authority beyond itself, both because modernization destroys as much as it creates and because the process of modernization itself produces the very yardsticks by which its worth must be measured. The building of roads increases trade; increasing trade encourages economic specialization; increased economic specialization creates the need for increased trade; and so on in a continuing cycle by which economic transformation promotes social transformation which, in turn, requires further economic transformation "justified" ultimately through convenient alterations at the ideological level.[23]

Undoubtedly Cary, the "Modernist" writer, was trying to ground the preference for civilization in something that he did not see as purely arbitrary and ad hoc in the negative sense: an aesthetics of personal choice which universalizes Modernist aestheticism by making every individual into an artist of sorts, a source of improvisatory energy and artistic value which he is responsible for bestowing on his own activities. For this reason, Rudbeck is presented as wasting

a good deal of time standing under bridges with Tasuki in common admiration of the timber work, under the illusion that he is doing necessary and important work. He is on the road every day, simply to enjoy it. He can't keep away from this keen new pleasure. (*MJ*, p. 83)

Yet, for all his interest in the road and in the *zungos* he builds along its route, Rudbeck never even attempts to produce even an instrumental justification for them himself. Cary is presenting the work of imperial administration in "Marlovian" terms – work which becomes an unanalyzable end-in-itself – yet does so by depriving his readers of a self-conscious narrator like Marlow who tells us that work has this function. *Mr. Johnson* satirizes the "responsibility system" by repeatedly dramatizing the failure of British administration to lead. Thus, Rudbeck simply builds road while only reluctantly performing his job as judge; Tring puts a temporary end to road-building out of a "holier-than-thou" commitment to fiscal responsibility – his route to a higher position within the bureaucracy; Bulteel, who is squeamish about Rudbeck's creative use of budget lines, nevertheless urges him to carry on the road-building more carefully, by indirectly suggesting later in the book that he might feel free to reintroduce the accountant's fiction "Suli," payments to whom disguise the actual costs of the road project on the books. Yet this form of official "criminality/creativity" never receives the punishment that Johnson's improvisations ultimately do, simply because the white officials hold ultimate legal power, and thus are free to exempt "bureaucratic irregularities" from inclusion within the category of "criminality." For this reason, Rudbeck's deceptions come to be defined eventually as valuable work; Johnson's, unfairly, as criminal venality.

However, the white officials themselves also represent competing ideas about imperial responsibility. Like Kipling, Cary presents "legality" itself as a way of life requiring the occasional public spectacle of disobedience to reinforce its legitimacy. The "responsibility system" carries the seeds for the undoing of rule-governed legality, partly because rule-violation can be overlooked when its results are suitably impressive. Thus, when Tring, standing in for Rudbeck while the latter is on leave, acts the overeager, rule-abiding official in the first half of the novel, bringing Rudbeck's books "to account" and then alerting higher-ups to irregularities in Rudbeck's methods, he is implicitly defining his own sphere of "responsibility" in a narrowly legalistic way. Yet, for exactly this reason – his adherence to the letter of the law – Tring poses a threat to the whole structure – and certainly, to Rudbeck's career. The irony is laid on thickly in the passage where Bulteel gently reminds Tring of how the rules need to be relaxed sometimes in order for any work to be done ("Tring, we've got to be trusted or the whole thing would come to bits" [*MJ*, p. 114]). The incoherence of the whole "responsibility system" is underlined here: Bulteel gently upbraiding Tring for interpreting his "responsibilities" in his own way by making it necessary for the bureaucracy to discipline Rudbeck for interpreting his "responsibilities" in his own way. In fact, Bulteel is astonished to find an ADO so naïve (or, perhaps, crafty) as to treat the rules as something white officials actually must obey to the letter:

He is going to explode when again he catches Tring's mild blue eye and suddenly doubts his judgment of the boy. "Is he so simple?" he thinks; "I've always said he would get on and perhaps this is the very way he is going to get on. Certainly I'm no judge – I'll never be a governor." (*MJ*, p. 114)

The ironic point here is that, as District Officer, Bulteel is a "governor" in the broadest political sense, despite the fact that he is clearly reluctant to come down too hard on his subordinate here out of fear that he will implicate himself in covering up the very corruption Tring is certain he has uncovered. Cary depicts British officialdom as both mindlessly incapable of understanding the purposes of empire and yet quite gifted in the skills of bureaucratic self-protection.

As we have already seen, from at least the middle of the nineteenth century, the outspoken promoters of colonialism had justified empire as a project to bring the benefits of free trading capitalism to Africans sunk in "primitive" darkness. In fact, the actual history of Sir George Goldie's Niger Company shows that it is vain to base the justification of colonialism on the hope for long-term profits from primary production. Indeed, the profits that once flowed into Niger Company coffers were beginning to dwindle as early as the 1890s, as the palm oil trade suffered from a worldwide glut of producers (part of an historical pattern of boom and bust which has afflicted virtually all primary-product producers in the Third World since at least the sixteenth century). Cary nonetheless assumes that his reading audience sees the stimulation of free trade as the essential economic purpose served by British rule over Nigeria. His character Rudbeck, in fact, seems to be dimly aware that infrastructural transformation is a precondition for an increase in trade. Yet his protean subordinate Johnson, who is responsible for improvising the ideology of the "responsibility system," is also the one character in the novel who manages to prove that it is possible to make money directly from the new road. Unfortunately for him, however, he does so atavistically, by implementing his own system of the very toll-taking which Livingstone deplored ninety years earlier as the time-honored African custom of demanding *hongo* for the right of passage.

What is striking about Johnson's various money-making schemes is that they can never be acknowledged as legitimate by British authority. This may seem a bit surprising in light of the fact that "free trade" ideology conventionally describes the capitalist system as itself a "lawless" system of traders acting to maximize their individual self-interest, but a system which carries within it a disciplinary mechanism to regulate and impose limits to individual behavior – the "invisible hand" of the market. However, despite the fact that capitalism provides a latitude for individual initiative, all of Johnson's business activities in this book are eventually defined as "illegal": his toll-taking, because he does not own the road which he helped build; his buying and selling of hides for Sargy Gollup's store, because he engages in monopolistic buying practices. By acting as middleman in two senses – buying hides from bush pagans at the compound and then selling them to himself at much higher prices in his role as buyer for Gollup's store – Johnson makes a great deal of money and reveals, however inadvertently, that he nevertheless does understand quite a bit about how lawless trade works in practice. Moreover, it is not at all clear why anyone who had not been taught otherwise would naturally see this as criminal activity either. Much like Conrad's *Secret Agent*, which is a meditation on the fluid boundary between legality and criminality, the way in which a certain type of criminality comes to be legitimized by being differentiated from other forms officially marked as illegitimate, Cary's *Mr. Johnson* proposes that we see modern European capitalist "civilization" as a type of criminality which is no longer outlawed, but which defines itself in opposition to a new type of criminality – theft of newly private property – which it nonetheless helps produce. "Crime" is not simply an unwelcome aftereffect of the coming of what calls itself "civilization" but rather a defining systemic feature of it. Legalistic punishment consolidates through a public scapegoating ritual emerging notions of "private" versus "public" property, on the one hand, and "legitimate trade" versus "extortion," on the other.

Cary's satire on the "responsibility system" is taken one step further than that here: Johnson comes to parody the autonomy of the district officer charged with making up his theory of rule as he goes along. Moreover, his fall from grace has an equivocal meaning as well: representing the fall of the responsibility system but treated within categories of understanding more appropriate to tribal forms of life – Johnson as the "fallen chief" whom it becomes dangerous to know. This double meaning is underscored in Johnson's inability to understand why Rudbeck fires him for taking tolls. Cary focuses a conflict near the end of the book between two incompatible notions of propriety: one based on a capitalist ethic of personal acquisitiveness and one based on an older ethic of public expenditure. Implicitly invoking the latter, Johnson comes to see himself as a kind of vassal, his greatness measured not by how much he has saved but by how much he has spent on his friends and on his own chief Rudbeck. Thus, he cannot understand why he should be punished for taking money when he has spent much more of what he has acquired on Rudbeck's road:

He has never troubled himself about money; he has much more interesting things to think about. But he knows very well that he has given all his devotion to Rudbeck and that what he may have spent on some trifling necessities for himself is nothing to what he has paid out for Rudbeck's road. (*MJ*, p. 175)

One might say, then, that Rudbeck's firing of Johnson – although Rudbeck is incapable of understanding it this way – is a scapegoating ritual which establishes, in a transparently inadvertent and unjust way, the dominance of a certain acquisitive ethos by defining the boundaries of private property and outlawing the practice of expenditure for the acquisition of prestige, outlawing, in effect, the convertibility of material wealth into "charismatic" wealth. Johnson's firing effectively marks the metaphorical passing of a "tribal" way of life within the new order established by British rule in Nigeria, despite the fact – and this is the devastating irony – that British administrators are ostensibly the custodians of just such a "tribal" way of life.

The subsequent decline of Johnson late in the novel into a much more conventionally "European" criminal (he is ultimately convicted of murdering Sargy Gollop while trying to steal money from Sargy's cash register) can be read as tragedy, for it metaphorically augurs the passing of an improvised ethic of personal dependency which was the chief prop of the imperial system. Yet, even the execution of Johnson at the end of the book is equivocal in meaning. In his role as judge, Rudbeck tries his best to find an extenuating piece of evidence that would compel a verdict of something less harsh than execution. He fails, of course, because Johnson is reluctant to give up what is of primary importance to him. His dependency relation on Rudbeck his chief, of greater value to him than his own life. Thus, Johnson's responses at his trial seem designed by Johnson not to extenuate his guilt but to accentuate it, thus absolving Rudbeck – preserving his exalted place in Johnson's eyes – through Johnson's own self-degradation and ultimate self-negation. Thus, when Rudbeck, in a moment of rare self-doubt, confesses to Johnson that his report on his firing was a bit unfair, Johnson reassures him that it was not:

"Oh, yes, sah." Johnson shakes his head while he quickly seeks a means of restoring Rudbeck's opinion of himself, and also, of course, his own idea of Rudbeck. "Oh, no, sah – I much more bad den ever you tink – I do plenty of tings behin' you back – I steal plenty times out of de cash drawer – I sell you paper to Waziri – I too bad – I damn bad low trash, good for damn nutting tall." (*MJ*, p. 223)

Rudbeck, of course, is quite dissatisfied with this explanation because unwilling to see himself in the exalted role to which he has been assigned and for which he is clearly unfit, despite the fact that the script of Indirect Rule inevitably casts all white officials in just such double roles – agents pretending to be mere instruments, leaders pretending to be mere supervisors. As Cary says,

He is still dissatisfied, not with Johnson's explanation, for he knows that Johnson is actually a thief and a murderer, but with everything. He feels more and more disgusted and oppressed, like a man who finds himself walking down a narrow, dark channel in unknown country, which goes on getting darker and narrower; while he cannot decide whether he is on the right road or not. (*MJ*, p. 224)

Moreover, Johnson literalizes his dependency on the idea of Rudbeck with a desperate plea for Rudbeck to dispatch him personally, a plea which manages to implicate the father in the crimes for which he is punishing the son: "You my father and my mother. I tink you hang me youself" (*MJ*, p. 224). In effect, Johnson is asking Rudbeck to dispense with the letter of the law as well, to overlook the rules temporarily in order to seal the personal nature of their bond. And Rudbeck does do so in a final scene which rings equivocal changes on the Kiplinguesque notion of rebellion as reconfirmation of authority's legitimacy. Thus, Rudbeck defies official procedures by shooting Johnson in the head and then covers up the fact that he has not followed the rules by writing a misleading report. Yet, this "defiance" of orders takes a form suspiciously close to compliance with orders: Rudbeck does, after all, execute Johnson as thoroughly as he would have had he had him hanged. The death of Johnson can thus be read as a final moment of rule-following, in which, despite temptations, the British official enables the "responsibility system" of imperial administration to swallow up all defiant gestures by insuring that they serve the ultimate goal of upholding the rules. On the other hand, it can also be read as a moment of transgression, in which the dependency relationship, an unrepresentable sense of true responsibility, is acknowledged – albeit ironically – through the intimacy of an execution which is "highly irregular" in form. The execution of Johnson mimics the murder of Sargy Gollup; law-enforcement takes the form of crime. By carrying the undecidability of the novel through to the end, Cary plots an implicitly dialectical history of colonialism in which undecidable meaning marks a transition from a passing age of colonial dependency to a new age of independence about to be born.

4

While little concerned in an overt way with the formal bureaucracy of rule, Orwell's *Burmese Days* nevertheless dramatizes a fact about the British Empire usually only reluctantly acknowledged by its supporters: that all Britons, whether officially titled or not, are and must act like rulers in the colonies, and, consequently, must submit themselves to a rigid code of behavior designed to uphold the sahib's "prestige" – the "pukka sahib's code," as it is called here. In the Burma of Orwell's novel, this code binds whites tightly to rigid formulae that provide them with ready interpretations of Burmese behavior while simultaneously prescribing their own behavior as fully as was the young Eric Blair's when he found himself forced by social pressure to shoot an elephant one day in Burma.[24] *Burmese Days* is thus about the government to which the governors must submit, about how the imperial policemen are policed.

*Burmese Days* is also a story about rule violation – in fact, about imperial service as displaced European class war which can never be acknowledged as such – and consequently, a book whose most important moments dramatize the acute embarrassment attendant on it in blackly satirical terms. It is about the generalization of official codes to regulate the behavior of all English people in the colony, presenting Orwell's vision of Empire as a coercive system of behavior to which all sahibs must subscribe, regardless of whether or not they belong to the official governing bureaucracy. Moreover, it is a novel which directly challenges the mystique of useful work celebrated both in the managerial ideology of Cromer and Lugard and in the literary works of Rudyard Kipling. Orwell tackles it directly here:

There is a prevalent idea that the men at the "outposts of Empire" are at least able and hardworking. It is a delusion. Outside the scientific services – the Forest Department, the Public Works Department and the like – there is no particular need for a British official in India to do his job competently. Few of them work as hard or as intelligently as the postmaster of a provincial town in England. The real work of administration is done by native subordinates; and the real backbone of despotism is not the officials but the Army.[25]

Not only does Orwell detach the notion of imperial work from the value of efficiency, but he underlines a truth that the ideology of useful work was designed to obscure: that the true "work" of Empire is ultimately nothing but the exercise of harsh military rule over the colonized. Thus, Orwell's book is not about the work that is rule so much as it is about the impossibility of performing truly useful work when your job consists of upholding a system of grinding tyranny.

The metaphorically significant setting in this novel, therefore, is not the district office or other such official outpost of Empire, but rather the Anglo-Indian Club. Moreover, the novel features as its chief villain, the wonderful U Po Kyin, a scheming Burmese official on the lower level of the official bureaucracy whose elaborate machinations are designed with the one ultimate object of getting himself elected to the Club. In that sense, *Burmese Days* is a satirical novel which closes with a final dark irony: the one Burman who orchestrates the appearance of rebellion does so for the ultimate goal of being admitted to membership in the very place which defines the empty ideal of both British conviviality and imperial social order. *Burmese Days* is a novel in which a show of subversion is produced by ambitious bureaucrats in the interest of preserving and reinforcing the status quo.

The "pukka sahib's code" here consists chiefly of stereotyped axioms declaimed over drinks, the ironies highlighted by a skeptical narrator ("No Anglo-Indian will ever deny that India is going to the dogs, or ever has denied it – for India, like *Punch*, never was what it was" [*BD*, p. 29]): in short, a set of prescribed truths about Burma, Burmans, and the proper self-presentation of whites before Burmans, sometimes repeated ritualistically as part of the communal rituals of the whites in the Club, but more often than not simply assumed to bind whites to a rule-governed confraternity in which the rules often remain unspoken. This code, in Orwell's view, subjects whites to something like a system of thought control: "You are a creature of despotism, a pukka sahib, tied tighter than a monk or a savage by an unbreakable system of tabus" (*BD*, p. 69).

The whites are tightly reined in by the code for reasons that have more to do with self-protection than with the goal of governing wisely, however. Not only do the English figures here fear engulfment by restive yellow crowds if they do not maintain their difference and consequently their "prestige," but white "society" has no ordering principle, consisting as it does chiefly of a population of rather unpleasant individuals of different social classes bound together by nothing more than the socially coerced agreement to drink together to beguile the hot afternoons and evenings. The pukka sahib's code attempts to enforce the appearance of "civilized" order on an otherwise unruly mob of white Europeans.

V. G. Kiernan is just one of many European critics of empire who have discussed the way in which the Empire provided "plebeian" Europeans with the experience of belonging to a privileged group, an aristocracy of sorts which they could never join at home in England. As we have already discussed, the sense of earned, privileged conviviality was one of the things which made bureaucratic service in outposts of the Empire so attractive to would-be middle-class professionals. Certainly, while Kipling is the best-known celebrator of this ideology of professional community, we have seen an implicit celebration of white community in the "professional" ethos examined in this book: in Marlow's refined irony, which gathers his listeners together in an implicit community of sophisticated, "knowing" professionals; in Lawrence's celebration of his band of "wild men"; and, of course, in its most highly idealized form, in the exalted credentialing strategies of bureaucratic leaders such as Cromer and Lugard. For these figures, community is based, though, on the assumption of professional competence and specialized expertise. Lawrence's "wild men" presumably earned their place in his encomium through their specific actions in Arabia.

In the non-white dependencies of the Empire, however, this sense of earned privilege was more often than not articulated with a mystique of racial privilege – by definition something that can hardly be called an "earned" quality of character. As V. G. Kiernan argues,

Mystique of race was Democracy's vulgarization of an older mystique of class. It gave white settlers an agreeable sensation of being one large family, as an aristocracy always is, a counterfeit of the equality that western Europe had dreamed of for so long, and to so little avail. This had an insidious attraction for muddle-headed plebeians arriving from Europe, where on a larger scale classes were being drawn together in brotherly harmony by a common sensation of superiority to the lesser breeds outside; above all to plebeians from England, accustomed to breathe an air composed of oxygen, nitrogen, and snobbery.[26]

The celebration of "whiteness" as a criterion of group membership was necessarily fraught with paradox. After all, one cannot be credited with having earned a white skin; one is born with it. Nor does one earn the aristocratic forebears one must possess for admission into the Carlton Club either (unless, of course, you are Disraeli, who was known to have invented exalted forebears when he found it politically expedient). It is clear that "whiteness" in the colonial context had, in fact, as much to do with behavior – with upholding a code – as it did with the unearned fact of skin color. Indeed, "whiteness" was often treated as a quality of "character," requiring him who would be recognized as "white" to learn how to command the outward signs of "whiteness" in order to demonstrate the quality before the "lesser breeds." Moreover, this fact tells us much about how close the evolving professional ethos was to the aristocratic ideology from which it originally derived. E. M. Forster lampoons this notion of race as a moral or characterological criterion in a classic moment in *A Passage to India*, when his schoolmaster Fielding reminds the other Club members – to their consternation – that whites are not white but actually "pinko-grey." For the members of the Club, "whiteness" is an honorary recognition conferred only on those who follow the pukka sahib's code, those who play "white men."

Yet there is no getting away from that fact that "whiteness" itself in the colonies was bound up with physical qualities, and thus there is no getting away from the historical fact that it was repeatedly used as a blunt criterion of exclusion. Thus, in Orwell's novel, for instance, no dark-skinned Indian or racially-other Burman can earn it, at least not for most of the novel. Only at the very end does the treacherous U Po Kyin "earn" the status of honorary "white man." Moreover, the fact that he does so by the end of the book helps to make the chief satirical point of the novel: with the admission of the novel's chief villain, the "prestige" which whites ostensibly bring to the Club is baldly revealed as fraudulent. The mask has been torn from the face of "prestige," revealing nothing but naked "power."

The physicality of skin color is intimately connected with the othering of Orwell's white "hero" Flory within the Anglo-Indian community in Burma, also. Like the young Kipling's own tawny color and clipped sing-song way of pronouncing English words, which, according to Philip Mason, had a decisive impact on him early in life, making him the victim of something that resembled racial discrimination when he was a schoolboy in England, and encouraging his eventual development into a great celebrator of the "clubs" from which he was initially barred, Flory's birthmark becomes in *Burmese Days* the very obvious physical representation of his own outcast status within the Club, a fleshly metonymy for his "unsteady" and possibly "subversive" opinions, marking him as an insider with questionable allegiances to the outside.[27] As Orwell insists, Flory's birthmark itself accounts for his cautiousness and unwillingness to risk dislike even from those who are unworthy (*BD*, p. 64): producing what Freud would call a "reaction formation," similar to Kipling's, by which the racially or linguistically "othered" dispels doubts about his right to membership – proves his own "whiteness" – by defending the very rules of exclusion which originally produced his own ostracism. In *Burmese Days*, Orwell, who knew his subject well, traces this psychological peculiarity to the English public school in which the bullied overcome their feelings of ostracism by leaping at the first chance to bully someone else in turn:

He thought of some of the early effects of his birthmark. His first arrival at school, aged nine; the stares and, after a few days, shouts of the other boys; the nickname Blueface which lasted until the school poet (now, Flory remembered, a critic who wrote rather good articles in the *Nation*) came out with the couplet:

> New-tick Flory does look rum,
> Got a face like a monkey's bum,

whereupon the nickname was changed to Monkey-bum. And the subsequent years. On Saturday night the older boys used to have what they called a Spanish Inquisition. The favourite torture was for someone to hold you in a very painful grip known only to a few illuminati and called Special Togo, while someone beat you with a conker on a piece of string. But Flory had lived down

"Monkey-bum" in time. He was a liar and a good footballer, the two things absolutely necessary for success at school. In his last term he and another boy held the school poet in Special Togo while the captain of the eleven gave him six with a spiked running shoe for being caught writing a sonnet. It was a formative period. (*BD*, p. 64)

The difference between this and similar scenes in Kipling is tone. For Flory as for Kipling's Stalky, the route to social acceptance is through vengeance that is usually displaced from the original object of venom. Orwell detaches it from the self-sacrificial heroic code, however, according to which the "real subaltern" must run even more physical risks than the men he commands. To Orwell, the notion that the public school ethos might be grounded in some sacred ideal of self-sacrifice is poppycock. The bully simply does what he does out of motives of self-protection. He revenges himself by bullying then retreats for protection to the Club, as the vicious racist Ellis in *Burmese Days* does in order to flee a crowd of Burmese rioters angered by his blinding of a schoolboy one day in a characteristic fit of spleen (in fact, the scene in which Ellis attacks the upper-class Burmese public schoolboys reemphasizes Orwell's theme of imperial rule as British class war displaced in the colonies).

Unlike an eccentric imperial hero like Lawrence, however, whose "irregularity" of character marks him out as the perfect man for a certain type of imperial job, Flory remains a deeply flawed anti-hero in *Burmese Days*. The one white figure capable of testing the limits of the Club's tolerance for deviance, he is also incapacitated by his history and status as victim which his social class background (he did not go to one of the great public schools), his history in Burma, and, above all, his birthmark give him. Thus, he not only capitulates to social pressure by allowing himself to be bullied into signing a petition early in the novel to bar his closest friend, the Indian Dr. Veraswami, from being admitted to the Club, but he allows his broad-minded appreciation of Burmese culture, a feature he shares with none of the other whites in the Club, to become as incapacitating as it is liberating. Despite his interest in Burmese culture, his appreciation for Dr. Veraswami, and his distrust of conventional Anglo-Indian types like Ellis and Westfield, Flory cannot redeem himself because he cannot surmount this determining history.

In fact, the failure of Flory to become a hero may tell us a great deal about why *Burmese Days* was not well received in England when it was published. The novel offers no self-congratulatory hope, no shred of redemptive possibilities, for any of its English characters. No Fielding stalks this text, representing the broad-minded attitudes of which the

English who are not part of the official governing order are capable. Flory himself concentrates his own hope of redemption in his – very mistaken – hope of marriage to one of the most atrociously conventional *memsahibs* that English fiction has produced: Elizabeth Lackersteen. Indeed, in misunderstanding Elizabeth, Flory misunderstands the meaning of the English domestic "virtues" he wishes her to represent, and consequently, falls victim in the end to misplaced hope.

Orwell's characterization of Elizabeth is a savagely satirical one, precisely because he characterizes her as English middle-class conventionality masquerading as a redeemable innocence (which is, in fact, nothing but appalling ignorance). Arriving in Burma in search of a man to marry and equipped with a tellingly binary way of classifying all experiences (the "beastly" and the "lovely"), Elizabeth first meets Flory when he "saves" her from an aggressive, snorting water buffalo. Elated with his luck, Flory is immediately infatuated with her and, vainly hoping that she might share his interest in Burmese culture, takes her that first night to see a Burmese *pwe*. The highlight of the performance occurs when the best Burmese dancer takes the stage:

> The music struck up, and the *pwe* girl began dancing again. Her face was powdered so thickly that it gleamed in the lamplight like a chalk mask with live eyes behind it. With that dead-white oval face and those wooden gestures she was monstrous, like a demon. The music changed its tempo, and the girl began to sing in trochaic rhythm, gay, hot, fierce. The crowd took it up, a hundred voices chanting the harsh syllables in unison. Still in that strange bent posture the girl turned round and danced with her buttocks protruded towards the audience. Her silk *longyi* gleamed like metal. With hands and elbows still rotating she wagged her posterior from side to side. Then – astonishing feat, quite visible through the *longyi* – she began to wriggle her two buttocks independently in time with the music. (*BD*, p. 106)

When a flustered Elizabeth insists on leaving immediately, Flory experiences the first of his own many moments of acute embarrassment (a scene of embarrassment recapitulated near the end of the novel, when the "powdered oval" face of his jilted Burmese concubine, Ha Mla May, materializes at the church door during Sunday services), while remaining ignorant of the fact that Elizabeth's conventionality makes her a more rigid rather than less rigid adherent to the pukka sahib's code. Thus,

> It was not the *pwe* girl's behaviour, in itself, that had offended her; it had only brought things to a head. But the whole expedition – the very notion of *wanting* to rub shoulders with all those smelly natives – had impressed her badly. She was perfectly certain that that was not how white men ought to behave. (*BD*, p. 107)

Unlike Adela Quested, who arrives in India with the utopian intent –
later betrayed, of course – of "understanding" India in its own terms,
Elizabeth Lackersteen has a response to Burma which is conditioned by
her need to fall back on a code the very details of which she doesn't know,
but which she comes to Burma already fully equipped to invoke.[28]

This is possible only because the pukka sahib code is based on a very
"English," very domestic, model of class separation. Thus, raised for
two years in Paris by an artist mother who had taken her out of the
physical comfort of England, Elizabeth comes out to live with her aunt
and uncle in Burma after her mother's death, feeling relieved that she
doesn't have to spend the rest of her life among unwashed bohemians.
Tellingly, her own innocence of the world combined with years of living
in near-poverty make her especially prone to take infection from the
atmosphere of wealth aboard ship on her way to Burma:

> It was so lovely after those two graceless years to breathe the air of wealth again.
> Not that most of the people here were rich; but on board ship everyone behaves
> as though he were rich. She was going to India, she knew. She had formed quite
> a picture of India, from the other passengers' conversation; she had even
> learned some of the more necessary Hindustani phrases, such as *"idher ao,"*
> *"jaldi,"* *"sahiblog,"* etc. In anticipation she tasted the agreeable atmosphere of
> Clubs, with punkahs flapping and barefooted white-turbaned boys reverently
> salaaming; and maidans where bronzed Englishmen with little clipped mous-
> taches galloped to and fro, whacking polo balls. It was almost as nice as being
> really rich, the way people lived in India. (*BD*, p. 96)

To note that this is a dream of class transfiguration is to state the
obvious. What the passage underlines, though, is how much this particular dream of social class transfiguration owes to exclusionary practices. The pleasures that this fantasy arouses are occasioned by the
agreeable spectacle of separation: the punka-pullers, the salaaming
turbaned boys, polo on the "maidan," the grassy expanse (among other
things, a clear field of fire) which, under the *Raj*, marked off the "white"
area of the Indian town from the "native" areas. The pleasures evoked
in this passage are inextricably bound up with the agreeable spectacle of
those who cannot share it, much as the pleasures of a cozy Christmas
dinner in a middle-class London household are enhanced by the presence of street urchins just outside the window, in the snow, looking on in
hungry envy.

Orwell performs an act of demystification here, calling his reader's
attention to the central importance of exclusionary practices which are
themselves definitional. Not only does his novel undermine the notion of

"white prestige," principally by repeatedly putting the defense of it in the mouths of white characters such as Ellis who would never be seen as superior to anyone, but he challenges the notion of the superiority of aristocratic life, the domestic English social class fantasy reshaped into a colonial fantasy of "whiteness." Thus, Elizabeth's early dream of a mustachioed, polo-playing Englishman on the maidan later materializes almost point for point in the form of Lieutenant Verrall, a mustachioed, polo-playing subaltern who, according to Orwell's narrator, "sat his horse as though he were part of it" and looked "offensively young and fit" (*BD*, p. 184). To underline Verrall's role, Orwell characterizes him as a thoroughly empty-headed brute who avoids all contact with other whites at the Club until the day he gets a close look at Elizabeth and launches himself on a determined campaign of "trifling" with her. A conventional rake whose conventionality somehow escapes the notice of Elizabeth and her aunt until after he dishonors her and flees ahead of his own troops and his many creditors, Verrall spends most of his time while in Kyauktada expressing contempt for the other members of the Club. Thus, he comes to stand as a metonymy for the relationship of the English Club members to Burma. In fact, one of the finest comic scenes in the book occurs between the splenetic Ellis and Verrall right after Verrall abuses a Club butler. Ellis, out of countenance over Verrall's presumption, lashes into him verbally, asking him why he kicked the butler. Verrall responds:

"Beggar gave me his lip. I sent him for a whiskey and soda, and he brought it warm. I told him to put ice in it, and he wouldn't – talked some bloody rot about saving the last piece of ice. So I kicked his bottom. Serve him right."

Ellis turned quite grey. He was furious. The butler was a piece of Club property and not to be kicked by strangers. But what most angered Ellis was the thought that Verrall quite possibly suspected him of being *sorry* for the butler – in fact, of disapproving of kicking *as such*. (*BD*, p. 208)

The mirror relationship between Ellis and Verrall necessarily accounts for the escalating violence of their verbal confrontation: kicking the Burmese butler is not at issue here, only the question of who has proprietorial rights to kick him. Indeed, the many similarities among the white characters in this book are underlined through plot analogies which highlight the fact that white society in Burma is a viciously competitive scramble for advantage. As Ellis's racist attitude toward Dr. Veraswami duplicates Verrall's class contempt for the other English characters, Flory's tawdry relationship to the Burmese concubine he eventually discards, Ha Mla May, is duplicated in the exploitive sexual relationship Verrall has with Elizabeth Lackersteen.

The central dramatic event of the novel – the riot – is precipitated by two events that are linked: the murder of a white man, Maxwell, by Burmans angered by his killing of two of their relatives, and the attack by the splenetic Ellis on some Burmese schoolboys which leaves one blinded (after his eyes are treated with a suitable noxious substance by a Burmese doctor). As a threat to white "prestige," however, the death of Maxwell is fittingly overblown by Orwell, who describes a scene of colonial hysteria which ensues after the news of the murder of a white man is received at the Club:

> Maxwell's death had caused a profound shock in Kyauktada. It would cause a shock throughout the whole of Burma, and the case – "the Kyauktada case, do you remember?" – would still be talked of years after the wretched youth's name was forgotten. But in a purely personal way no one was much distressed. Maxwell had been almost a nonentity – just a "good fellow" like any other of the ten thousand *ex colore* good fellows of Burma – and with no close friends. No one among the Europeans genuinely mourned for him. But that is not to say that they were not angry. On the contrary, for the moment they were almost mad with rage. For the unforgivable had happened – a *white man* had been killed. When that happens, a sort of shudder runs through the English of the East. Eight hundred people, possibly, are murdered every year in Burma; they matter nothing; but the murder of *a white man* is a monstrosity, a sacrilege. Poor Maxwell would be avenged, that was certain. But only a servant or two, and the Forest Ranger, who had brought in his body, and who had been fond of him, shed any tears for his death. (*BD*, p. 238)

The coercive nature of the pukka sahib's code is underlined in the reaction of the Europeans to the murder of Maxwell. Whatever the complexities of the situation, all whites, regardless of attitude, are forced into a defensive closing of ranks and minds against the Burmese, discarding any pretense of imperial legality in favor of group vengeance. Indeed, the loss of Maxwell as an individual is meaningless. The loss of the role – a white man – matters immensely, however, to the other whites for reasons that are never overtly conceded but nonetheless universally assumed. Moreover, when Ellis blinds the Burmese school-boy and precipitates a riot by angry Burmans, the Club quickly offers him refuge, regardless of the justice of the Burmese rioters' complaints against him.

Flory's dramatic exploits in turning the rioting crowd away from the Club would be treated in heroic terms if this were an imperial novel by, say, Haggard or Buchan. But the riot itself becomes a comic exercise here, at least partly because the narrative of Flory's heroism is followed quickly by the narration of Flory's subsequent disgrace in church, when the frowzy, discarded concubine, Ha Mla May, tutored carefully by U Po Kyin, arrives at the door to demand payment for services rendered in front of all the European members of the Club. Whatever credit Flory had earned with the other Europeans as a result of saving them from the mob evaporates instantly, as his Sunday reveries about a future life with Elizabeth are spoiled by Ma Hla May's "Pike-san pay-like" (a metaphorical enactment of British betrayal of a dependent people). Orwell is at his best in describing the scene of acute embarrassment which follows:

The scene had been so violent, so squalid, that everyone was upset by it. Even Ellis looked disgusted. Flory could neither speak nor stir. He sat staring fixedly at the altar, his face rigid and so bloodless that the birthmark seemed to glow upon it like a streak of blue paint. Elizabeth glanced across the aisle at him, and her revulsion made her almost physically sick. She had not understood a word of what Ma Hla May was saying, but the meaning of the scene was perfectly clear. The thought that he had been the lover of that grey-faced maniacal creature made her shudder in her bones. But worse than that, worse than anything was his ugliness at this moment. His face appalled her, it was so ghastly, rigid and old. It was like a skull. Only the birthmark seemed alive in it. She hated him now for his birthmark. She had never known till this moment how dishonouring, how unforgivable a thing it was. (*BD*, p. 274)

The richness of this scene comes from the way Orwell represents a moment of moral embarrassment in brutally physical terms. Ma Hla May's powdered face and Flory's birthmark are what trigger her revulsion. The psychological mechanism at work here is, of course, the mechanism of abjection.[29] Although quite willing at one time to play a European version of Ma Hla May herself by giving herself to the heartless Verrall, Elizabeth secures her difference from Flory's "grey-faced" concubine through the comforting physical reaction of disgust. "If she makes me vomit she cannot be me" is one way of putting her reaction. Disgust precludes threatening identification.

Flory's fleshly metonymy, his birthmark, produces an analogous reaction in the end. The bodily sign which marks his difference from others is, of course, precisely what humanizes him. Thus, Elizabeth's reaction to his birthmark is a reaction against sexuality itself: the sign of all people's shame made to signify a peculiarly individual shame for Flory here, the mark of the beast (i.e. the human). When Flory shoots himself in the head near the end of the novel, his birthmark fades instantly, returning him to the land of the human merely as the subject of cautionary Anglo-Indian narratives:

"Flory? Oh yes, he was a dark chap, with a birthmark. He shot himself in Kyauktada in 1926. Over a girl, people said. Bloody fool." (*BD*, p. 283)

As in a Jane Austen novel, the ability to feel embarrassment, to recognize the authority of a rule that has been violated, is the chief sign that one possesses "character." For Orwell, Flory's abject status and despairing suicide at least make him heroic in this limited sense, despite the melodramatic banality of committing suicide in despair over losing the respect of such a mean object as Elizabeth Lackersteen. Yet it is clear that the "natural" in this text both does and does not matter. Like the signs of racial difference, what matters finally about Flory's mark are the meanings attached to it, not any meanings that birthmarks have in and of themselves. Thus, it marks him for heroism, grows more visibly ugly in his acute embarrassment, fades with his death and return to the common lot of humanity, and is evoked at the end as a mark of distinction in the tiresome stories of Anglo-Indian hands.

The end asserts a return to normalcy, with Elizabeth now married to McGregor and filling "with complete success the position for which Nature had designed her from the first, that of a *burra memsahib*" (*BD*, p. 287). Orwell's novel, like Cary's and Forster's, ends with an assertion of an historically-impossible stasis, a resumption of the decorous, however compromised such notions are by the end of the novel. The death of Flory returns us to the beginning point, with the one individual character who possesses the qualities necessary to challenge the system of which he is a product consigned to the status of mere subject of the comforting narratives told by Anglo-Indians. True to the spirit of much interwar fiction, Orwell's *Burmese Days* cannot envision the end of a bureaucratic system of rule because it cannot envision the possibility of the heroic individual succeeding. Like Dekker's Max Havelaar, Orwell's Flory is the slightly absurd (if potentially noble) product of a system designed to thwart resistance from within.

*Burmese Days*, one of the angriest satirical novels of the interwar period, can be seen as an attempt to break with the formal conventions of the novel of imperial manners, so strikingly represented in the work of Forster and carried on in the thirties by Cary. True to the writerly persona he would carefully construct for himself during the ideological wars of the 1930s, Orwell seeks both to represent the manners of imperial officialdom and to subvert them by denying any moral efficacy to indirection. It matters to Orwell that the action of *Burmese Days* – especially the presentation of the overt racism of British officials and the collapse of social order occasioned precisely by the exercise of an attenuated form of Indirect Rule in Burma – is often direct and violent, and that imperial power often bears a hostile physicality analogous to the brute physicality of his protagonist Flory's birthmark. Because indirection and reticence are the chief identifying marks of the British colonial bureaucrat, Orwell renders these forms of behavior morally and politically inefficacious.

# Conclusion: work as rule

This book has been a book about management: the management of the self in the interest of the management of others, and the management of feeling to which the bureaucrat must submit. In asserting a connection between that mysterious thing the English call "character" and the colonial enterprise, I have suggested that the unique demands of the work that is rule led to the discursive construction of a type of bureaucratic subject designed to rule as unobtrusively as possible, a subject designed to meet the taxing psychological demands of Indirect Rule.

Adapting a notion of the subject made available to them by Victorian novelistic culture and already put into administrative practice in the Punjab of the Lawrences, turn-of-the-century promoters of empire such as Cromer and Lugard sought to formulate a system of rule for the colonies that would procure for imperial rule the appearance of innocence that grand moral projects commanded in the Victorian middle-class mind. By demanding much personal sacrifice from would-be administrators, the theory of Indirect Rule evolved into a philosophy of government over the conquered masquerading as a philosophy of the self-government of the bureaucrat. In designing this theory, the theorists of Indirect Rule were able to insure a role for a new kind of professional colonial manager in a twentieth-century world order characterized by gradual decolonization, for, when the goals of rule are conceived in instrumentalist terms, the means of rule – bureaucracy – becomes a powerful machine capable of generating new business for itself, as it generates new goals to replace its founding purpose, and supplies new gratifications in place of the old.

The imperial bureaucrat of Cromer's vision, however well adapted he may seem to coping with the novel demands of the era of national efficiency, was, to a great extent, a suitable product of Victorian middle-class culture. While the ideology of individual autonomy was widely celebrated publicly during the nineteenth century, the new forms of

193

industrial work being developed taught an implicit lesson that was antithetical to this public message (to those who were willing to pay attention to it): a lesson about the necessity of attenuating the subject's autonomy, about the tailoring of the subject to fit the corporate system rather than the reshaping of the system to accommodate the individual. A yawning gap opens in public consciousness as a result, as the celebration of individual greatness or heroism is used to cloak the scale of bureaucratic power. In this book, we have seen this most clearly in the work of Henry M. Stanley who often highlighted his own personal accomplishments by understating the importance of the material conditions – superior military force, superior firepower, superior organization, and so on – which were the underpinnings of that success.

Grounded in eighteenth-century radical traditions which supplied the language in which a newly emergent middle class cast its ultimately successful challenge to the social and political prerogatives of its aristocratic betters, the ideology of liberal individualism had undoubtedly become hegemonic by the end of the nineteenth century because the British middle class had attained social and political ascendancy by that time.[1] Indeed, the influence of this ideology can be felt almost everywhere great deeds are celebrated.[2] Yet the celebration of individual initiative would, as we have seen, ultimately engender fears about the ability of British society to work together toward common goals. In the era of "national efficiency," social ideals which are corporate in nature would come to seem unrealizable without attenuating individual initiative, without, in short, subjecting individual freedom to the needs of the system – whether the nation, the economy, or the corporation.

Often, these middle-class fears took the form of suspicions of working-class loyalty. Thus the suspicion that the working-class *homo economicus* would become a creature incapable of fidelity to anything other than his own economic self-interest inspired, among other things, the celebratory paternalism of the late-Victorian business class. Late-Victorian employers increasingly attempted to enforce a corporate ethic of loyalty built around new social rituals cast in the form of both carrots and sticks. Many arranged all-day railway excursions and picnics for their employees; others, such as the chocolate tycoons the Cadburys, organized enormous parties on the spacious grounds of their estates complete with games: forms of compulsory socializing designed to work against the atomistic effects of the cash nexus. These new social rituals inevitably developed along quasi-military lines. Typical of the new rituals was the company parade, in which a company's entire workforce was compelled to march in procession behind the firm's band. Inspired by the image of the well-drilled Army corps, these corporate rituals soon drew on military traditions to supply the chief metaphors for an emerging corporatist ideology adaptable to the interests of nationalists and businessmen alike.[3]

Social observers at the turn of the century were not slow to note how much the emerging social ethos used to justify these rituals resembled in form the military traditions of the aristocracy, and some observers began to wonder about why the industrial middle class seemed so devoted to it. From the mid-nineteenth century on, many forms of popular entertainment in Britain had been trumpeting what looked like the corporate values of loyalty and self-sacrifice traditionally associated (as Schumpeter would argue in 1919) with the military traditions of a class in political and social eclipse – the aristocracy.[4] Because Schumpeter saw militarism and the religion of nationalism as clear threats to bourgeois class interests (did not the carnage of World War I clearly prove that?), he wondered aloud about the infatuation of the European middle classes for social "atavisms" so clearly antithetical to their own class interests.

Like many post-war critics of militarism addicted to the Smithian ideals of free trade and individualist economic principles, Schumpeter was unable to see just how easily the corporate culture of the turn-of-the-century business world had already accommodated itself to the nationalist sentiments that drove the war effort in 1914–1918. To take just one example: scientific management in the workplace is not incompatible with attempts to organize leisure time in the interests of promoting loyalty to the firm. Nor is either of the above necessarily incompatible with nationalist ideology and its emphasis on group loyalty which is evoked especially hard in times of world war. As we have shown many times in this book, on a personal level the individual who submits to the discipline of a bureaucratic organization does not, thereby, necessarily sacrifice personal efficacy. In fact, the great advantage that bureaucracy can offer – whether in business or in the military – is the advantage of enhanced personal agency. As Kipling teaches over and over again, initial submission is often the price one has to pay for enhanced power and a degree of eventual autonomy.

Popular representations of imperial deeds in the nineteenth and early twentieth centuries often participated in the duality we are underlining. Newspaper battlefield reporting by figures such as G. A. Henty begins to be popular during the Crimean War (the last war Britain would fight with another well-armed and well-trained European power until 1914). This was followed by vivid accounts of heroic exploits which became staples of homefront journalism during the second half of the nineteenth century, as newspapers sent reporters and artists to cover battles in Egypt, the Sudan, Afghanistan, and any of the many places where Britain found itself at war with non-European people. By 1901, J. A. Hobson was deploring, in his *Psychology of Jingoism*, the extent to which the values of militarism had saturated not only the press but most other forms of British popular culture, and especially that most popular of English working- and middle-class entertainments, the music halls.[5] The explanation for this popularity is not hard to find, however. The popular culture industries of the late nineteenth century required dramatic material to feed the voracious appetites of their customers, and they often found it readily available in the near-constant (and usually success-ful) warfare that accompanied expansion. Not surprisingly to those of us who live in the world of Rupert Murdoch, newspapers of one hundred years ago found their most memorable stories, not in yawn-inducing tales of investment opportunities and the large-scale movements of capital – in other words, in the narratives of actual history – but, more often than not, in dramatic narratives of daring adventure overseas. As John Springhall has recently argued, "If the idea of Empire was to be sold to the great British public . . . then the propaganda appeal of lonely exploration along African rivers, of missionaries converting the heathen or, more importantly, of heroic military exploits, was obviously far greater than that of shareholders investing capital in chartered com-panies or of companies haggling with rival powers over treaty bound-aries."[6] The story of the movements of capital across the globe, as Hobson would discover, no matter how important, went largely under-reported to an increasingly literate British public, eclipsed instead by dramatic tales of individual heroism which were often embedded within increasingly shrill and jingoistic celebrations of military glory.

Baden-Powell, the military hero responsible for the successful relief of Mafeking during the Boer War, embodies the contradictions we have just noted between corporatist and individualist ideologies, not simply because he himself became the subject of popular adulation at the end of the Boer War but because he founded an organization designed to teach children how to channel individual efforts toward the accomplishment of corporate goals. In deliberately modeling his Boy Scout movement after the military, Baden-Powell was interested not simply in teaching boys how to develop "pluck," but in insuring that British middle-class youth were inculcated with the seemingly antithetical tribal values of national and group loyalty which he saw as essential to the survival of the British Empire. As Allen Warren has noted,

there is in Baden-Powell a consistent corporatism about politics both national and imperial and a constant reiteration of the need for social and political unity against dangers both external and subversive. "We are all bricks in the wall," is a constantly reiterated metaphor, and each citizen was urged to see him or herself as part of the national team playing the great game.[7]

The tensions between an ethic of group loyalty, so insistent a note struck by the popular culture of the era of national efficiency, and the celebration of individual initiative, which the lionization of Baden-Powell himself as military hero epitomizes, cannot be abolished, of course, simply by encouraging people to take heart in the realization "We are all bricks in the wall." In many ways the most representative institution of the age of "national efficiency," the Boy Scouting movement was founded to resolve a disciplinary contradiction that had bedeviled Dr. Thomas Arnold sixty years before: to teach boys how to follow so that they would one day know when and how to lead.

Public discourse in the period from 1880 until World War I is thus saturated with symptomatic metaphors that attempt imaginary resolutions of the very tensions we are underlining here. Perhaps even more popular than metaphors drawn from military life were sporting metaphors. Field sports were no longer seen as simply the peculiar rituals of upper-class life inculcated in well-heeled youth during their days at public school. By the end of the century, the ethos of field sports seemed to offer the perfect national model to which the members of all classes could aspire (at least to middle-class intellectuals): a model of individual initiative yoked to the service of corporate goals. As the liberal Charles Dilke put it in *Greater Britain* in 1891,

While Britons retain their national interest in sport the subjects which divide them into arid sects must necessarily be of only momentary concern. There will never be more than a formal disintegration of the empire while we are subject to the bond of a common interest in arts which spring directly from the instincts of the national character. The common love of the chase in any of its forms, the common joy in a well-fought maul in the football field, satisfied our optimistic observers that, whatever may betide us in politics, our British spirit is a thing of permanence.[8]

Had "instinct" not been discovered surely it would have to have been invented. Dilke invokes it here as a primal bond connecting a peculiarly upper-class form of sporting life with the life of the English nation as a whole. However little direct experience a working-class resident of Manchester may have had with hunting (or with rugby football, for that matter), Dilke assures his readers, these things remain part of his instinctual inheritance, part of the animal bond he shares with males of all the other classes. Thus, Dilke equates hunting with rugby, and treats both as crucially important bonding rituals.[9] Games offer the compelling spectacle of competitive violence – the rugby "maul" – which bonds competitors together in a common cause. Sports seem to offer the best of both worlds: plenty of incentives to the individual to perform at his personal best as well as a disciplinary mechanism which insures that the individual's "best" ultimately serves the cause of the group. Field sports thus provide perhaps the most compelling examples of the effective management of individual energy in the interest of corporate goals.

Lord Cromer sought to appeal, however, to the elite not to the masses, to that educated middle class in fact which, despite its cultural hegemony, was still a numerical minority within Britain at the turn of the century. The imperial bureaucrat, I have tried to suggest, was constructed – by Cromer and Lugard, by Victorian adventurers such as Stanley, by writers such as Kipling, and later, by charismatic bureaucrats such as Lawrence – at least partly in response to the threat that bureaucracy poses to the conventional notion of the autonomous heroic individual who seems to stalk the pages of popular newspapers and the *Boy's Own Paper*. In recruiting bodies to feed the machine of Empire, colonial bureaucracy threatened to annex individuals to the service of a project which required the sacrifice of the very individuality so prized and celebrated by the middle and upper classes. The ideology of Indirect Rule requires the successful management of the subject's own desires in the interest of the successful management of others: in particular, as we have shown, the sacrifice of the desire to stand out in the interest of the corporate need to remain less visible. As a code of moral and professional prescriptions for administrators, Indirect Rule is all about the management of the appearance of power; it demands a carefully staged economy of unsung heroism. Consequently it seems to promise, at least in theory, a happy resolution to the conflict we have been describing.

Moreover, most of the critics of the ideology of Indirect Rule examined here – writers such as Conrad, Cary, and Orwell – found themselves buying into the very ideology of the bourgeois subject as the only available stance from which to critique Imperial bureaucracy as a system. The celebration of the individual, especially in Modernist writers like Cary and Orwell, becomes the early twentieth century's only available response to the coerciveness of bureaucracy. Thus, even socialists such as Orwell were repelled by the unwholesome spectacle of popular glorification of militarism and jingoism, a spectacle they held responsible both for the horrors of World War I and for the inevitability of the Second World War.

Despite the concerns of these later writers with the nasty effects of the imperial system on the Europeans who serve it, they usually cast their chief complaints about the Empire's effect on the colonized in the same terms. Thus, even the chief critics of the imperial system in the early twentieth century often found themselves in implicit agreement with the goals articulated by major imperial figures such as Frederick Lugard: the goal of imperial rule ought to be to create autonomous indigenous subjects ready to accept the responsibilities of democratic self-governance one day. The ironic logic of Indirect Rule is thus played out in two fields: among colonial bureaucrats, who must submit to the rule of self-effacement in order to rule effectively, and among the colonized themselves, who, the script of Indirect Rule requires, must accept submission as the only condition of eventual independence.

The preoccupation of European missionaries, travelers, explorers, military leaders, and colonial administrators with the work that is rule, however, can be placed within a larger history of changing patterns of middle-class work in the advanced capitalist societies of Europe and the United States, for changes in the ideology of rule were in many ways responses to changes in the nature of middle-class work back home. Over the course of the twentieth century, much middle-class work has, in fact, become "ruling." Despite the widespread layoffs of middle managers in the United States during the most recent recession, the fact remains that the management of people is a significant part of the job that most middle-class business professionals now perform. The growth of the professional class during the early twentieth century and the refinement of its ethos paralleled and fed into a trend occurring within the business class itself: the separation of ownership and control which led to a dramatic expansion of what would eventually be called the "managerial" class within business culture. While this trend was noted by many intellectuals in the early twentieth century, it was first explicitly theorized in the 1920s in Berle and Means' *The Modern Corporation and Private Property* and popularized among intellectuals by one of the most influential (and alarming) books of the mid-twentieth century: James Burnham's *The Managerial Revolution* (1941).

Published just before the official entry of the United States into war with Germany and Japan, *The Managerial Revolution* boldly predicts the eventual replacement of capitalist society by a "managerial society" in which bureaucrats with specialized expertise monopolize social privilege and political power. While this trend has progressed further in the Soviet Union and fascist Italy and Germany by 1941 than it has in Britain or the United States, according to Burnham, it is a trend, he predicts, that will prove irresistible even in the latter countries. Indeed, the vast expansion of government investment in the US economy during the Depression years of the 1930s (in response to a dramatic scaling-back of private investment which contributed mightily to deepening the depression) provides Burnham with the chief evidence for his claim that managerialism is a universally irresistible trend.[10] Moreover, Burnham was writing at the very beginning of an even larger expansion in the role of government in the US economy which wartime military production necessitated.

Like Weber who laments the "iron cage" of bureaucracy, Burnham tinges his belief in the inevitable triumph of managerialism with pessimism and regret, a regret most evident in his discussion of the efficiency of Nazi Germany (he was writing in the dark days of 1940). The threat that managerialism poses for him is, finally, the threat of the triumph of totalitarian power, already realized in the Germany of 1940. Bureaucratic power combined with professional efficiency leads inevitably to the end of democracy, he believes. Not only will free labor disappear as the government increasingly becomes the only employer, but parliamentary sovereignty will increasingly become an anachronism as actual power shifts from parliaments to bureaus staffed by professionals.[11] In a chilling prediction, Burnham writes off political democracy as an historical atavism: "Parliament was the sovereign body of the limited state of capitalism. The bureaus are the sovereign bodies of the unlimited states of managerial society."[12]

Burnham's fear of the bureaucratic state may perhaps seem rather dated now. With the disintegration of the last totalitarian empire – the Soviet Union – most Americans and Europeans are arguably preoccupied less by the specter of the growing power of the megastate than they are by the increasing anachronism of nation-states themselves in a world which seems more and more like the world of Cobden turned nightmarish: a worldwide free-trading order of internationalized – and highly mobile – capital, in which the gap between rich and poor is growing rapidly (both between "developed" and "developing" states and within them); in which job security for most of the workforce is increasingly tenuous; in which individual nation-states command less and less power over their own economic fortunes; in which labor in the First World is disciplined by the continuing threat that jobs will be exported at a moment's notice to any of a dozen developing states; in which labor in the Third World is disciplined by artificial famine or military force.

Yet, if Burnham's vision now seems flawed because of his over-reliance on the model of the American New Deal – that historically unprecedented melding of government and managerial expertise that helped pull the United States out of the Great Depression – and the fortunately brief tenure of fascism in Europe, it is nonetheless an important symptomatic "moment" in the twentieth century conceptualization of bureaucracy. It was a vision that was seized upon by one of the most important British writers of the interwar period – George Orwell – precisely because it offered a plausible model of a modern social order ruled by professional expertise grafted onto the power of the militarized state. Like some of the best writers of his generation, Orwell first made a name for himself as a writer by critiquing an historically earlier and less efficient, but decidedly British, version of this model: the Empire. Moreover, as Hannah Arendt's *Origins of Totalitarianism* makes clear, one of the most compelling intellectual responses to the horrific events of 1939–1945 in the immediate post-war era was to see that war as the apocalyptic last chapter of a story that began to be written in the late nineteenth century: a story of the inevitable clash of imperial competitors, driven to the brink of world destruction by the inevitable momentum of national efficiency technology grafted onto nationalist and racist ideology. If the totalitarian nightmares of post-war intellectuals seem dated now, the issues they raised are of continuing relevance in a world still ruled by well-organized power.

# Notes

### INTRODUCTION

1 Franz Kafka, "In the Penal Colony," *The Penal Colony: Stories and Short Pieces*, trans. Willa and Edwin Muir (New York: Schocken, 1971), pp. 191–230.

### I   AGENTS AND THE PROBLEM OF AGENCY: THE CONTEXT

1 According to the *OED*, the earliest uses of the terms "bureaucracy" and "bureaucratic" in English (dating from the 1830s and 40s) are disparaging ones. Moreover, if Carlyle's use of the term in the *Latter-Day Pamphlets* can be regarded as typical of this period ("The continental nuisance called 'bureaucracy'" [1850]), then "bureaucracy" was also imagined as principally a foreign disease. *The Compact Edition of the Oxford English Dictionary* (Oxford: Oxford University Press, 1971), p. 1184.

2 Harry Braverman identifies the role of "scientific management" (or Taylorism) in the evolution of capitalist business management. Taylorism was a theory for reducing the highly individual craft skills of the preindustrial worker to the simpler, and highly undifferentiated, skills of the industrial proletarian: the role of scientific management "was to ensure that as craft declined, the worker would sink to the level of general and undifferentiated labor power, adaptable to a large range of simple tasks, while as science grew, it would be concentrated in the hands of management." Harry Braverman, *Labor and Monopoly Capital* (New York and London: *Monthly Review* Press, 1974), p. 121. Moreover, Braverman argues that Taylorism was not, as many have claimed, a radically new technique for organizing work appearing only at the end of the nineteenth century when Taylor himself began to promote his theories, but rather the logical continuation of a longer tradition of labor management, first developed in the earliest textile mills, theorized by the early political economists, and updated theoretically by the early-Victorian political economists Andrew Ure and Charles Babbage in England. Braverman, p. 85.

3 Max Weber, *Economy and Society*, ed. G. Roth and C. Wittich, trans. Fischoff et al. (New York: Bedminster, 1968), p. 956. My characterization of Weber's view of bureaucracy as "positive" needs clarification, needless to say. Despite

describing bureaucratic modernity as an "iron cage," Weber views bureaucratic forms of social organization as the characteristic feature of a "modernity" which is implicitly – if hesitatingly – valorized in his theories. In fact, it is the replacement of earlier forms of personalized rule ("charismatic," "feudal") with rule-governed bureaucratic domination within nation-states that Weber finds typically "modern." For a discussion of Weber's theories in relation to the Foucauldian thematic of power/knowledge, see Christopher Dandeker, *Surveillance, Power, and Modernity: Bureaucracy and Discipline from 1700 to the Present Day* (New York: St. Martin's, 1990).

4  Both Britain and the United States have inherited this sometimes misleading conceptual dichotomy in its late twentieth-century guise as the distinction between "public" and "private" sectors of the post-industrial economy, although both spheres in the late twentieth-century have long been thoroughly bureaucratized (indeed, the term "bureaucracy" is as adequate a label for the social organization of work in most industrial organizations as it is for government). For more on this, see Harold Perkin on the ideological reasons for the persistence of the language of class within post-industrial society. Harold Perkin, *The Rise of Professional Society: England Since 1880* (London: Routledge, 1989), p. 12.

5  "In 1830 the despotic or authoritarian element latent in Utilitarianism was not noted by the statesmen of any party. The reformers of the day placed, for the most part, implicit faith in the dogma of *laissez-faire* and failed to perceive that there is no necessary connection between it and that 'greatest happiness principle,' which may, with equal sincerity, be adopted either by believers in individual freedom or by the advocates of paternal government . . . And, oddly enough, the tendency of Benthamite teaching to extend the sphere of State intervention was increased by another characteristic . . . – that is, by the unlimited scorn entertained by every Benthamite for the social contract and natural rights." A. V. Dicey, *Lectures on the Relation Between Law and Public Opinion in England During the Nineteenth Century* (London: Macmillan, 1905). Quoted in Ellen Frankel Paul, *Moral Revolution and Economic Science* (Westport, CT: Greenwood, 1979), p. 280. See also David Roberts, *Victorian Origins of the British Welfare State* (New Haven: Yale University Press, 1960), pp. 29–31.

6  G. R. Searle, *The Quest for National Efficiency* (Oxford: Oxford University Press, 1971), pp. 206, 230, and 24 respectively.

7  Perkin, *Rise of Professional Society*, p. 121.

8  For the best discussion of how imperialism becomes connected to ideas of social reform at the turn of the century among figures as diverse as the Fabians, the Chamberlainites, and pro-imperial Liberals such as Churchill, see Bernard Semmel, *Imperialism and Social Reform* (Cambridge, MA: Harvard University Press, 1960).

9  A. P. Thornton, *The Imperial Idea and Its Enemies* (New York: St. Martin's, 1963), p. 15. That the "humanitarian" movement was encouraged by the confluence of interests between the moral project of freeing people from bondage and the economic project of internationalizing the practice of paid

"free" labor is clear from Victorian discussions of the aftermath of abolition on the economic viability of the British sugar colonies in the Caribbean. As an article in *The Times* of January 6, 1848 reveals, the wealthy middle-class readers of that newspaper were being deliberately encouraged to see a connection between the viability of Jamaica as a producer of salable sugar and the abolition of slavery elsewhere in the globe – especially among Jamaica's competitors such as Cuba, which was still practicing slavery in 1848 and thereby undercutting Jamaican prices. As *The Times* declared, "We have, then, two objects before us which are generally and reasonably sought by the community at large. We wish for a commodity at its natural price, and we wish to extinguish a certain method of producing this commodity." Cited in Deirdre David, *Rule Britannia: Women, Empire, and Victorian Writing* (Ithaca and London: Cornell University Press, 1995), pp. 13–14.

10 "Our national existence is involved in the well-doing of our manufacturers. If our readers . . . should ask, . . . To what are we indebted for this commerce? – we answer, in the name of every manufacturer and merchant of the kingdom – The *cheapness* alone of our manufactures. Are we asked, How is this trade protected, and by what means can it be enlarged? The reply still is, By the *cheapness* of our manufactures. Is it inquired how this mighty industry, upon which depends the comfort and existence of the whole empire, can be torn from us? – we rejoin, Only by the *greater cheapness of the manufactures of another country*." Richard Cobden, *The Political Writings of Richard Cobden*, vol. 1 (London: Fisher Unwin, 1903; reprinted New York: Kraus, 1969), p. 219.

11 "National interest" is a difficult animal to pin down at this time. One of the things which the "national efficiency" movement of the turn of the century undoubtedly did, though, was to accelerate the development of a recognizably modern form of British nationalism. See the Conclusion for a further discussion of this issue.

12 Ronald Robinson and John Gallagher, *Africa and the Victorians* (New York: St. Martin's, 1967), pp. 4–29.

13 On Disraeli's use of "imperialism," see C. C. Eldridge, *England's Mission: the Imperial Idea in the Age of Gladstone and Disraeli, 1868–1880* (Chapel Hill: University of North Carolina Press, 1973), p. xv. For a useful historical discussion of the bureaucratic reorganization of European armies in the nineteenth and early twentieth centuries, see Dandeker, *Surveillance, Power, and Modernity*, pp. 66–109.

14 See Stanley Weintraub on the resignation of Lord Hardinge and his replacement as Commander-in-Chief by the Queen's cousin, the Duke of Cambridge, who barely escaped himself from this job with his royal prestige intact. *Victoria: an Intimate Biography* (New York: Dutton, 1987), p. 243. On Crimea, see Olive Anderson, *A Liberal State at War* (London: Macmillan; New York: St. Martin's, 1967).

15 Perkin makes the point that the new civil service exam which was required of most would-be employees of the British government after 1870 was

initially devised to favor the products of the major public schools and Oxbridge rather than the broad middle class. By designing the reform bill this way, its sponsors insured its eventual passage through an initially reluctant House of Lords and through a House of Commons still dominated by the landed class. Perkin, *Rise of Professional Society*, p. 90. In those early days, knowing one's Horace was the best route to a civil service appointment. Of course, the British national government remained extremely small throughout the nineteenth century. Roberts, citing statistics from *The Times* of 1846, notes that the French government of that day had 932,000 civilian employees. This compares with a total of 21,305 civilian officials employed by the British government in 1833, a figure which had changed very little by 1846. Roberts, *Victorian Origins*, pp. 13–14. On the impact of the Northcote–Trevelyan Report of 1854 on Colonial Office reform, see Brian L. Blakeley, *The Colonial Office: 1868–1892* (Durham, NC: Duke University Press, 1972), pp. 3–19.

16  J. R. Seeley, *The Expansion of England* (London: Macmillan, 1888), p. 8.

17  Benjamin Disraeli, "Crystal Palace Speech" (June 24, 1872), in *Selected Speeches*, ed. T. E. Kebbel (London: Longmans, Green and Co., 1882), p. 534.

18  Searle, *Quest for National Efficiency*, p. 54.

19  Perkin, *Rise of Professional Society*, p. 155.

20  Ibid.

21  Semmel, *Imperialism and Social Reform*, pp. 64–82.

22  Blakeley, *Colonial Office*, p. 90.

23  George Chesney's "Battle of Dorking" frightened many of his English readers, because it depicted an invasion of the English homeland and was published in the wake of Germany's defeat of France.

24  Paul Kennedy, *The Rise and Fall of the Great Powers: Economic Change and Military Conflict from 1500 to 2000* (New York: Random House, 1987), pp. 151–8.

25  For the best overall discussion of this, see Searle, *Quest for National Efficiency*. The best-known voices in the 1880s warning of imperial decline were James Anthony Froude in *Oceana* (New York: Scribner, 1886), and J. R. Seeley.

26  See Thomas Pakenham's discussion of this episode in *The Scramble for Africa, 1876–1912*, pp. 218–238.

27  The works I am referring to include J. A. Hobson, *Imperialism: A Study* (London: George Allen and Unwin, 1938 [1902]), V. I. Lenin, *Imperialism, the Highest Stage of Capitalism, Collected Works*, vol. 22 (London: Lawrence and Wishart, n.d.), pp. 185–304 and Joseph Schumpeter, *Imperialism*, trans. Heinz Norden (New York: Meridian, 1955 [1920]). For a more detailed discussion of the debate on the motives driving imperial expansion at the turn of the century than I have space for here, see my *Desire and Contradiction: Imperial Visions and Domestic Debates in Victorian Literature* (Manchester: Manchester University Press, 1990), pp. 113–127.

28  Perkin, *Rise of Professional Society*, p. 2.

29 On Cromer's "knowing" the "Oriental" as a member of a "subject race," see Edward Said, *Orientalism* (New York: Vintage, 1979), especially pp. 36–49. In the wake of Foucault's work, there has been an explosion of literature on the topic of the construction of the "object" of knowledge which is designed to confirm the expertise of the knowing "subject." Said's *Orientalism* is perhaps the best-known treatment of this theme in colonial discourse, and certainly Said's discussion of European "redemptive fantasies" about the East underlines the important point that Europe – especially in the nineteenth century – came to conceive of the work of empire as an almost inexhaustible project of moral reform. For a more recent study of how the institutional structure of the modern professions contributes to the self-interested "discovery" of new objects of knowledge, see Christopher Lasch, *The True and Only Heaven: Progress and Its Critics* (New York and London: Norton, 1991).

30 Hannah Arendt, *The Origins of Totalitarianism* (New York: Harcourt Brace and Co., 1958), p. 212.

31 Ibid., p. 216.

32 Robinson and Gallagher, *Africa and the Victorians*, p. 60.

33 Joseph Conrad, *Heart of Darkness* (New York: Norton, 1988), p. 10.

34 Evelyn Baring, Earl of Cromer, *Political and Literary Essays, 1908–1913*, vol. I (London: Macmillan, 1913), p. 5.

35 Ibid., vol. I, p. 12.

36 Ibid., vol. III, p. 10.

37 Arendt, *Origins of Totalitarianism*, p. 215.

38 Ibid., p. 213.

39 Valerie Pakenham, *Out in the Noonday Sun: Edwardians in the Tropics* (New York: Random House, 1985), p. 50.

40 See especially the essay "What is Noble" in *Beyond Good and Evil*, trans. Walter Kauffmann (New York: Random House, 1966), pp. 199–237.

41 John Kucich, *Repression in Victorian Fiction* (Berkeley: University of California Press, 1987), p. 23. This aspect of the self-abnegating bureaucratic ideal – its capacity to liberate erotic fantasy of the self-negating sort – is discussed in greater detail in Chapters 3 and 5.

42 In his more autobiographical writings such as *Modern Egypt*, Cromer generally depicts himself as a modest but right-thinking higher-up at the center of grand events, one whose role is largely invisible to both the Egyptian and British public. See Chapter 4.

43 Charlotte Brontë, *Jane Eyre* (New York and London: Norton, 1987), p. 60.

44 Lewis Wurgaft, *The Imperial Imagination: Magic and Myth in Kipling's India* (Middletown, CT: Wesleyan University Press, 1983), p. 35.

45 Cited in Wurgaft, p. 37.

46 See Kathryn Tidrick's discussion of this issue in *Empire and the English Character* (London: I. B. Tauris and Co., 1992), pp. 6–47. It is important to note, however, that India was one of the places in the British Empire in which British rule was almost never indirect.

47 Ibid., p. 209.

48 Kathryne S. McDorman, "Two Views of Empire: Margery Perham and Joyce Cary Analyze the Dual Mandate Policy," *Research Studies* 50 (September/December 1983), pp. 153–160.

49 Lord Frederick Lugard, *The Dual Mandate in British Tropical Africa* (London: Archon, 1965 [1922]), p. 58.

50 Tidrick, *Empire and the English Character*, pp. 196–197. As we will discuss in Chapter 6, Lugard's system of Indirect Rule in Nigeria came under a great deal of criticism for institutionalizing and reinforcing the political power of the reactionary Emirs in Northern Nigeria. Lugard's successor, Hugh Clifford, who admired Lugard before he succeeded him as Governor-General of Nigeria, eventually denounced Lugard's system for perpetuating in Nigeria "the medieval conditions which at present prevail." Quoted in Valerie Pakenham, *Out in the Noonday Sun*, p. 42.

51 Probably the most notorious instances of this are to be found in the tricks which Henry M. Stanley was known to play on African chiefs in the Congo in order to arrange treaties highly favorable to his railroad project. The American George Washington Williams detailed Stanley's techniques in his famous "Open Letter" to King Leopold of Belgium in 1890: "All the sleight-of-hand tricks had been carefully rehearsed, and he [Stanley] was now ready for his work. A number of electric batteries had been purchased in London, and when attached to the arm under the coat, communicated with a band of ribbon which passed over the palm of the white brother's hand, and when he gave the black brother a cordial grasp of the hand the black brother was greatly surprised to find his white brother so strong, that he nearly knocked him off his feet in giving him the hand of fellowship. When the native inquired about the disparity of strength between himself and his white brother, he was told that the white man could pull up trees and perform the most prodigious feats of strength. Next came the lens act. The white brother took from his pocket a cigar, carelessly bit off the end, held up his glass to the sun and complaisantly smoked his cigar to the great amazement and terror of his black brother. The white man explained his intimate relation to the sun, and declared that if he were to request him to burn up his black brother's village it would be done. The third act was the gun trick. The white man took a percussion cap gun, tore the end of the paper which held the powder to the bullet, and poured the powder and paper into the gun, at the same time slipping the bullet into the sleeve of the left arm. A cap was placed upon the nipple of the gun, and the black brother was implored to step off ten yards and shoot at his white brother to demonstrate his statements that he was a spirit, and, therefore, could not be killed. After much begging the black brother aims the gun at his white brother, pulls the trigger, the gun is discharged, the white man stoops . . . and takes the bullet from his shoe!" George Washington Williams, "Open Letter," quoted in Conrad, *Heart of Darkness*, pp. 104–105.

52 D. H. Lawrence, Introduction to "Multatuli" (Edward Douwes Dekker), *Max Havelaar, Or the Coffee Auctions of the Dutch Trading Company*, trans. Roy Edwards (Amherst: University of Massachusetts Press, 1982), p. 11.

53 For a discussion of Holland's central role in the European economic order of the seventeenth century, see Immanuel Wallerstein, *The Modern World-System*, vol. 1 (New York: Academic Press, 1974), especially pp. 224–357.

### 2 WHY AFRICA NEEDS EUROPE: FROM LIVINGSTONE TO STANLEY

1 Thomas Pakenham, *Scramble for Africa*, p. 20.

2 The reason is twofold: if the project is to be sold to Africans, they must be encouraged to see alternatives to the sale of human beings; if the project is to be sold to the most influential sectors of the British public (the intended audience for the book), this public must be promised a vast potential market for British goods – especially Manchester cloth. On the reconceptualization of Africa as a market, see Mary Louise Pratt, *Imperial Eyes: Travel Writing and Transculturation* (London and New York: Routledge, 1992), p. 69. On the "imperialism of humanitarianism," see Thornton, *Imperial Idea*, p. 15.

3 For a summary of early British commercial and exploratory missions in Sub-Saharan Africa, see Judith Blow Williams, *British Commercial Policy and Trade Expansion, 1750–1850* (Oxford: Clarendon Press, 1972), pp. 94–114. On the abolitionist movement and the penetration of Africa, see Patrick Brantlinger, "Victorians and Africans: the Genealogy of the Myth of the Dark Continent," in *"Race," Writing, and Difference*, ed. Henry Louis Gates (Chicago and London: University of Chicago Press, 1986), pp. 185–222 and Howard Temperley, *British Antislavery, 1833–1870* (London: Longman, 1972). The most interesting and inclusive contemporary reading of early European African travelogues is contained in Mary Louise Pratt's *Imperial Eyes*. See also J. M. Coetzee, *White Writing* (New Haven and London: Yale University Press, 1988). The argument that Britain's interest in Tropical Africa was primarily economic is made by J. Forbes Monro in his *Britain in Tropical Africa, 1880–1960* (London: Macmillan, 1984). But Monro identifies this "neo-mercantilist" official attitude with the late nineteenth and early twentieth centuries: "Britain acquired colonial possessions in Tropical Africa for essentially defensive reasons: to ensure, in the face of neo-mercantilist tendencies of other European states, that some parts of the African continent would remain open to British trade and investment" (p. 19).

4 Brantlinger, "Victorians and Africans", p. 195.

5 Dorothy O. Helly contends that Horace Waller, Livingstone's friend and the editor of his posthumously published *Last Journals*, was as responsible as his rival Stanley for popularizing Livingstone the courageous abolitionist. Helly, *Livingstone's Legacy: Horace Waller and Victorian Mythmaking* (Athens, OH and London: Ohio University Press, 1987).

6 Tim Youngs, " 'My Footsteps on these Pages': the Inscription of Self and 'Race' in H. M. Stanley's *How I Found Livingstone*," *Prose Studies*, Spring 1990, p. 236.

7 Ibid., p. 239.

8 On this transition, see Philip D. Curtin, *The Image of Africa: British Ideas and Action, 1780–1850* (London: Macmillan, 1965), p. vi.

9 Brantlinger notes that both books were bestsellers: Livingstone's book sold 70,000 copies within a few months, eventually going to three editions; Stanley's sold over 140,000. Brantlinger, "Victorians and Africans," p. 195.

10 I do not mean to overstate this. The narrative is certainly organized around a presumption of designed plot: we readers are largely assumed to know that Livingstone undertakes his journey to Loanda in the interest of scientific and geographic exploration, missionary activity, and abolition. But it differs from Stanley's travelogue in that the narrative lacks many of the overt markers of destination that Stanley's book has in abundance.

11 On the differences between these two travel genres, see Pratt, *Imperial Eyes*, pp. 7 and 86–88.

12 Ibid., pp. 60–65 and 69–85.

13 Helly, *Livingstone's Legacy*, pp. 5–6. Other Victorian explorers like Sir Richard Burton, who could be vociferously critical of the sentimentality of the Victorian middle class, did attempt such a "rereading" of slavery, at least in Arabia. Burton's defense of what he called the "mild" institution of Arab slavery in his *Pilgrimage to El-Medinah and Mecca* (1856), though, is a form of overstatement in its own right: laying disproportionate emphasis on the serendipitous possibility (much greater, it seems, in Arab lands than in, say, South Carolina in the nineteenth century) of slaves using their connections with an important house as a means of upward social mobility. See my "Playing the Muslim: Sir Richard Burton's *Pilgrimage* and Negative Cultural Identity," in *Borders of Culture, Margins of Identity* (New Orleans: *Xavier Review* Press, 1994), pp. 85–94.

14 David Livingstone, *Missionary Travels and Researches in South Africa* (New York: Harper, 1858), p. 164. Hereafter: "Livingstone."

15 On reciprocity in the colonial sphere, see Peter Hulme, *Colonial Encounters* (Cambridge: Cambridge University Press, 1987).

16 David Livingstone, *Dr. Livingstone's Cambridge Lectures* (Cambridge: Deighton, Bell and Co., 1858), p. 21.

17 The fervent belief that markets grow "naturally" without having to be created is perhaps understandable in a representative of Manchester textile interests – the chief industry of the so-called "First Industrial Revolution" in Britain. Manchester's cloth did in fact displace indigenously-made (but more expensive) cloth rather effortlessly in a great many markets around the world, but, of course, this was largely because the market for cloth has existed everywhere from time immemorial. The same may be said of the market for weapons. By contrast, the typical products of a later stage of the Industrial Revolution (coal, steel, railway rolling stock, and so forth) often

did not address needs that were self-evident to the people to whom they were to be sold: the market for such goods needed to be deliberately created in most parts of the non-industrialized world or, as in the case of the Indian Railway, imposed on a subject population by the imperial government and paid for by forced taxation. See E. J. Hobsbawm, *Industry and Empire* (New York: Penguin, 1981), pp. 56–78.

18 As Robinson and Gallagher note, the "official view" of Africa within the Colonial and Foreign Office bureaucracies until well into the 1880s was that Africa was not going to repay colonial or imperial efforts. Robinson and Gallagher, *Africa and the Victorians*, pp. 16–17.

19 Ibid., p. 30.

20 The self-enclosure of Euro-American travel discourse has been much discussed recently, especially in the wake of the publication of Edward Said's *Orientalism* in 1978. In his recent book, Tim Youngs incisively highlights the way in which British travel discourse on Africa is grounded in "domestic" anxieties about social class: "what travellers describe in Africa is mainly Britain . . . the portrayal of the wilderness contains an apprehension of the city . . . accounts of feudal systems in Africa constitute a commentary on the changes in British society . . . that the traveller's report on his or her relation to companions and to Africans is a displacement of or compensation for anxieties about one's position in the British class system." *Travellers in Africa: British Travelogues, 1850–1900* (Manchester: Manchester University Press, 1994), p. 6.

21 Thomas Pakenham, *Scramble for Africa*, pp. 316–334.

22 Henry M. Stanley, *Through the Dark Continent*, vol. 1 (New York: Dover, 1988 [1878]), p. 38. All other references to this work are preceded by "Stanley"; volume and page numbers are indicated in parentheses hereafter.

23 Martin Green discusses the dissociation of capitalist business values from "heroic" values in Victorian domestic culture in his *Dreams of Adventure, Deeds of Empire* (New York: Basic Books, 1979), pp. 15–27. It is worth noting that Stanley uses the proprietorial phrase "my *Wangwana*" throughout this text without remarking on its oxymoronic connotations: "my freemen."

24 "From the details furnished in this and the two preceding chapters, a tolerably correct idea may be gained by the intending traveller, trader, or missionary in these lands, of the proper method of organization, as well as the quality and nature of the men whom he will lead, the manner of preparation and the proportion of articles to be purchased. In the Appendix will be found the price list and names, which will afford a safe guide." Stanley, vol. 1, p. 87.

25 Renato Rosaldo, "Imperialist Nostalgia," *Representations* 26 (Spring 1989), pp. 107–122.

26 Stanley seems to have been particularly impressed by the natural abundance of Uganda. His discussion of his journey through Mtesa's kingdom is punctuated by numerous lyrical celebrations of the richness of Africa's land and the beauty of African bodies nurtured on this land. For instance, in

speaking of the people of Uganda: "Their very features seem to proclaim, 'We live in a land of butter and wine and fulness, milk and honey, fat meads and valleys.' The vigour of the soil, which knows no Sabbath, appears to be infused into their veins. Their beaming lustrous eyes – restless and quick-glancing – seem to have caught rays of the sun. Their bronze-coloured bodies, velvety smooth and unctuous with butter, their swelling sinews, the tuberose muscles of the flanks and arms, reveal the hot lusty life which animates them." Of course, this "Eden" is ruled by a benevolent "Eve" – Mtesa – whose laudable "curiosity" about European ways is read by Stanley as a sign of the incompleteness which only repletion – paradoxically – can generate. See Stanley, vol. 1, p. 381. Stanley's narrative, like the exploration narratives of such famous Victorian explorers as Speke, Burton, Cameron, and Grant and the missionary narratives of Livingstone and others, constitutes a discourse on the "problems" of Africa, since so much of this writing is taken up with detailing and suggesting solutions to the vexing problems of persistent "savagery," geographic isolation, economic "backwardness," and political Balkanization these explorers see all around themselves in Africa (or precipitate by their presence).

27 "The grand redeeming feature of Mtesa, though founded only on self-interest, is his admiration for white men." *Stanley*, vol. 1, p. 318.

28 Frank McLynn, *Stanley* (London: Constable, 1989), p. 315.

29 See John Bierman, *Dark Safari: The Life Behind the Legend of Henry Morton Stanley* (New York: Knopf, 1990), pp. 192–195 and 268–269 and Thomas Pakenham, *Scramble for Africa*, p. 319.

30 See Karl Marx, *Capital*, vol. 1, ed. Frederick Engels, trans. Samuel Moore and Edward Aveling (New York: International Publishers, 1967 [1867]), especially pp. 71–83.

31 Henry M. Stanley, *The Congo and the Founding of Its Free State* (New York: Harper and Bros., 1885), pp. 406–407.

3 KIPLING'S "LAW" AND THE DIVISION OF BUREAUCRATIC LABOR

1 Philip Mason, *Kipling: the Glass, the Shadow, and the Fire* (New York: Harper, 1975), pp. 48–49.

2 Green, *Dreams of Adventure*, p. 283. In his important study, John McClure argues that Kipling "seems to have modelled his early style on the modes of discourse characteristic of the imperial service elite." John A. McClure, *Kipling and Conrad: the Colonial Fiction* (Cambridge, MA: Harvard University Press, 1981), p. 6. The volume *The Day's Work*, published in 1898, contains perhaps the best-known stories of this sort, but this remained a preoccupation of Kipling's throughout his career.

3 Rudyard Kipling, "The Conversion of Aurelian McGoggin," in *Plain Tales from the Hills* (New York: Charles Scribners, 1916), pp. 127–128.

4 See my argument about Conrad's *Nostromo* in Chapter 4.

5 On *Kim* as a novel which deliberately invests imperial work with the values

associated conventionally with "play," see my *Desire and Contradiction*, pp. 42–50.

6 C. S. Lewis, "Kipling's World," in *Kipling and the Critics*, ed. Elliot L. Gilbert (London: Peter Owen, 1966), pp. 99–117.

7 On division of labor as the "glue" of industrial social order, see especially E. P. Thompson, "Time, Work-Discipline, and Industrial Capitalism," *Past and Present* 38 (1967), pp. 56–96; Harry Braverman, "Capitalism and the Division of Labor," in *Classes, Power, and Conflict*, eds. Anthony Giddens and David Held (Berkeley: University of California Press, 1982), pp. 148–156; and Weber, *Economy and Society*, pp. 115–140.

8 See Bernard S. Cohn, "Representing Authority in Victorian India," in *The Invention of Tradition*, ed. E. J. Hobsbawm and Terence Ranger (New York and Cambridge: Cambridge University Press, 1983), pp. 165–210.

9 The Kipling of *The Day's Work* stories, and, above all, *Kim*. For a discussion of Kipling as an apostle of work, see Lewis, "Kipling's World".

10 Rudyard Kipling, "At the End of the Passage," in *In the Vernacular: The English in India*, ed. Randall Jarrell (Gloucester, MA: Peter Smith, 1970), p. 78. Hereafter: "Passage."

11 Kipling even uses the now familiar mechanical metaphor "cog" in his story "William the Conqueror" from *The Day's Work* (1898), a story in which one of the main character's successors is described as "another cog in the machinery." Rudyard Kipling, "William the Conqueror," *The Day's Work*, *The Collected Works of Rudyard Kipling* (New York: AMS, 1970), vol. VI, p. 175. Kipling's work – especially in this volume – is remarkable for the fantasy of bureaucratic rationality and infinite substitutability in which it is drenched. While I agree up to a point with John McClure's claim that Kipling "modelled his early style on the modes of discourse characteristic of the imperial service elite," Kipling goes beyond simply representing elaborate fantasies of bureaucratic rationality to actually suggest that the language of "official" order serves the goal of professional self-protection.

12 The homosocial bonding in *The Light That Failed* is given a literal resolution when Kipling's blind protagonist Dick Heldar, unable to establish a suitable dependency relationship with the inaccessible Maisie, finds it at the end of his "passage," on the battlefield of the Sudan, his head cradled in the arms of his male "mother" Torpenhow; male bonding in *Stalky and Co.*, on the other hand, is accomplished through the rituals of insult and rough practical joking which, like the insult-trading of the English officials in "At the End of the Passage," strain the bonds of community in the act of affirming them.

13 Hummil's attraction to death suggests comparison with Freud's tentative reformulation of his own therapeutic project in *Beyond the Pleasure Principle* (Freud for obvious professional reasons never gets to the point of rejecting the therapeutic mission of psychoanalysis outright). If, as Freud claims in that essay, "the aim of all life is death," then "life" must be something like a "disease" inevitably resulting in "death." If so, then the role of therapy cannot be "cure," for death can be the only cure for the disease that is life.

This insight threatens to dismantle, needless to say, the binary logic of the therapeutic project for psychoanalysis: the founding distinction between "disease" and "health" must be rejected, for if "life" is coextensive with "disease," there can be no such thing as "health" in the conventional sense. Instead, Freud introduces an immanentist conception – the "organism must find its own route to death" – in order to preserve some role for the professional expert in treating the "ill," despite the fact that the "ill" have become, by his own implicit admission, identical with all who live. Sigmund Freud, *Beyond the Pleasure Principle*, trans. James Strachey (New York: Norton, 1961).

14 Green, *Dreams of Adventure*, pp. 264–296.

15 This emerges from Robert Caserio's reading of *The Light That Failed*. "Kipling in the Light of Failure," in *Rudyard Kipling*, ed. Harold Bloom (New York: Chelsea House, 1987), pp. 117–144.

16 The "sacrifice" of the "signified." The classic statement of this, of course, is to be found in Jacques Lacan's *écrits*. See "The Agency of the Letter in the Unconscious or Reason since Freud," in *écrits: A Selection*, trans. Alan Sheridan (New York and London: Norton, 1977), pp. 146–178.

17 J. A. Mangan, "Social Darwinism and Upper-Class Education in Late Victorian England," in *Manliness and Morality: Middle-Class Masculinity in Britain and America, 1800–1940*, eds. J. A. Mangan and James Walvin (Manchester: Manchester University Press, 1987), p. 139.

18 Rudyard Kipling, *The Complete Stalky and Co.* (London: Macmillan, 1929), p. 65. The first of these stories were published under this title in 1899. Hereafter: "*Stalky*."

19 Noel Annan, "Kipling's Place in the History of Ideas," in *Kipling's Mind and Art*, ed. Andrew Rutherford (London: Oliver and Boyd, 1964), p. 102 and Shamsul Islam, *Kipling's "Law": A Study of His Philosophy of Life* (London: Macmillan, 1975), p. 37. Kipling's use of "The Law" seems to owe something to his familiarity with St. Paul's Epistle to the Romans, quoted at the head of this chapter. "The Law" in St. Paul serves a purpose analogous to that which it serves in Kipling's fiction: an inference, a systemic intention, which organizes and systematizes what comes to be seen as manifest evidence of law-abiding activity, "The Law" is a putative "intention," inaccessible to direct observation, known only by its effects, but implicitly powerful and authoritative for precisely that reason.

20 Islam, *Kipling's "Law"*, p. 41

21 Ibid., p. 45.

22 Calling the system "nature" at this point would be reductive: while encouraging us to conceive of the jungle life depicted here as "Edenic" in some limited sense, this identification would preclude an allegorical reading of the text in which the "animals" could be identified with "humans" and their behavior taken as a parable of human social behavior. This is the problem that limits James Harrison's otherwise fine reading of the text. See Harrison, "Kipling's Jungle Eden," in *Critical Essays on Rudyard Kipling*, ed.

Harold Orel (Boston: G. K. Hall, 1989), pp. 77–92. While there is no question that *The Jungle Books* assert an antagonistic relationship between jungle society and human society (although not, importantly, between the jungle and British imperial administration), overstressing this dichotomy disables the allegorical reading which the text, nonetheless, also seems to encourage.

23 Kant, *Prolegomena to any Future Metaphysics That Will Be Able to Present Itself As a Science*, trans. Peter G. Lucas (Manchester: Manchester University Press, 1953).

24 Rudyard Kipling, *The Jungle Books* (London: Penguin, 1987 [1894–1895]), p. 14. Hereafter: "*Jungle*."

25 Mason traces all of Kipling's toying with rebellion to a desire to restore equipoise and affirm law. Mason, *Kipling*, p. 45. It can hardly be simply an accident that the emphasis on the autonomy of art found in late-Victorian Aestheticism overlaps historically with Victorian anthropology's fascination with totemism. Kipling's own ancestral ties to late-Victorian aestheticism are solid: his father, a well-known artist, illustrated the first edition of the first *Jungle Book*; his maternal uncle was David Burne-Jones the Pre-Raphaelite painter.

26 Martin Green, in a recent book, notes how the preoccupation of adventure fiction with vengeance is consonant with its concern with law: he argues that violence in adventure fiction is often exercised in the interest of rule-governed order. Martin Green, *Seven Types of Adventure Tale* (University Park, PA: Pennsylvania State University Press, 1991), pp. 123–144.

### 4 CROMER, GORDON, CONRAD AND THE PROBLEM OF IMPERIAL CHARACTER

1 Charles Gordon, *Khartoum Journal*, ed. Lord Elton (New York: Vanguard, 1961).

2 The telegraph, which began to be widely used for diplomatic communication only in the 1870s, was an item of modern technology which would seem to promise the eventual obsolescence of the "responsibility system" by making daily supervision from the Foreign Office of all agents in the field an actual possibility for the first time in history. In fact, however, the "responsibility system" would have a long and contentious career in both theory and fact well into the twentieth century.

3 Tidrick, *Empire and the English Character*, p. 16.

4 The Earl of Cromer, *Modern Egypt* (New York: Macmillan, 1908), vol. 1, p. 571.

5 Ibid., vol. 1, p. 428.

6 Ibid., vol. 1, p. 431.

7 Ibid., vol. 1, p. 430.

8 Ibid., vol. 11, p. 10.

9 On the agency of "anonymous effects" in Darwin and Foucault, see Phillip

Barrish, "Accumulating Variation: Darwin's *On the Origin of Species* and Contemporary Literary and Cultural Theory," *Victorian Studies* 34.4 (Summer 1991), pp. 431–453.

10 Among the many contemporary exposés of the "Congo situation" perhaps the most influential was E. D. Morel's *History of the Congo Reform Movement,* eds. Wm. Roger Louis and Jean Stengers (Oxford: Clarendon Press, 1968). Mark Twain contributed a savagely satirical piece on the Congo with his *King Leopold's Soliloquy: A Defense of his Congo Rule* (Boston: The P.R. Warren Co., 1905). One should also mention Conrad's own "Congo Diary," in *Congo Diary and Other Uncollected Pieces,* ed. Zdzislaw Najder (New York: Doubleday, 1978). In a recent essay, Michael Levenson makes the claim that "after Kafka Conrad is our most searching critic of bureaucracy." "The Value of Facts in *Heart of Darkness,*" in Joseph Conrad, *Heart of Darkness,* ed. Robert Kimbrough, 3rd ed. (New York: Norton, 1988), p. 397.

11 A notable exception: Michael Levenson's "The Value of Facts in *Heart of Darkness.*" According to Levenson, "*Heart of Darkness* is a drama of officialdom" that juxtaposes the ruthless colonial bureaucrat – the Manager – against the "charismatic" rogue-agent Kurtz (p. 395). Where Levenson focuses insightfully on the role of Kurtz as "charismatic" figure, I am primarily interested here in Kurtz as a necessary fiction for Marlow the company man. Fredric Jameson's very provocative reading of Conrad is also a source of inspiration for this chapter. See Jameson on "rationalization" as the "instrumentalization of the world" in *The Political Unconscious* (Ithaca, NY: Cornell University Press, 1981), pp. 219–220.

12 Apparently Conrad himself acquired his piloting job in the Congo in 1890 much the way Marlow does: by putting an influential woman to work in his behalf and by being available at the moment his predecessor, Captain Johannes Freiesleben, is killed in Africa. Jeffrey Meyers, *Joseph Conrad: A Biography* (New York: Scribner's, 1991), p. 95.

13 Homi Bhabha discusses Conrad's use of ideological ambivalences within the context of the "yarn" as a containment strategy: "It is the ideal of English civil discourse that permits Conrad to entertain the ideological ambivalences that riddle his narratives. It is under its watchful eye that he allows the fraught text of late nineteenth-century imperialism to implode within the practices of early modernism. The devastating effects of such an encounter are not only contained in an (un)common yarn; they are concealed in the propriety of a civil 'lie' told to the Intended (the complicity of the customary?): 'The horror! The horror!' must not be repeated in the drawing-rooms of Europe." "Signs Taken for Wonders," in *"Race," Writing, and Difference,* ed. Henry Louis Gates, Jr. (Chicago: University of Chicago Press, 1986), p. 168.

14 On this transferential relationship, see my *Desire and Contradiction,* p. 85.

15 Irony in *Heart of Darkness* is a – by now – familiar Modernist strategy deployed to distance the narrator from the political implications of his own narrative project. However, my contention is that this distance is closed over

and over by Conrad, who, instead, estranges himself from his narrator Marlow. Although it might seem anomalous that the Manager sets out to remove Kurtz, his most profitable agent in the field, the novel suggests two plausible and linked reasons for this: 1) that the Manager is personally consumed with envy and fear that outweigh his allegiance to the profit motive that drives the Company, and 2) that the Manager knows that his claim that Kurtz procures ivory through "unsound methods" will find a receptive audience in higher bureaucratic circles of the company, given the evidence that Kurtz's "methods" may retard the company-sponsored spread of "civilization" (i.e. the brutal system of wage slavery described by Marlow in Part I) and, consequently, endanger the prospects for long-term profitability. Moreover, the book clearly implies that Marlow suspects the Manager of deliberately sinking the boat before his arrival, forcing a three-month delay while the boat is rebuilt, and then taking great satisfaction, once Marlow's party arrives at Kurtz's station, from the discovery that the delay has considerably weakened Kurtz.

16 These parallels are reinforced by formal symmetries between Marlow's descriptions of Kurtz as, say, disembodied voice, and the frame narrator's description of Marlow's "worn, hollow" face, flickering in the light of a match flame (p. 48). That Kurtz is well aware of the threat Marlow represents to his rule is underlined over and over again: it accounts for why Kurtz orders the attack on the boat; and accounts for the atmospherics in the jungle on the night of Kurtz's escape. When Marlow confronts the sick Kurtz, who had just crawled on all fours into the jungle to encourage the Africans to attack the whites, he quickly improvises a very satisfactory business arrangement which prevents this imminent massacre: implicitly agreeing to "assure" Kurtz's "reputation" in Europe ("Your success in Europe is assured in any case") in return for Kurtz's giving himself up to the Company (and to powerlessness and ultimate death). That Marlow chooses to speak about this confrontation as a quasi-metaphysical appeal to Kurtz in the name of the only thing Kurtz could recognize as "higher" than himself – his "reputation" – does not detract from the plausibility of this reading, as Marlow in this passage rather obviously congratulates himself for having fastened on a brilliantly practical solution to a vexing problem ("one gets sometimes such a flash of inspiration"). *Heart of Darkness*, pp. 64–65. Moreover, the form of Marlow's telling of this story enhances Conrad's point through the use of carefully symmetrical alternations of Kurtz's grandiose and unfocused ambitions cast in past tense verbs ("I had immense plans!") with Marlow's very concrete threats ("I will throttle you for good") formulated in future tense verbs.

17 "Although the almost oppressive force of Marlow's narrative leaves us with a quite accurate sense that there is no way out of the sovereign historical force of imperialism, and that it has the power of a system representing as well as speaking for everything within its dominion, Conrad shows us that what Marlow does is contingent, acted out for a set of like-minded British

hearers, and limited to that situation." Edward Said, *Culture and Imperialism* (New York: Alfred A. Knopf, 1994), p. 24.

18  See Padmini Mongia: "Once Marlow enters the narrative, Jim's limitations, which the opening highlights, are made small errors in an imperialist *Bildungsroman*, necessary to the full development of the hero who triumphs, finally, over himself." "Narrative Strategy and Imperialism in Conrad's *Lord Jim*," in *Studies in the Novel* 24.2 (Summer 1992), p. 181.

19  See Jameson's complaint about *Lord Jim* in *The Political Unconscious*, p. 264: "*Lord Jim* remains stubbornly deflected onto the problematic of the individual act, and puts over and over again to itself questions that cannot be answered."

20  Mongia is a good example of the former. The latter position is that of Zakia Pathak, Saswati Sengupta, and Sharmila Purkayastha in "The Prisonhouse of Orientalism," *Textual Practice* 5.2 (Summer 1992) pp. 211–216.

21  Morse Peckham, *Explanation and Power* (Minneapolis: University of Minnesota Press, 1979), p. 34.

22  Joseph Conrad, *Lord Jim* (New York: Signet, 1961 [1900]), p. 27. Hereafter: "*LJ*."

23  Peckham, *Explanation and Power*, p. 53.

24  I do not use the phrase "making Jim a man" loosely here. The novel both infantilizes and feminizes Jim in the beginning. Both strategies are brought together in the early description of Jim's pre-*Patna* view of the sea: Jim, as Conrad's narrator tells us, was "penetrated" by the "certitude of unbounded safety and peace that could be read on the silent aspect of nature like the certitude of fostering love upon the placid tenderness of a mother's face." *Lord Jim*, p. 19.

25  That is why the critic can justifiably argue, as I do here, that *Lord Jim* exposes Marlow to the reader's inferential reading process while reducing Jim to a cypher – a cypher, nonetheless, whose meaning seems to be filled in by Marlow's authoritative inferences.

26  "Is it sheer coincidence that a state of exile – literal or metaphoric – often accompanies an interest in the primitive? I think not. The state of exile is an informing fact and a fundamental condition. It is the most literal sign – but only the most literal – of the site . . . of transcendental homelessness." Marianna Torgovnick, *Gone Primitive: Savage Intellects, Modern Lives* (Chicago: University of Chicago Press, 1990), p. 188.

27  "The Prisonhouse of Orientalism," p. 212.

28  This is why, finally, the common critical claim that Conrad was a "pessimist" is misleading. "Pessimistic" he may have been, but not because he was adrift on an existential sea. On the contrary, he was a person who seemed to combine the marine officer's concern with the "right way" of conduct with a tragic insight into the fact that codes of conduct are not anchored in and therefore sanctioned by metaphysical reality: a view which "desacralizes" both "The Real" (in Jameson's sense: that which lies outside of narrative) and narrative itself, which develops a "sacred" or, at least, "destined"

quality in such well-known English novels as, for instance, *Jane Eyre*. Here, the main character's seemingly "aimless" wanderings are retrospectively "intentionalized" when they are organized into a narrative in which she is assigned (and eventually accepts) the place of subject after St. John Rivers tells her her own story near the end of the novel. See *Jane Eyre*, pp. 334–336. On the larger theoretical issues involved, see also Peter Brooks, *Reading for the Plot: Design and Intention in Narrative* (New York: A.A. Knopf, 1984).

29 Lyotard identifies "science" as perpetually in conflict with "narrative." Thus, he distinguishes sciences he calls "modern" from sciences he calls "postmodern" according to how they legitimate or fail to legitimate themselves. "I will use the term modern to designate any science that legitimates itself with reference to a metadiscourse of this kind making an explicit appeal to some grand narrative, such as the dialectics of Spirit, the hermeneutics of meaning, the emancipation of the rational or working subject, or the creation of wealth . . . [new paragraph] Simplifying to the extreme, I define postmodern as incredulity toward metanarratives. This incredulity is undoubtedly a product of progress in the sciences: but that progress in turn presupposes it." Jean-François Lyotard, *The Postmodern Condition: A Report on Knowledge*, trans. Geoff Bennington and Brian Massumi (Minneapolis: University of Minnesota Press, 1979), pp. xxiii and xxiv.

30 Joseph Conrad, *Nostromo* (New York: Bantam, 1989 [1904]), p. 98.

31 Jameson's "History" (in *The Political Unconscious*).

32 Jeremy Hawthorn, *Joseph Conrad: Language and Fictional Self-Consciousness* (Lincoln, NE: University of Nebraska Press, 1979), p. 60.


5   T. E. LAWRENCE AND THE EROTICS OF IMPERIAL DISCIPLINE

1 A. P. Foulkes, *Literature and Propaganda* (London and New York: Methuen, 1983).

2 It cannot be surprising, then, that the book opens with a listing of the major English figures involved in organizing the Arab Revolt, then concludes with the odd statement, "It would be impertinent in me to praise them." T. E. Lawrence, *Seven Pillars of Wisdom: A Triumph* (New York and London: Doubleday, 1991 [1935]), p. 24. Hereafter: "*SP*."

3 John E. Mack notes that Thomas always insisted that Lawrence collaborated willingly in the creation of his own legend. *A Prince of Our Disorder* (Boston: Little, Brown, 1976), p. 275.

4 Lawrence's complicated diplomatic machinations in the post-war period have sparked many heated debates. For one thing, Lawrence seems to have played an ambiguous role regarding Zionism. At a meeting of the Eastern Committee of the War Cabinet in October 1918, Lawrence called for a sovereign Syria and argued that Zionists would only be accepted by Arabs under British sovereignty: no independent Jewish state would be acceptable to the Arabs. Two months later, in December, 1918, Lawrence arranged a meeting between Feisal and Chaim Weizmann and helped draw up the

agreement between the two which stipulated that the Arabs would accept a Jewish state provided Britain fulfilled its pledge to grant independence to an Arab state as well. For another, Lawrence's continued support for the Hashemite dynasty became increasingly anachronistic in the post-war era. Lawrence used his influence to insure the installation of Hussein as king of the Hejaz, his son Feisal as king of the newly created state of Iraq, and his oldest son Abdullah as king of Transjordan (the latter two states were governed in actuality by Britain under League of Nations mandate until after World War II). Yet Feisal was given Iraq only because Lawrence was unable to get the British government to establish a Greater Syria, and Hussein's days as ruler in the Hejaz were numbered from as early as May 1919, when Ibn Saud's forces began their attacks. The only remaining Hashemite state – the modern Jordan – is still ruled by a descendant of Hussein who, despite Lawrence's efforts on behalf of his family in the immediate aftermath of World War I, enjoys relatively little influence within the Arab world today.

5  This is a matter of some dispute. For an account largely critical of Lawrence's role at these conferences, see Suleiman Mousa, *T. E. Lawrence: An Arab View*, trans. Albert Boutros (New York: Oxford University Press, 1966), pp. 212–256. The very term "mandate," which came into fashion with imperial leaders in the League of Nations era, captures the carefully designed ambiguity of Britain's self-conception perfectly: Britain herself accepts a solemn "duty" to manage territories ostensibly on their way to earning independence. These territories are ruled no longer for the antique pleasure of conquest but out of a paternal sense of "duty," with the ultimate goal of bringing the day of political independence closer. For more on this issue, see Chapter 6.

6  Lawrence explained his reasons for enlisting in the RAF under a pseudonym to George Bernard Shaw: many people enlist "because they haven't done well in the fight of daily living, and want to be spared the responsibility of ordering for themselves their homes and food and clothes and world – or even the intensity of their work." Cited in Mack, *A Prince of Our Disorder*, p. 322. For a discussion of the evidence that Lawrence was employed in intelligence-gathering for the Foreign Office in the months before the official beginning of the war in August 1914, see Philip Knightley and Colin Simpson, *The Secret Lives of Lawrence of Arabia* (New York: McGraw-Hill, 1969), pp. 44–58. Whatever claims one wishes to make about his official role in those early days, it is clear that Lawrence was anything but unknown within the military and Foreign Office bureaucracies before organizing the Arab Revolt. A protégé of David Hogarth's, he had already taken a position of "considerable influence" by 1914, and would refer to Generals Kitchener and Maxwell and to Winston Churchill ("Winny") in very familiar terms in his dispatches. Knightley and Simpson, p. 45. He was certainly a "subaltern" only in the sense that his official military rank was lieutenant.

7  Kathryn Tidrick identifies Lawrence as one of the chief exponents of

Indirect Rule: "To take an even more famous imperial hero, perhaps the most famous of all, it could be said of T. E. Lawrence that his whole life was a testimony to the fascination of the secret power of the will. In the desert, as his wartime dispatches show, he was entranced by the conviction that he was controlling the Arabs without their even realizing it; in his self-imposed obscurity after the war he busied himself secretly, though not too secretly, with pulling strings. His prescription for success in the desert – 'Wave a Sherif in front of you like a banner and hide your own mind and person' – could be taken as a motto for Indirect Rule." Tidrick, *Empire and the English Character*, p. 210.

8 Quoted in Jeremy Wilson, *Lawrence of Arabia* (New York: Macmillan, 1989), p. 194.

9 Perhaps the most controversial aspect of Lawrence's career has to do with the question of just how active a role he had in constructing Arab national consciousness. Mousa claims not only that Lawrence understated the role of Arab nationalist groups in Syria in constructing a nationalist ideology, but that Lawrence overstated his own military importance at the expense of important Arab leaders (most of Mousa's book is given over to making this argument). Dawn comes to the defense of Lawrence, attacking Mousa for relying too heavily on oral evidence (gathered mainly in the 1950s and 60s) "when it had been severely subjected to the usual effects of aging and the passing of time and to heavy pressure to distance oneself from the British as a result of the anti-Hashemite trend in Arab politics." C. Ernest Dawn, "The Influence of Lawrence on the Middle East," in *T. E. Lawrence: Soldier, Writer, Legend*, ed. Jeffrey Meyers (New York: St. Martin's, 1989), p. 78.

10 In his use of Arab clothing, Lawrence is closer to Doughty than to Burton. In fact, in his Introduction to *Travels in Arabia Deserta*, he cites Doughty as a predecessor whose donning of native clothing emphasized his "Englishness" rather than deracinated him, as Burton's practice of disguise did. Lawrence, "Introduction," Charles Doughty, *Travels in Arabia Deserta* (New York: Boni and Liveright, 1921), p. xx.

11 Said notes Lawrence's tendency to reduce Arab experience to his own experience on behalf of Arabia: "Whereas Aeschylus had represented Asia mourning its losses, and Nerval had espressed [sic] his disappointment in the Orient for not being more glamorous than he had wanted, Lawrence becomes both the mourning continent and a subjective consciousness expressing an almost cosmic disenchantment . . . Indeed what Lawrence presents to the reader is an unmediated expert power – the power to be, for a brief time, the Orient. All the events putatively ascribed to the historical Arab Revolt are reduced finally to Lawrence's experiences on its behalf." *Orientalism*, p. 243. Mack devotes a good deal of attention to Lawrence's early interest in medieval romances. Moreover, he sees Lawrence's overall political project – the imposition of Hashemite Bedouin rulers on the Arabs of the cities – as flawed precisely by his tendency to romanticize the Bedouin. Mack, *A Prince of Our Disorder*, pp. 208–209.

12  Kaja Silverman, *Male Subjectivity at the Margins* (New York: Routledge, 1992), p. 300.

13  Lawrence employed as personal servants the fun-loving lovers Farraj and Daud. Deciding to take them on initially because "they looked so young and clean," Lawrence indulged their sometimes annoying pranks, and eventually grew quite attached to both, although there is no evidence that his fondness ever took an overtly sexual form. Their attachment to each other created the occasion for a number of Lawrentian musings on the positive effects of homosexual bonding on military morale: "Such friendships often led to manly loves of a depth and force beyond our flesh-stupid conceit." *Seven Pillars*, p. 237. Neither survived the war, Daud dying at Azrak and the mortally wounded Farraj meeting his end at the hands of Lawrence himself who, in conformity with the battlefield code of the Arab Army, shot him in the head to spare him the tortures of an even more ghastly death at the hands of the vengeful Turks who were fast approaching. The whole scene of Farraj's death is heavily overdetermined, in fact, the atmosphere of homosocial mercy killing investing the scene with the meaning of an implicit sexual encounter. The episode begins when Lawrence and Farraj, having reconnoitered Turkish positions near Amman dressed as gypsy women, are forced to flee Turkish soldiers making sexual advances. In flight, Farraj is badly wounded by Turkish fire and Lawrence stops briefly to prepare to perform his duty to him. Then, in one of the most moving scenes in a book noted for its richly "novelistic" effects, Lawrence performs this mercy killing as a *Liebestod*, the details of Farraj's "scaly hand" and "grey shrinking face" working to humanize while distancing the comrade who is about to be dispatched to the land of the dead: "I knelt down beside him, holding my pistol near the ground by his head, so that he should not see my purpose; but he must have guessed it, for he opened his eyes, and clutched me with his harsh, scaly hand, the tiny hand of these unripe Nejd fellows. I waited a moment, and he said, 'Daud will be angry with you,' the old smile coming back so strangely to this grey shrinking face. I replied, 'salute him from me.' He returned the formal answer, 'God will give you peace,' and at last wearily closed his eyes." *Seven Pillars*, p. 517.

14  The term "homosocial" is not quite accurate here, since it defines a form of bonding based on the repression of homoerotic expression (and, indeed, "homosocial" groups seldom tolerate homoerotic expression). Lawrence, though, wants to have it both ways: his text argues that corps morale is fostered both by homoerotic bonding and by its repression or refusal.

15  See Lawrence's letter to Lionel Curtis comparing himself to his libidinous barracks fellows in the Army: "Physically, I can't do it: indeed I get in denial the gratification they get in indulgence." Quoted in Mack, 342. Lawrence's brother Arnold acknowledged that Lawrence had a tendency to develop intense friendships with men which substituted for sexual love relationships. Mack, p. 93.

16  Burton was probably the best-known Victorian celebrator of Bedouin valor.

17 One might also add that this definition conveniently allows Lawrence himself to occupy the identity of "the Arab."

18 Geoffrey Galt Harpham defines asceticism as a deliberate strategy for procuring imaginative gratification. As he claims, asceticism "in the loose sense . . . refers to any act of self-denial undertaken as a strategy of empowerment or gratification." Moreover, in Harpham's view, ascetic renunciation is the very ground for the experience of desire itself: "What ethics, literary criticism, and even psychoanalysis call desire is a speculative construct inferred from repression rather than an independent energy that exists prior to repression. Repression is not a fate befalling desire but a condition of desire itself, and of everything else in mental life. 'Desire' cannot be opposed to 'conscience' or to other regulatory agencies, for both the impulse and its opposition arise simultaneously at the origin of consciousness, and assume from the first the relational form thematized by asceticism as temptation." Geoffrey Galt Harpham, *The Ascetic Imperative in Culture and Criticism* (Chicago and London: University of Chicago Press, 1987), pp. xiii and 54.

19 Kaja Silverman, p. 306.

20 Lean's film treats this scene as precisely this kind of heroic recognition scene.

21 Knightley and Simpson raise legitimate questions about whether the Deraa rape actually occurred at all. Knightley and Simpson, pp. 241–248. That it is a scene of great fantasmatic power in the book can hardly be doubted, however.

22 Silverman's discussion of Lawrence's ability to deracinate himself, to find himself in the place of the Other, is relevant here. "That text [*Seven Pillars*] dramatizes the curious paradox whereby a white man, ostensibly working on behalf of imperial Britain, comes to assume the psychic coloration of the Arabs he seeks to organize." The indeterminacy that this oscillation occasions in the political allegiances of the text is, I think, starkly underlined in the Deraa episode. Silverman, *Male Subjectivity*, p. 299.

23 Silverman discusses Lawrence's masochism as an aspiration to power that works both through identifications with the Other and through leadership: "the double mimesis." Silverman, *Male Subjectivity*, pp. 316–317.

24 Mack, *A Prince of Our Disorder*, p. 176.

25 Before seeking anonymity in the 1920s, Lawrence was involved in two major events – the Versailles Peace Conference of 1919 and the Cairo Conference of 1921 – which leave the question of his ultimate political allegiances murky.

### 6   RESURRECTING INDIVIDUALISM: THE INTERWAR NOVEL OF IMPERIAL MANNERS

1 Tidrick, *Empire and the English Character*, p. 229.

2 John E. Flint, "Frederick Lugard: The Making of an Autocrat," in *African Proconsuls: European Governors in Africa*, eds. L. H. Gann and Peter Duignan (New York and London: Macmillan, 1978), pp. 294–299.

3 Quoted in ibid., p. 301.
4 Harry A. Gailey, "Sir Hugh Clifford (1866–1941)," in *African Proconsuls*, pp. 282–283.
5 Flint, "Frederick Lugard," p. 309.
6 The suspicion of educated Africans as actual or potential "troublemakers" seems to have dominated the upper echelons of the British colonial service down to the period of post-World War II decolonization.
7 Flint, "Frederick Lugard," p. 309.
8 For a history of this period, see Umar Badruddin, *The Indian National Movement*, trans. by Azizul Islam (Dhaka, Bangladesh: University Press, 1993).
9 This part of his life is covered in Bernard Crick's *George Orwell: A Life* (Boston: Little, Brown, 1980), pp. 76–103.
10 Bhabha, "Signs Taken for Wonders," p. 168. In a recent essay, Satya P. Mohanty urges the possibility of an epistemological stance she calls "post-positivist 'realism.'" While acknowledging the reality of cultural bias and, to a certain extent, the incommensurability of discourses, "postpositivist realism" nevertheless avoids the extreme skepticism of postmodernist relativism by acknowledging "the possibility of fallibility, self-correction, and improvement" within its own account. Satya P. Mohanty, "Colonial Legacies, Multicultural Futures: Relativism, Objectivity, and the Challenge of Otherness," *PMLA* 110.1 (January 1995), p. 115.
11 E. M. Forster, *A Passage to India* (New York: HBJ, 1984 [1924]), p. 87. Hereafter: "Forster."
12 The notion of "incommensurable" discourses is borrowed from Richard Rorty, *Philosophy and the Mirror of Nature* (Princeton: Princeton University Press, 1979), pp. 348–349.
13 See Alan Bishop's description of this period of Cary's career in *Gentleman Rider: A Life of Joyce Cary* (London: Michael Joseph, 1988), pp. 104–175. As Cary quickly discovered upon being assigned to Borgu as ADO in 1917, the immensity of his responsibilities made a mockery in practice of the theoretical ideal of Indirect Rule. Bishop, p. 148.
14 McDorman, "Two Views of Empire," p. 153.
15 This double attitude is especially clear in his essay "Policy for Aid," in which he discusses how Britain, in banning the Islamic practice of cutting off prisoners' hands as a punishment for theft, actually contributed to increasing criminality. As Cary says, "I think the charge [that the British were undermining religion and morality] was true. There *was* more theft. It was certainly true about crime in general. As soon as we stopped the slave raids, put down inter-tribal war and opened the roads to traders, court cases increased everywhere and prisons had to be enlarged." "Policy for Aid," in Joyce Cary, *Selected Essays*, ed. A. G. Bishop (New York: St. Martin's, 1976), p. 98.
16 The theoretical issue is important to post-structuralist theory. Jonathan Culler, for instance, discusses Derrida's notion of *différance* in terms of the

distinction between active and passive meanings of difference. As he says, "*Différance* thus designates both a 'passive' difference already in place as the condition of signification, and an act of differing which produces differences." Culler, *On Deconstruction: Theory and Criticism After Structuralism* (Ithaca, NY: Cornell University Press, 1982), p. 97.

17 Joyce Cary, *Mr. Johnson* (New York: New Directions, 1989 [1939]), p. 13. Hereafter "*MJ*."

18 Published in 1922, Lugard's *The Dual Mandate* is steeped in the evolutionary assumptions of late-Victorian culture. Thus, the project itself assumes that "primitive" tribal cultures can evolve because, like all prominent Victorian thinkers, Lugard assumes a single universal cultural continuum ranging from "the primitive" to "the civilized." What makes *The Dual Mandate* a recognizably modern text is the way it focuses the discussion of "improvement" almost wholly on the material basis of African life which, Lugard believes, it is the special duty of Britain to work toward improving. See especially "Conclusion," pp. 606–619.

19 The most influential discussion of colonialism in terms of European "Oedipal" models is Octave Mannoni's *Prospero and Caliban*, which, in the spirit of much European ethnographic literature, generalizes about "the African" from a particular experience among certain Africans – in Mannoni's case, the Malagasy. *Prospero and Caliban*, trans. Pamela Powesland (New York: Praeger, 1964). According to Mannoni, a European treats an objective position of dependence as a sign of inferiority while a Malagasy only feels inferior when "the bonds of dependence are in some way threatened" (p. 40). Fanon disputes the validity of Mannoni's ethnographic claims on the grounds that what Mannoni takes to be evidence of psychological and cultural differences is actually explainable as symptoms of the inequalities of power imposed by colonialism. Frantz Fanon, "The So-called Dependency Complex of Colonized Peoples," in *Black Skin, White Masks*, trans. Charles Lam Markmann (New York: Grove Press, 1967), pp. 83–108. One might argue that the works of Kipling – especially books such as *Stalky and Co.* – are really about the "dependency complex" of colonizing people, in that *Stalky* foregrounds the psychological importance to the main characters of negative recognition from the patriarchal "Head," who is anything but an absent, abstract figure in most of the stories of that collection.

20 The "natives" can hardly be characterized accurately as "unspoilt," for the bush pagans, of whom Bamu's family are the best representatives here, are presented as suspicious, close-minded, and interested only in "fleecing" people they call "strangers" – a depiction which hardly qualifies them for the conventional role of noble savages. Moreover, the Emir's fear of roads is rooted, ultimately, in nothing but his own political self-interest as well, his fear that the coming of strangers will corrode his power – as, of course, it does.

21 Like many of the Modernists of his generation, Cary is "primitivizing" the

"civilized." As Marianna Torgovnick reminds us, "the primitive does what we ask it to do." Moreover, in an era of postcolonial cultural hybridity (which *Mr. Johnson* attempts to imagine), it becomes practically impossible to isolate the "primitive" from the "modern." Torgovnick, pp. 9 and 38.

22 Dennis Hall, *Joyce Cary: A Reappraisal* (New York: St. Martin's, 1983), p. 45, argues that Johnson is depicted as both "benefactor" and "menace" to Nigerian society.

23 "The price of modernization is alienation. The anthropologist Stanley Diamond sees in the modernizing process a breakdown in the 'cultural integration' of what we call primitive societies, where traditionally an entire series of values – religious, economic, social, and magical – combine in the meaning of any single activity. To the extent that the individual in such a society serves several functions simultaneously – warrior, artisan, village elder, etc. – modernization limits the range of this participation through its inevitable division of labor. It also undermines such aspects of primitive or traditional society as the tolerance of deviance in culturally institutionalized forms, the celebration of the sacred and the natural in ritual, the respect for and direct engagement with the natural environment, and the right to socioeconomic support as a natural inheritance rather than as a privilege subject to the individual's value in terms of labor." David Spurr, *The Rhetoric of Empire* (Durham, NC: Duke University Press, 1993), pp. 73–74.

24 In "Shooting an Elephant," Orwell describes the British governor as "seemingly the leading actor of the piece, but in reality . . . only an absurd puppet pushed to and fro by the will of those . . . behind." *Inside the Whale and Other Essays* (London: Penguin, 1962), p. 95. As Jomo Kenyatta noted during his rebel days in Kenya, "The system of Government in Kenya is based on strict racial discrimination . . . The white man looks upon his own authority and prestige as of the greatest importance." Quoted in V. G. Kiernan, *The Lords of Humankind* (Boston: Little, Brown, 1969), p. 230.

25 George Orwell, *Burmese Days* (New York: HBJ, 1962 [1934]), pp. 68–69. Hereafter, "*BD*."

26 Kiernan, *Lords of Humankind*, p. 230.

27 Mason, *Kipling*, p. 49.

28 Ronald Hyam has an interesting discussion of how the British government began a deliberate policy of encouraging the immigration of white English-women to India in order to increase social distance between the English and Indians in the nineteenth century. Perhaps as many as 90 percent of the British in India had made marriages with locals by the mid-eighteenth century. Many "Anglo-Indians" resulted from these liaisons. Intermarriage was virtually at an end by the beginning of the nineteenth century, though, after a rebellion in Santo Domingo and the slaughter of whites there led to hysterical fears that the same would happen in India if the distance between ruler and ruled were not increased. With the Mutiny, the opening of the Suez Canal and the coming of many white women, the social disapproval of "mixing" became universal among whites in India by the end of the

century. Ronald Hyam, *Empire and Sexuality: The British Experience* (Manchester: Manchester University Press, 1990), pp. 116–119.

29 "The abject has only one quality of the object – that of being opposed to *I*," Julia Kristeva, *Powers of Horror*, trans. Leon S. Roudiez (New York: Columbia University Press, 1982), p. 1.

### CONCLUSION: WORK AS RULE

1 The *OED* locates the first use of the term "individualism" in 1827 in English; the second was in de Tocqueville's negative use of it as a descriptor of a peculiarly American sin.

2 For a discussion of nineteenth-century liberals and their support for imperial projects, see Patrick Brantlinger, *Rule of Darkness: British Literature and Imperialism, 1830–1914* (Ithaca, NY: Cornell University Press, 1988), pp. 19–32.

3 F. M. L. Thompson, *The Rise of Respectable Society: A Social History of Victorian Britain, 1830–1900* (London: Fontana, 1988), p. 213.

4 Thus, Schumpeter would argue that the European bourgeoisie generally fell prey to "mental patterning" by an aristocratic class whose military traditions are a holdover from pre-capitalist days. Yet, "the dead always rule the living." Schumpeter, *Imperialism*, pp. 94–98.

5 J. A. Hobson, *The Psychology of Jingoism* (London: G. Richards, 1901).

6 John Springhall, "Up Guards and at Them!" in John D. Mackenzie, ed., *Imperialism and Popular Culture* (Manchester: Manchester University Press, 1986), p. 49.

7 Allen Warren, "Citizens of the Empire: Baden-Powell, Scouts and Guides, and an Imperial Idea, 1900–1940," in Mackenzie, ed., *Imperialism and Popular Culture*, p. 238.

8 Charles Dilke, *Greater Britain*, quoted in *The Cultural Bond*, ed. J. A. Mangan (London: Frank Cass and Co., 1992), p. 5.

9 Indeed, the term sport primarily referred to the chase throughout the nineteenth century; it would only gradually come to be lumped into a common category with field sports by the end of the century.

10 Burnham performs one of the most egregious misuses of historical evidence extant when he reads the anomalous investment situation in the United States of the 1930s as a confirmation of his predictions. See *The Managerial Revolution* (New York: John Day, 1941), pp. 252–272. See Orwell's reservations about Burnham's qualified admiration for Nazi Germany in his "Second Thoughts on James Burnham," in *The Orwell Reader*, Introduction by Richard H. Rovere (New York: Harcourt, 1956), pp. 335–354. Orwell's change of attitude toward Burnham is a complicated story which cannot be told in detail here.

11 Burnham, *Managerial Revolution*, p. 132.

12 Ibid., p. 148.

# Bibliography

Anderson, David M. and David Killingray. *Policing the Empire: Government, Authority, and Control, 1830–1940*. Manchester: Manchester University Press, 1991.

Anderson, Olive. *A Liberal State at War*. London: Macmillan; New York: St. Martin's, 1967.

Annan, Noel. "Kipling's Place in the History of Ideas." *Kipling's Mind and Art*. Ed. Andrew Rutherford London: Oliver and Boyd, 1964.

Arendt, Hannah. *The Origins of Totalitarianism*. New York: Harcourt Brace and Co., 1958.

Badruddin, Umar. *The Indian National Movement*. Trans. Azizul Islam. Dhaka, Bangladesh: University Press, 1993.

Baring, Evelyn, Earl of Cromer. *Modern Egypt*. 2 vols. New York: Macmillan, 1908.

*Political and Literary Essays, 1908–1913*. 2 vols. London: Macmillan, 1913.

Barrish, Phillip. "Accumulating Variation: Darwin's *On the Origin of Species* and Contemporary Literary and Cultural Theory." *Victorian Studies* 34.4 (Summer 1991) pp. 431–453.

Bhabha, Homi. "Signs Taken for Wonders." *"Race," Writing, and Difference*. Ed. Henry Louis Gates, Jr. Chicago and London: University of Chicago Press, 1986.

ed. *Nation and Narration*. London and New York: Routledge, 1990.

Bierman, John. *Dark Safari: The Life Behind the Legend of Henry Morton Stanley*. New York: Knopf, 1990.

Bishop, Alan. *Gentleman Rider: A Life of Joyce Cary*. London: Michael Joseph, 1988.

Bivona, Daniel. *Desire and Contradiction: Imperial Visions and Domestic Debates in Victorian Literature*. Manchester: Manchester University Press, 1990.

"Playing the Muslim: Sir Richard Burton's *Pilgrimage* and Negative Cultural Identity." *Borders of Culture, Margins of Identity*. New Orleans: *Xavier Review* Press, 1994, pp. 85–94.

Blakeley, Brian L. *The Colonial Office: 1868–1892*. Durham, NC: Duke University Press, 1972.

Brantlinger, Patrick. *Rule of Darkness: British Literature and Imperialism, 1830–1914*. Ithaca, NY: Cornell University Press, 1988.

"Victorians and Africans: the Genealogy of the Myth of the Dark Continent." *"Race," Writing, and Difference*. Ed. Henry Louis Gates. Chicago and London: University of Chicago Press, 1986, pp. 185–222.

Braverman, Harry. "Capitalism and the Division of Labor." *Classes, Power, and Conflict*. Eds. Anthony Giddens and David Held. Berkeley: University of California Press, 1982, pp. 148–156.

*Labor and Monopoly Capital*. New York and London: *Monthly Review* Press, 1974.

Brontë, Charlotte. *Jane Eyre*. New York and London: Norton, 1987.

Brooks, Peter. *Reading for the Plot: Design and Intention in Narrative*. New York: A.A. Knopf, 1984.

Burnham, James. *The Managerial Revolution*. New York: John Day, 1941.

Cary, Joyce. *Mr. Johnson*. New York: New Directions, 1989.

*Selected Essays*. Ed. A. G. Bishop. New York: St. Martin's, 1976.

Caserio, Robert. "Kipling in the Light of Failure." *Rudyard Kipling*. Ed. Harold Bloom. NY: Chelsea House, 1987, pp. 117–144.

Cobden, Richard. *The Political Writings of Richard Cobden*. Vol. 1. London: Fisher Unwin, 1903; reprinted New York: Kraus, 1969.

Coetzee, J. M. *White Writing*. New Haven and London: Yale University Press, 1988.

Cohn, Bernard S. "Representing Authority in Victorian India." *The Invention of Tradition*. Ed. E. J. Hobsbawm and Terence Ranger. New York and Cambridge: Cambridge University Press, 1983, pp. 165–210.

*The Compact Edition of the Oxford English Dictionary*. Oxford: Oxford University Press, 1971.

Conrad, Joseph. "Congo Diary." *Congo Diary and Other Uncollected Pieces*. Ed. Zdzislaw Najder. New York: Doubleday, 1978.

*Heart of Darkness*. New York: Norton, 1988.

*Lord Jim*. New York: Signet, 1961.

*Nostromo*. New York: Bantam, 1989.

Crick, Bernard. *George Orwell: A Life*. Boston: Little Brown, 1980.

Culler, Jonathan. *On Deconstruction: Theory and Criticism After Structuralism*. Ithaca, NY: Cornell University Press, 1982.

Curtin, Philip D. *The Image of Africa: British Ideas and Action, 1780–1850*. London: Macmillan, 1965.

Dandeker, Christopher. *Surveillance, Power, and Modernity: Bureaucracy and Discipline from 1700 to the Present Day*. New York: St. Martin's, 1990.

David, Deirdre. *Rule Britannia: Women, Empire, and Victorian Writing*. Ithaca, NY and London: Cornell University Press, 1995.

Dicey, A. V. *Lectures on the Relation Between Law and Public Opinion in England During the Nineteenth Century*. London: Macmillan, 1905.

Disraeli, Benjamin. *Selected Speeches*. Ed. T. E. Kebbel. London: Longmans, Green and Co., 1882.

Doughty, Charles. *Travels in Arabia Deserta*. New York: Boni and Liveright, 1921.

Eldridge, C. C. *England's Mission: the Imperial Idea in the Age of Gladstone and Disraeli,*

*1868–1880*. Chapel Hill: University of North Carolina Press, 1973.

Elias, Norbert. *The History of Manners*. Trans. Edmond Jephcott. New York: Pantheon, 1978.

Fanon, Frantz. *Black Skin, White Masks*. Trans. Charles Lam Markmann. New York: Grove Press, 1967.

Flint, John E. "Frederick Lugard: The Making of an Autocrat." *African Proconsuls: European Governors in Africa*. Eds. L. H. Gann and Peter Duignan. New York and London: Macmillan, 1978, pp. 290–312.

Forster, E. M. *A Passage to India*. New York: HBJ, 1984.

Foulkes, A. P. *Literature and Propaganda*. London and New York: Methuen, 1983.

Freud, Sigmund. *Beyond the Pleasure Principle*. Trans. James Strachey. New York: Norton, 1961.

Froude, James Anthony. *Oceana*. New York: Scribner, 1886.

Gailey, Harry A. "Sir Hugh Clifford (1866–1941)." *African Proconsuls: European Governors in Africa*. Eds. L. H. Gann and Peter Duignan. New York and London: Macmillan, 1978, pp. 265–289.

Gates, Henry Louis, Jr., ed. *"Race," Writing, and Difference*. Chicago and London: University of Chicago Press, 1986.

Gordon, Charles. *Khartoum Journal*. Ed. Lord Elton. New York: Vanguard, 1961.

Green, Martin. *Dreams of Adventure, Deeds of Empire*. New York: Basic Books, 1979.
*Seven Types of Adventure Tale*. University Park, PA: Pennsylvania State University Press, 1991.

Hall, Dennis. *Joyce Cary: A Reappraisal*. New York: St. Martin's, 1983.

Harpham, Geoffrey Galt. *The Ascetic Imperative in Culture and Criticism*. Chicago and London: University of Chicago Press, 1987.

Harrison, James. "Kipling's Jungle Eden." *Critical Essays on Rudyard Kipling*. Ed. Harold Orel. Boston: G. K. Hall, 1989, pp. 77–92.

Hawthorn, Jeremy. *Joseph Conrad: Language and Fictional Self-Consciousness*. Lincoln, NE: University of Nebraska Press, 1979.

Helly, Dorothy O. *Livingstone's Legacy: Horace Waller and Victorian Mythmaking*. Athens, OH and London: Ohio University Press, 1987.

Hobsbawm, E. J. *Industry and Empire*. New York: Penguin, 1981.

Hobson, J. A. *Imperialism: A Study*. London: George Allen and Unwin, 1938.
*The Psychology of Jingoism*. London: G. Richards, 1901.

Hulme, Peter. *Colonial Encounters*. Cambridge: Cambridge University Press, 1987.

Hyam, Ronald. *Empire and Sexuality: The British Experience*. Manchester: Manchester University Press, 1990.

Islam, Shamsul. *Kipling's "Law": A Study of His Philosophy of Life*. London: Macmillan, 1975.

Jameson, Fredric. *The Political Unconscious*. Ithaca, NY: Cornell University Press, 1981.

Kafka, Franz. "In the Penal Colony." *The Penal Colony: Stories and Short Pieces*. Trans. Willa and Edwin Muir. New York: Schocken, 1971, pp. 191–230.

Kant, Immanuel. *Prolegomena to any Future Metaphysics That Will Be Able to Present Itself As a Science*. Trans. Peter G. Lucas. Manchester: Manchester University Press, 1953.

Kennedy, Paul. *The Rise and Fall of the Great Powers: Economic Change and Military Conflict from 1500 to 2000*. New York: Random House, 1987.

Kiernan, V. G. *The Lords of Humankind*. Boston: Little, Brown, 1969.

Kipling, Rudyard. "At the End of the Passage." *In the Vernacular: The English in India*. Ed. Randall Jarrell. Gloucester, MA: Peter Smith, 1970.

*The Collected Works of Rudyard Kipling*. New York: AMS, 1970.

*The Complete Stalky and Co.* London: Macmillan, 1929.

*The Jungle Books*. London: Penguin, 1987.

*Plain Tales from the Hills*. New York: Charles Scribners, 1916.

Knightley, Philip and Colin Simpson. *The Secret Lives of Lawrence of Arabia*. New York: McGraw-Hill, 1969.

Kristeva, Julia. *Powers of Horror*. Trans. Leon S. Roudiez. New York: Columbia University Press, 1982.

Kucich, John. *Repression in Victorian Fiction*. Berkeley: University of California Press, 1987.

Lacan, Jacques. "The Agency of the Letter in the Unconscious or Reason since Freud." *écrits: A Selection*. Trans. Alan Sheridan. New York and London: Norton, 1977, pp. 146–178.

Lane, Christopher. *The Ruling Passion: British Colonial Allegory and the Paradox of Homosexual Desire*. Durham, NC: Duke University Press, 1995.

Lasch, Christopher. *The True and Only Heaven: Progress and Its Critics*. New York and London: Norton, 1991.

Lawrence, T. E. *Seven Pillars of Wisdom: A Triumph*. New York and London: Doubleday, 1991.

Lenin, V. I. *Imperialism, the Highest Stage of Capitalism, Collected Works*. Vol. 22. London: Lawrence and Wishart, n.d.

Levenson, Michael. "The Value of Facts in *Heart of Darkness*." Joseph Conrad. *Heart of Darkness*. Ed. Robert Kimbrough. 3rd ed. New York: Norton, 1988, pp. 391–405.

Lewis, C. S. "Kipling's World." *Kipling and the Critics*. Ed. Elliot L. Gilbert. London: Peter Owen, 1966, pp. 99–117.

Livingstone, David. *Dr. Livingstone's Cambridge Lectures*. Cambridge: Deighton, Bell and Co., 1858.

*Missionary Travels and Researches in South Africa*. New York: Harper, 1858.

Lugard, Lord Frederick. *The Dual Mandate in British Tropical Africa*. London: Archon, 1965.

Lyotard, Jean-François. *The Postmodern Condition: A Report on Knowledge*. Trans. Geoff Bennington and Brian Massumi. Minneapolis: University of Minnesota Press, 1979.

Mack, John E. *A Prince of Our Disorder*. Boston: Little, Brown, 1976.

Mackenzie, John M. *Propaganda and Empire: the Manipulation of British Public Opinion, 1880–1960*. Manchester: Manchester University Press, 1984.

Mackenzie, John M. ed. *Imperialism and Popular Culture.* Manchester: Manchester University Press, 1986.

Mangan, J. A. *The Games Ethic and Imperialism: Aspects of the Diffusion of an Ideal.* New York: Viking, 1986.

ed. *The Cultural Bond.* London: Frank Cass and Co., 1992.

Mangan, J. A. and James Walvin, eds. *Manliness and Morality: Middle-Class Masculinity in Britain and America, 1800–1940.* Manchester: Manchester University Press, 1987.

Mannoni, Octave. *Prospero and Caliban.* Trans. Pamela Powesland. New York: Praeger, 1964.

Marx, Karl. *Capital.* Vol. I. Ed. Frederick Engels. Trans. Samuel Moore and Edward Aveling. New York: International Publishers, 1967.

Mason, Philip. *Kipling: the Glass, the Shadow, and the Fire.* New York: Harper, 1975.

McClintock, Anne. *Imperial Leather: Race, Gender, and Sexuality in the Colonial Contest.* New York and London: Routledge, 1995.

McClure, John A. *Kipling and Conrad: the Colonial Fiction.* Cambridge, MA: Harvard University Press, 1981.

McDorman, Kathryne S. "Two Views of Empire: Margery Perham and Joyce Cary Analyze the Dual Mandate Policy." *Research Studies* 50 (September/December 1983), pp. 153–160.

McLynn, Frank. *Stanley.* London: Constable, 1989.

Meyers, Jeffrey. *Joseph Conrad: A Biography.* New York: Scribner's, 1991.

ed. *T. E. Lawrence: Soldier, Writer, Legend.* New York: St. Martin's, 1989.

Miller, D. A. *The Novel and the Police.* Berkeley: University of California Press, 1988.

Mohanty, Satya P. "Colonial Legacies, Multicultural Futures: Relativism, Objectivity, and the Challenge of Otherness." *PMLA* 110.1 (January 1995), pp. 108–118.

Mongia, Padmini. "Narrative Strategy and Imperialism in Conrad's *Lord Jim.*" *Studies in the Novel* 24.2 (Summer 1992), pp. 173–186.

Monro, J. Forbes. *Britain in Tropical Africa, 1880–1960.* London: Macmillan, 1984.

Morel, E. D. *History of the Congo Reform Movement.* Eds. Wm. Roger Louis and Jean Stengers. Oxford: Clarendon Press, 1968.

Morgan, Susan. *Place Matters: Gendered Geography in Victorian Women's Travel Books about Southeast Asia.* New Brunswick, NJ: Rutgers University Press, 1996.

Mousa, Suleiman. *T. E. Lawrence: An Arab View.* Trans. Albert Boutros. New York: Oxford University Press, 1966.

"Multatuli" [Edouard Douwes Dekker]. *Max Havelaar, Or the Coffee Auctions of the Dutch Trading Company.* Trans. Roy Edwards. Amherst: University of Massachusetts Press, 1982.

Nietzsche, Friedrich. "What is Noble." *Beyond Good and Evil.* Trans. Walter Kauffmann. New York: Random House, 1966, pp. 199–237.

Orwell, George. *Burmese Days.* New York: HBJ, 1962.

*Inside the Whale and Other Essays.* London: Penguin, 1962.

*The Orwell Reader*. Introduction by Richard H. Rovere. New York: Harcourt, 1956.

Pakenham, Thomas. *The Scramble for Africa, 1876–1912*. New York: Random House, 1991.

Pakenham, Valerie. *Out in the Noonday Sun: Edwardians in the Tropics*. New York: Random House, 1985.

Pathak, Zakia; Saswati, Sengupta, and Sharmila, Purkayastha. "The Prison-house of Orientalism." *Textual Practice* 5.2 (Summer 1992), pp. 211–216.

Paul, Ellen Frankel. *Moral Revolution and Economic Science*. Westport, CT: Greenwood, 1979.

Peckham, Morse. *Explanation and Power*. Minneapolis: University of Minnesota Press, 1979.

Perkin, Harold. *The Rise of Professional Society: England Since 1880*. London: Routledge, 1989.

Pick, Daniel. *War Machine: the Rationalisation of Slaughter in the Modern Age*. New Haven and London: Yale University Press, 1993.

Pratt, Mary Louise. *Imperial Eyes: Travel Writing and Transculturation*. London and New York: Routledge, 1992.

Roberts, David. *Victorian Origins of the British Welfare State*. New Haven: Yale University Press, 1960.

Robinson, Ronald and John Gallagher. *Africa and the Victorians*. New York: St. Martin's, 1967.

Rorty, Richard. *Philosophy and the Mirror of Nature*. Princeton: Princeton University Press, 1979.

Rosaldo, Renato. "Imperialist Nostalgia." *Representations* 26 (Spring 1989), pp. 107–122.

Rutherford, Andrew, ed, *Kipling's Mind and Art*. London: Oliver and Boyd, 1964.

Said, Edward. *Culture and Imperialism*. New York: Alfred A. Knopf, 1994.

*Orientalism*. New York: Vintage, 1979.

Schumpeter, Joseph. *Imperialism*. Trans. Heinz Norden. New York: Meridian, 1955.

Searle, G. R. *The Quest for National Efficiency*. Oxford: Oxford University Press, 1971.

Seeley, J. R. *The Expansion of England*. London: Macmillan, 1888.

Semmel, Bernard. *Imperialism and Social Reform*. Cambridge, MA: Harvard University Press, 1960.

*The Liberal Idea and the Demons of Empire*. Baltimore and London: Johns Hopkins University Press, 1993.

Silverman, Kaja. *Male Subjectivity at the Margins*. New York: Routledge, 1992.

Spurr, David. *The Rhetoric of Empire*. Durham, NC: Duke University Press, 1993.

Stanley, Henry M. *The Congo and the Founding of Its Free State*. New York: Harper and Bros., 1885.

*Through the Dark Continent*. Vols. ii and ii. New York: Dover, 1988.

Temperley, Howard. *British Antislavery, 1833–1870*. London: Longman, 1972.

Thompson, E. P. "Time, Work-Discipline, and Industrial Capitalism." *Past and*

*Present* 38 (1967), pp. 56–96.

Thompson, F. M. L. *The Rise of Respectable Society: A Social History of Victorian Britain, 1830–1900*. London: Fontana, 1988.

Thornton, A. P. *Empire and the English Character*. London: I. B. Tauris and Co., 1992.

Tidrick, Kathryn. *Heart-Beguiling Araby*. Cambridge: Cambridge University Press, 1981.

*The Imperial Idea and Its Enemies*. New York: St. Martin's, 1963.

Torgovnick, Marianna. *Gone Primitive: Savage Intellects, Modern Lives*. Chicago: University of Chicago Press, 1990.

Twain, Mark. *King Leopold's Soliloquy: A Defense of his Congo Rule*. Boston: The P.R. Warren Co., 1905.

Wallerstein, Immanuel. *The Modern World-System*. Vol. I. New York: Academic Press, 1974.

Weber, Max. *Economy and Society*. Ed. G. Roth and C. Wittich. Trans. Fischoff et al.. New York: Bedminster, 1968.

Weintraub, Stanley. *Victoria: an Intimate Biography*. New York: Dutton, 1987.

Williams, Judith Blow. *British Commercial Policy and Trade Expansion, 1750–1850*. Oxford: Clarendon Press, 1972.

Wilson, Jeremy. *Lawrence of Arabia*. New York: Macmillan, 1989.

Wurgaft, Lewis D. *The Imperial Imagination: Magic and Myth in Kipling's India*. Middletown, CT: Wesleyan University Press, 1983.

Youngs, Tim. " 'My Footsteps on these Pages': the Inscription of Self and 'Race' in H. M. Stanley's *How I Found Livingstone*." *Prose Studies*, Spring 1990, pp. 231–245.

*Travellers in Africa: British Travelogues, 1850–1900*. Manchester: Manchester University Press, 1994.

# Index